YOUNG MR. OBAMA

YOUNG MR. OBAMA

*Chicago and the Making of a
Black President*

Edward McClelland

Bloomsbury Press
New York Berlin London

Published by Bloomsbury Press, New York

"Illinois Blues" by Skip James copyright © 1968 renewed 1994 Wynwood
Music Co., Inc. All Rights Reserved. Used by Permission.

All papers used by Bloomsbury Press are natural, recyclable products made
from wood grown in well-managed forests. The manufacturing processes
conform to the environmental regulations of the country of origin.

LIBRARY OF CONGRESS CATALOGING-IN-PUBLICATION DATA

McClelland, Ted.
Young Mr. Obama : Chicago and the making of a black president /
Edward McClelland. —1st U.S. ed.
p. cm.
Includes index.
ISBN 978-1-60819-060-7 (alk. paper)
1. Obama, Barack.   2. Presidents—United States—Biography.
3. African American lawyers—Illinois—Chicago—Biography.
4. African American politicians—Illinois—Chicago—Biography.
5. African American legislators—Illinois—Biography.   6. Chicago
(Ill—Politics and government—1951-   7. Illinois—Politics and
government—1951-   I. Title.
E908.M39 2010
973.932092—dc22
[B]
2010007976

First U.S. edition 2010

1 3 5 7 9 10 8 6 4 2

Typeset by Westchester Book Group
Printed in the United States of America by Worldcolor Fairfield

To the Arden family: Patrick, Esther, Liam, and Joseph

CONTENTS

Prologue: "Hello, Chicago!"   I

Chapter 1:   The Gardens   5

Chapter 2:   Harold   25

Chapter 3:   The Asbestos Piece   41

Chapter 4:   Project Vote!   62

Chapter 5:   The Young Lawyer   75

Chapter 6:   Hyde Park   88

Chapter 7:   The First Campaign   103

Chapter 8:   State Senator Obama   122

Chapter 9:   Defeat   145

Chapter 10:   "I'll Kick Your Ass

              Right Now"   169

Chapter 11:   "You Have the Power to

              Make a U.S. Senator"   193

Chapter 12:   The Godfather   210

Chapter 13:   The Obama Juice   227

Epilogue: The Birthplace of Post-Racial

              Politics   261

Acknowledgments   265

Index   267

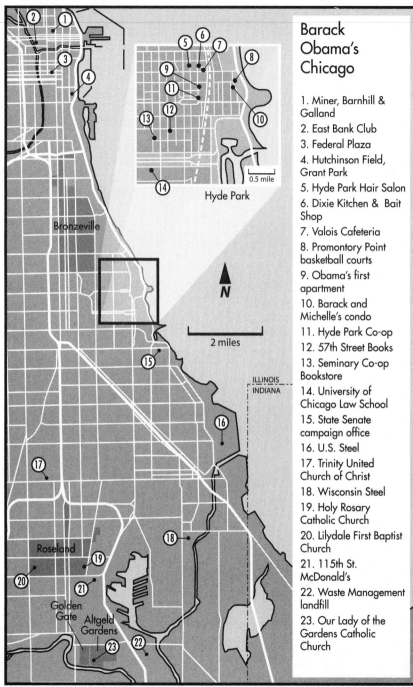

Barack Obama's Chicago

1. Miner, Barnhill & Galland
2. East Bank Club
3. Federal Plaza
4. Hutchinson Field, Grant Park
5. Hyde Park Hair Salon
6. Dixie Kitchen & Bait Shop
7. Valois Cafeteria
8. Promontory Point basketball courts
9. Obama's first apartment
10. Barack and Michelle's condo
11. Hyde Park Co-op
12. 57th Street Books
13. Seminary Co-op Bookstore
14. University of Chicago Law School
15. State Senate campaign office
16. U.S. Steel
17. Trinity United Church of Christ
18. Wisconsin Steel
19. Holy Rosary Catholic Church
20. Lilydale First Baptist Church
21. 115th St. McDonald's
22. Waste Management landfill
23. Our Lady of the Gardens Catholic Church

Bronzeville

Hyde Park

0.5 mile

N

2 miles

ILLINOIS
INDIANA

Roseland

Golden Gate

Altgeld Gardens

DOUGLAS HUNTER

Prologue

"HELLO, CHICAGO!"

THE GATES TO GRANT PARK's Hutchinson Field were thrown open at a quarter past six, over an hour ahead of schedule. The crowd massing against the metal barriers wouldn't wait any longer. The first of sixty thousand Obama supporters—those lucky enough to score tickets in an Internet lottery—cantered across the softball diamonds, carefree as streakers, racing for a spot near the floodlit stage. It was standing-room-only for the final Obama rally of the 2008 presidential campaign.

They were young, most of them. There was a sense of conquest as they filled the sunken field and raised American flags of all sizes, from desktop squares to bedsheet banners. The last generational shift in American politics had taken place on the same grass they were trampling. The riots at the 1968 Democratic National Convention broke apart the New Deal coalition and began a forty-year-long conservative backlash whose ashes would be blown away by the end of this night. Then, Chicago had stood for dissent and disunion. It was the stage where a nation acted out its angriest divisions since the Civil War. Once again, the whole world was watching Grant Park, but this time, it would represent the values of the man who had chosen this spot, a man who, four years before, on the second-biggest night of his life, had declared,

"There's not a liberal America and a conservative America—there's a *United States* of America."

"It's the transformative night of my generation," said a twenty-six-year-old Chicagoan. "Obama is going to be the first post–baby boomer president. He's getting us past the sixties. All this stuff about Bill Ayers and the racial issue, I don't give a shit. There's more important stuff out there, like the economy and alternative energy."

They came from all over the world. A half dozen Sudanese Lost Boys, all gangly six-footers like the half-African candidate, stood together on a patch of infield dirt. An Irish immigrant wore a faded-looking T-shirt: BARACK OBAMA FOR ILLINOIS STATE SENATE, 13TH DISTRICT '96. No such campaign memorabilia had ever existed. The T-shirt came from Urban Outfitters. Every few minutes, the young Irishman checked his BlackBerry. His father was texting him with election returns from in front of a TV in Dublin.

No one anticipated Obama's victory with more satisfaction than Chicago's African-Americans. They had raised the man to power. Twenty-three years before, he had arrived in this city as a stranger, unsure even of his place in its black community. But he had organized its poorest residents, had gotten his picture in *Jet* (whose offices overlooked Grant Park) by becoming president of the *Harvard Law Review*, and then returned to the South Side to marry one of its most beautiful, accomplished daughters and represent his fellow blacks in the state senate. Along the way, some had questioned whether he really was black, or just a deep-down white man whose blackness was only skin deep, an accident of ancestry. But now that he was hours away from winning the most powerful office on Earth, they were eager to claim him, and his triumph, as their own. In the VIP tent sat Jesse Jackson and Oprah Winfrey. Almost as much as Obama, they represented what ambitious African-Americans could achieve in Chicago. Like him, they had arrived in the city in their twenties and risen to worldwide fame.

In the crowd stood Ronnie Wickers, better known as "Ronnie Woo-Woo." An original Wrigley Field bleacher bum, he had altered his Cubs uniform to read OBAMA 08 and changed his stadium cheer for the candidate.

"Obama! Woo! Obama! Woo! Obama! Woo!" he wheezed, substituting "Obama" for "Cubs."

"I'm sixty-seven years old," Wickers said. "Obama's like Jackie Robinson. An African-American got a chance to play baseball back in the day. Obama, he's got a chance to prove himself."

The sunken meadow was walled on three sides by skyscrapers, whose illuminated windows formed constellations for city dwellers. VOTE 2008 spelled out the windows of the Associates Center. The CNA Building was a Lite-Brite Stars and Stripes. Diamond Vision screens, as big as billboards, were flashing CNN's carnival-colored election maps. Whenever a state turned blue, a hundred thousand voices rose. (The crowd outside the park was just as big as the crowd inside. Those who hadn't won a golden ticket stood along Michigan Avenue, begging like Deadheads looking for a miracle. "Anyone need a guest?" "I need one. I'm not a scalper.") When Ohio went for Obama, the roar was as loud as any cheer for a Bears touchdown in Soldier Field, a few blocks to the south. Mathematically, Ohio didn't clinch the election, but that was the moment everyone knew, because Ohio had tripped up John Kerry in 2004.

It became official at ten o'clock Central Time. Obama's partisans counted down the seconds until the polls closed on the West Coast: "Ten-nine-eight-seven-six-five-four-three-two-one."

It's not the jubilation from that moment that remains in people's minds. It's the tears. Jesse Jackson, who had grown up in segregated South Carolina, moved to even more segregated Chicago, and sought this same office when it was impossible for a black man to win, watched his protégé with reddened eyes. Oprah Winfrey, born in Mississippi, pregnant at fifteen, leaned on a stranger's shoulder. Out in the meadow, Amie Sipp cried too, after she gave up trying to call her father, who was celebrating on the South Side.

"It means change," the thirty-year-old woman said. "Equal opportunity. No matter what color you are, you can do whatever you want to do, no limitation."

When Obama finally emerged for his victory speech, his first words were "Hello, Chicago!" It was both a greeting to the city where he had made his political career and a note of gratitude. Obama is a remarkable politician, but if he hadn't come to Chicago, he wouldn't have been standing on a stage, about to address the entire world. His home state of Hawaii is more diverse, the California of his college days more tolerant, New York more cosmopolitan, and Massachusetts more sophisticated. But only in Chicago could a black man have become president of the United States. His rise to power had begun just a few miles away, on the South Side, in the midst of the largest black community in the United States. It couldn't have happened anywhere else.

Chapter 1

THE GARDENS

ALTGELD GARDENS—known to its older residents as "the Gardens," to its younger residents as "the G," and as "Alligator Gardens" to the cops who have to deal with its drug trade and its shootings—is a housing project in the remotest reaches of Chicago's South Side. Long, low, two-story apartment buildings, built of mud-brown Chicago brick, cover acres of bottomland along the banks of the Calumet River, which defines the city limits. The Gardens looks more like a military camp than a high-rise slum. In fact, it was built in the 1940s, to house blacks with wartime jobs in the nearby steel mills. It was a first home for upwardly mobile laborers, many just arrived in Chicago from Arkansas or Mississippi who would move on to bungalows and two-flats in the city's Black Belt.

Forty years later, Altgeld was something much less hopeful: a reservation for Chicago's poorest blacks. Most housing projects are in the inner city. Altgeld's location seemed designed to keep its residents unemployed and destitute. The Loop was twenty miles north, the Sears Tower invisible over the horizon. The L had never made it down this far; the nearest station was forty blocks away. Half the residents didn't own cars, which made it nearly impossible to find a job that might allow them to buy a car. Babies were born to public-aid mothers and grew up to raise their own children on public aid. There was a grocery store in a crumbling strip mall, but its aisles were so dirty and disorganized, its meat and vegetables so close to spoiling, that anyone with the means left the Gardens to shop at an A&P in Roseland, the closest real neighborhood.

In a way, Altgeld Gardens was the perfect place for Chicago's poorest. It was part of the Calumet region, a crescent of South Chicago and northwest Indiana that collects whatever the rest of Chicagoland doesn't want to look at, touch, or smell. The steel mills were here, broadcasting soot so thick it sifted onto cars and stuck in steelworkers' throats, to be washed away in mill gate taverns. The Gardens lay along a kink in the Calumet River called the Acme Bend, after the tin-roofed factory that lay across the channel and tainted the water with its waste. The dumps were here, too, so when the wind blew in from Lake Michigan, it carried an acrid, mulchy odor that weakened the residents' lungs.

Toward the end of South Langley Avenue, near where the street dead-ends into the river, was the poorest church in the Archdiocese of Chicago. Our Lady of the Gardens was nicknamed OLG by its parishioners, but to residents who depended on its food pantry or its clothing exchange, the church was simply "the Catholic," as though it were another of the welfare institutions they dealt with on a weekly basis. OLG's fifty families—all of them either from the Gardens or from Golden Gate, a nearby working-class neighborhood—could rarely muster even $200 for the Sunday collection plate. A grammar school, which charged $300 a year, offered a chance for the brightest students to win a scholarship to a Catholic school in the suburbs, although most ended up at all-black Carver High, a Chicago public school.

No diocesan priest would accept a posting at OLG, so throughout the 1970s and the early 1980s, the pastor was a black man from the Carribean island of St. Kitts. Father Stanley Farier belonged to the Society of the Divine Word, whose mission was working with people so poor that only Jesus would acknowledge them.

"It was like a village in itself," Farier would remember years later, after he had left the priesthood. "Self-enclosed, often abandoned in a sense, transportation-wise. When I was there in the seventies, you would tell people where you worked, and they would say, 'Oh, Altgeld Gardens.' It had that kind of a name: drug ridden, crime ridden, and poverty ridden. There was a gang problem, too. There was no job that you could get in Altgeld, except teaching in the school. If you had a job outside, if you didn't have a car, you couldn't hold down a job."

Because they had no jobs, the people of Altgeld Gardens were scarcely affected by the crisis that struck the Calumet region in the early 1980s: the steel mill closings. The southeast side of Chicago once forged so much steel that it was known as the Ruhr of America, although that was hardly fair, since weapons built of Chicago steel defeated weapons built on the original Ruhr. At its wartime peak, in 1944, the U.S. Steel plant on Lake Michigan employed eighteen thousand men and women—nearly a division of industrial labor. But U.S. Steel had a newer plant in Gary, Indiana, and, slowly, the company allowed its Chicago mill to die of old age. In 1980, it still employed seven thousand steelworkers. Three years later, only a thousand remained. Nearby Wisconsin Steel expired even more abruptly. One afternoon, the workers were simply told to go home, because the mill was bankrupt. The furnaces went cold, the gates were padlocked, the innards sold for scrap.

The steelworkers refused to admit the jobs weren't coming back. But Jerry Kellman, a dark-haired, tight-featured, intense community organizer, could see it. Raised in a Jewish family in the New York City suburbs, Kellman had followed a radical's path to the South Side. While attending the University of Wisconsin— where he demonstrated against the school's ROTC program—he road-tripped to the 1968 Democratic National Convention in Chicago. After watching Mayor Richard J. Daley's police go wild on his fellow protesters, Kellman decided Chicago was not a place he ever wanted to live. But he returned a few years later, to learn about organizing poor people from one of Daley's nemeses, Saul Alinsky. Alinsky had founded the community organizing movement in the 1930s by working with progressive Catholic churches to organize meat packers in the city's notorious stockyards.

Alinsky's model of building political power was based on the local Democratic Machine and was one of the Machine's few rivals in an era when Chicago was becoming a one-party town. The churches were the dominant institutions in most people's lives; if you asked a Chicagoan where he lived, he'd name his parish, not his neighborhood. Liberal priests believed in Pope Leo XIII's encyclical on labor: A worker had a right to organize for a wage that would "maintain himself, his wife and children in reasonable comfort." As a result, Alinsky's Industrial Areas Foundation received large grants from the archdiocese.

Kellman stayed on in Chicago and was working for a group that organized Latino churches when he got an idea for his own campaign. Why not work with churches in the Calumet region to find new jobs for steelworkers who'd been thrown out of work by the recession that coined the term "Rust Belt"? Kellman, who had converted to Catholicism the year before, set about visiting parishes on the South Side and in the south suburbs. Alinsky's model could still work in the mid-1980s, even though religious and neighborhood ties were weaker by then.

"I need board members," he told the priests, "you, and two parishioners."

At OLG, Father Dominic Carmon, the Blessed Word priest who had succeeded Stanley Farier as pastor, appointed Loretta Augustine and Yvonne Lloyd—two middle-aged mothers who helped the church sodality raise its meager budget by putting on plays and organizing fund-raising cruises on the lake. Augustine was the grade school's Girl Scout leader, sang in the choir, and sat on the school's board.

"I can't think of any two people I'd rather have than the two of you," Carmon told the women.

The Calumet Community Religious Conference, as Kellman's new organization was called, was an immediate success, winning a $500,000 state grant to open a job bank at a local college. But Augustine and Lloyd felt out of place at the meetings, which were held at a suburban church. The job bank was nice, they thought, but the Gardens didn't have any steelworkers. The Gardens had people who had never held a job in their lives.

"Loretta and I would go to the meetings, and we'd sit there, and we knew what was needed," Lloyd would recall years later. "The Gardens was going down and there was so many problems over there. But they were focused on stuff suburban people focused on, like how much you fine someone if they didn't cut their grass, and the garbage cans had to be put out on the curb. I didn't care about that. I had enough kids to pick up garbage cans and put 'em in the yard."

Father Carmon was concerned about the landfill. The residents constantly complained that the fumes made them ill. One of his fellow priests had developed cancer.

Kellman agreed that his South Side and suburban churches were unequally yoked. He decided to split the urban parishes into a separate group, which he named the Developing Communities Project. He realized the group needed a black organizer. While he searched for one, he placed it under the aegis of a colleague named Mike Kruglik. Kruglik was an experienced organizer, but he was also Jewish, Princeton educated, and spoke with a sharp-voweled white ethnic accent. Even though the DCP's board members knew Kruglik was temporary, they bridled at his leadership.

"I know you're trying," Lloyd told Kruglik, "but you're in the city, and most of the churches in the city are black, and they're not gonna listen to what you say, because they feel like you're not in tune with the things that we need to survive."

Throughout early 1985, Kellman was searching frantically for a permanent organizer, taking out ads in the Chicago papers, trade journals, even the *New York Times*. He brought more than one black candidate before the board, but none of them had the right combination of brains and idealism. The problem, Kellman reflected, was that anyone smart enough to be an organizer was too smart to be an organizer. The bright ones had better opportunities. He was frustrated, the women were frustrated, the priests were frustrated.

"I have some people in mind," he told a board meeting, "but so far, I haven't found a black organizer."

"You're gonna have to go back," a black priest told him, " 'cause there's somebody out there."

In a reading room at the New York Public Library, an unemployed, twenty-three-year-old Barack Obama picked up a magazine called *Community Jobs*, a "do-gooder publication," as he thought of it, that carried classified ads for community organizers. He had quit his job as an editor at a business news service because it made him feel like a corporate sellout and was trying to break into organizing by taking part-time gigs in Harlem with the New York Public Interest Research Group, an organization affiliated with Ralph Nader.

Obama had tried once before to get a job in Chicago, writing to the city's newly elected black mayor, Harold Washington. He never heard back. If he couldn't work in city hall, close to the mayor, maybe he could work on the South Side. Obama was looking for a job in an African-American community, and the South Side—home to nearly a million blacks—was the largest African-American community in America. He mailed his résumé to Kellman.

Kellman was impressed enough to schedule an interview with Obama the next time he visited New York. They met in a Lexington Avenue coffee shop, where Kellman was relieved to see that, in spite of his foreign-sounding name, Obama was an African-American. It was immediately obvious to Kellman that he'd found the right candidate, so he started pitching Obama on the job, telling him about the devastation in the Calumet region. The steel mills were hot, dangerous, and dirty, he said, but people desperately wanted to work there, because it was a job for life. Now that the mills were gone, disillusionment and bitterness were corroding the community. The worse he made it sound, the more Obama would feel needed there, Kellman figured. Obama was so desperate to become an organizer in a black community that Kellman could have talked him into a job in Newark. They struck a deal at the table: Obama would start at $10,000 a year, plus a car allowance. A week later, he was headed to Chicago in a $2,000 Honda beater.

Loretta Augustine and Yvonne Lloyd first saw their new organizer at a rally in a suburban high school, thrown to celebrate the

CCRC's half-million-dollar job grant. It was a big night, with eight hundred people packed into the gym to hear a speech by Cardinal Joseph Bernardin, the archbishop of Chicago.

Oh, my God, Augustine thought as Kellman introduced her to the gangly young man, he's got this kid. Is he even going to be up for this? He looks so young.

Obama won her over quickly. In the short time he'd had to prepare, he'd done some research on the South Side. As soon as he started talking, describing his vision for the neighborhoods, Augustine looked at Lloyd and they nodded to each other.

"Loretta, that's the one," Lloyd said.

"Sure is," Augustine replied.

Obama admitted to the women that he knew nothing about community organizing, but at least he was honest about that, they thought, and he was respectful. In spite of his obvious intelligence and his Ivy League degree, he didn't condescend. Later, Lloyd and Augustine took him on a tour of the neighborhood's boarded-up houses. They could tell he was going to fit in at the Gardens when he sat down with an OLG nun who was a notoriously bad cook and ate her pie. Not even the church ladies would do that.

Obama's new office was two rooms in the rectory of Holy Rosary Church, on 113th Street. A soaring, vaulted church, with its own convent and grade school, Holy Rosary had once been a corner-stone of the Roseland neighborhood, filled with prosperous fami-lies. Now it was struggling to serve a multiracial congregation composed of blacks, Latinos, and older whites. In the 1970s, no Chicago neighborhood changed from white to black more rapidly than Roseland, which had taken its name from the flowers planted by its original Dutch settlers. The shopping strip on Michigan Avenue told the story: The tall marquee of Gately's Department

Store was still bolted to a brick storefront, but the business had closed a few years before, unable to compete with suburban malls. The shoe emporium followed, then the hardware store, then the restaurants. They were replaced by wig shops and sneaker boutiques, owned by Koreans who drove in from the suburbs each morning to raise the gates on their ghetto businesses—like a daily invasion of locusts, some residents thought resentfully. While the streets west of the railroad tracks still maintained a middle-class, even stately appearance, the drug trade was part of the new commerce on Michigan Avenue.

Kellman told Obama to spend his first month conducting "one-on-ones," interviews with neighborhood residents and with pastors who might be enticed to join the DCP. The idea was to learn the far South Side's story and identify an issue that might become the basis of a "piece"—organizer-speak for a project. At first, as he made the rounds of churches, spending ten or twelve hours a day chatting up pastors and trying to set up appointments over the phone, Obama felt as frustrated as his hapless grandfather back in Hawaii, peddling insurance to unwilling customers. He didn't know the first thing about politics or the black church, whose pastors can be independent, entrepreneurial, and jealous of the power they hold over their congregations. To grow in the black community, DCP would have to enlist Protestant churches—who mistrusted the organization's Catholic roots. Older pastors were unimpressed with Obama. The kid was just out of college, he had a funny name, and when they asked him the all-important question "What church do you belong to?" he didn't have an answer.

Obama found his first ally at Lilydale First Baptist Church. Reverend Alvin Love had arrived just two years before as a twenty-eight-year-old in his first pulpit, so he could relate to Obama's problems with the well-established pastors. The old bulls hadn't welcomed him, either. Lilydale's congregation had migrated from an inner-city neighborhood, taking over a Lutheran church left behind by the fleeing Dutch, so it represented Roseland's changes, as well as its current problems: The church was often covered in graffiti, and burglars had stolen the PA system and the silverware.

When Obama sat down in Love's study, the pastor didn't take him as anything other than a young African-American. But Obama was self-conscious about his exoticness: his Muslim name, his lack of roots in Chicago or the black community in general.

"I know you're wondering about this funny accent," Obama said, even though Love hadn't detected an accent. "My father is from Kenya and my mother is from Kansas. Some folks call me Yo Mama. Some folks call me Alabama."

Love chuckled, then Obama asked him, "What do you think about the neighborhood? What do you want to see happen?"

"We've got a drug problem," Love said, "and people here need jobs."

The two men talked about their upbringings—Obama's in Hawaii and Indonesia, Love's in Mississippi during the civil rights movement and on the West Side of Chicago during the riots after Martin Luther King's assassination. Obama, who had been reading Taylor Branch's *Parting the Waters: America in the King Years*, was fascinated by the civil rights movement, an episode in black history that he'd missed out on. This brother's looking for a connection with our community, Love thought. He agreed to attend a pastors' meeting at Holy Rosary. Most of his parishioners drove in from other parts of town, so it wouldn't hurt to belong to something that connected Lilydale with Roseland. He thought it might be good for the church and the neighborhood. At the meeting, the pastors discussed how their churches could fight the neighborhood's crime and drug problems. Only eight attended, and six were Catholic priests, but Obama was starting to build the DCP.

Obama was also working with the laid-off steelworkers whose plight had inspired Kellman to start a community organization in the first place. He and Loretta Augustine became fixtures at union halls, where he learned that steelworkers could be just as stubborn as inner-city pastors.

Steel had a century-long history on the southern shore of Lake Michigan. The steelworkers' union had shed blood, when ten men were gunned down by police during a 1937 strike. Its sacrifices were rewarded with wages that made its members blue-collar aristocrats. The sons of those strikers lived in brick bungalows, towed powerful speedboats up to their Wisconsin cottages, and were proud to be part of an industry that called itself "the backbone of America"—the first step in building skyscrapers. They had inherited steelmaking from their fathers, and refused to believe they wouldn't be able to pass it on to their children. Obama and Augustine interviewed men who wore diamond rings and heavy gold chains. Their plan: to ride out the layoffs on unemployment and union benefits. In the past, they'd always gone on strike, come back to work, and made more money than before. They had no skills that could be used outside a steel mill. One man ran a steel-straightening machine. He pushed a button, a bar of steel went in. He pushed the button again, the bar came out.

Obama talked to the workers about retraining and set up interviews with job counselors. Many of the steelworkers ended up as computer programmers. The less fortunate landed near-minimum-wage jobs at the Sherwin-Williams paint factory or the Jay's Potato Chips plant, or Brach's candy. Not even the most ambitious, though, made as much money as they'd earned pouring steel. As

Obama listened to the frustrated workers pour out their stories, he tried to translate them into an "issue"—a project that would bring jobs to the South Side and prove to the local pastors that the DCP could deliver money to their neighborhoods. Augustine, Lloyd, and another DCP board member named Margaret Bagby helped him come up with one.

Barack Obama's very first followers were a trio of middle-aged women who sat on the DCP's board. Their backgrounds could not have been more different from Obama's—or more similar to the great majority of blacks who had grown up in the segregated America of the 1940s and '50s. Augustine was a native South Sider; Lloyd a Southerner, from Nashville; Bagby a country girl from a small Michigan town that was a remnant of the Underground Railroad. All three lived in Golden Gate, the neighborhood of aluminum-clad ranch houses alongside Altgeld, and all three were married to men with blue-collar jobs: Augustine's husband was a postal clerk, Lloyd's was a cop, Bagby's a UPS driver. Augustine, the youngest, was a cherubic woman who had lived several years in Altgeld during the early years of her marriage. But by the time Obama arrived to head the DCP, that marriage was breaking apart, and she was spending more and more time on community activism. That was one reason she became the group's president. Lloyd, thin and sardonic, was the mother of eleven children, several of them born before Obama. Bagby, a quiet, heavyset woman who had joined the DCP after seeing several steelworker neighbors lose their jobs, also had sons older than the kid organizer.

At one point, all the women asked themselves the same question: Why am I following this child? When Kellman had been their organizer, they dutifully obeyed his orders, figuring it was for the good of the neighborhood. With Obama, it was different.

They wanted to do what Barack told them to do because Barack told them to do it. The DCP was responsible for its own funding, through church dues and grants, which meant going to foundation boards and asking for money.

"We've got to have funding," Obama would tell the group in meetings at Holy Rosary, and then he'd tick off the names of organizations that might give them money—the Woods Charitable Trust, the Joyce Foundation, the Wieboldt Foundation—astonishing everyone with his knowledge of the bureaucracy and the research he'd done during the few spare hours he wasn't hauling his ass from meeting to interview to meeting to church service. Lloyd wondered if he ever slept.

"Barack, why don't you make the presentation?" Lloyd would ask him wearily before yet another plea for funds.

"Oh, no," Obama would say. "This is your neighborhood. You feel this inside. You're going to have to go and talk to these people."

That was a tenet of community organizing he'd learned from Kellman: You could lead people but you couldn't do the work for them. Obama would call downtown to set up the appointments, and then he'd drill the women there at Holy Rosary, telling them exactly what to say to those white board members who had millions of dollars to hand out. His favorite words of advice were "Stay focused. If everyone around you is acting the fool, screaming and hollering, you stay focused." On the day of big presentations, he'd drive them to the meeting, all jammed into that rusty blue Honda they thought was the hooptiest car they'd ever seen.

And damn if they didn't get the money every time.

That was Obama's dual nature at work. He was black enough to fit in on the South Side but white enough to believe that if he walked into a room and asked people for money, they would give it to him. To women who'd always thought of their race as a limitation, Obama's attitude was a new way of looking at life.

Augustine became especially close to Obama—close enough to discuss her personal problems with him when he visited her house on DCP business. She thought he was the soberest, hardest-working young man she'd ever met. That $10,000 a year was blood money, because he was working eighty hours a week to earn it. You'd never see him in a pair of jeans, only college-boy chinos and little zip-up boots. You'd never even see him eat, he was so focused. On the way to meetings, Obama would stop his car at restaurants. While the women piled their plates with chicken and mashed potatoes, he ordered a spinach salad.

"Food weighs me down," Obama explained. "It keeps me from thinking. Makes me sluggish."

When he was forced to cater a meeting, he brought in sand-wiches and chips from Subway. Not only does he have no taste for good food, Lloyd thought, he's cheap, too.

Augustine figured Obama was carrying 140 pounds on his six-foot-one frame. She was so worried about his eating that she invited him to her house for Thanksgiving.

"I'll be all right," he assured her.

None of them knew anything about Obama's personal life be-cause he never invited them to his apartment. Obama didn't live on the far South Side. He lived in Hyde Park, a few blocks from the University of Chicago, in a timeworn courtyard building with ill-fitting windows, chipped paint, and crooked venetian blinds. It was inexpensive, and it was in an academic ghetto, similar to the neighborhood he'd recently left in New York. Obama quickly discovered the Seminary Co-op Bookstore, an underground war-ren with sections devoted to such esoteric topics as "Critical

Theory & Marxism" and "Christian Theology," and paid $10 for a share, or membership. He lived as ascetically as a philosophy Ph.D. candidate, spending his meager free time reading serious books on history and politics. Kellman gave him a copy of *The Power Broker*, a thousand-page biography of urban planner Robert Moses; he considered it the best book ever written on how power-hungry politicians and greedy developers can destroy urban neighborhoods. After finishing *Parting the Waters*, Obama told Kellman, "That's my story." But even Kellman became so concerned about Obama's bookishness and overwork that he urged his protégé to get a social life. He didn't want the young man to burn out.

Obama and Kellman met regularly at the McDonald's on 115th Street, across the street from the Sherwin-Williams plant. The more Kellman got to know his new hire, the more he understood why Obama sympathized with people whose backgrounds were so different from his own. Like the residents of Altgeld Gardens and Roseland, he was an outsider, too. Growing up as an American in Indonesia, and then as a black kid in Hawaii, without a mother or a father, he understood what it was like to be different from the surrounding society. Outsiders can take one of two paths: They can ease their dislocation by conforming, or they can rebel. By quitting his suit-and-tie job to become an organizer, Obama had rebelled. He had thrown in his lot with the outsiders. That was why he worked so well with people facing poverty and discrimination. The difference between Obama and the folks in Altgeld was that he could go back to the inside whenever he wanted. He had an Ivy League education. He had opportunities. Kellman was always expecting Obama to quit organizing for a better-paying career.

The Mayor's Office of Employment and Training, known as the MET, was a citywide network of storefronts that posted job listings on bulletin boards and counseled the out-of-work on résumé writing, interview skills, and training programs. Like every other city service (except the police department), it was out of reach to residents of Altgeld Gardens. The closest branch was on Ninety-fifth Street, in South Chicago. That was an hour-long ride on two buses, and it was in a neighborhood that many blacks considered hostile territory—the Tenth Ward, stronghold of Alderman Edward Vrdolyak, leader of the white bloc that was always trying to thwart Mayor Washington in the city council. Jobs, as Obama had learned from his interviews with the steelworkers, were the Calumet region's greatest need. But the Regional Employment Network, that $500,000 job training program, wasn't doing a damn thing for Altgeld. First of all, it was in the suburbs. Second, Altgeld's people had no education, no marketable skills. Some couldn't even read. When Yvonne Lloyd had worked as a census taker, she'd encountered four generations crammed into a single apartment, all of them illiterate. They needed entry-level jobs. So why not bring a MET office to Altgeld?

It was the Developing Communities Project's first brainstorm. Obama wrote a letter to Maria Cerda, the MET's director, and wangled a meeting in her city hall office. Cerda agreed to visit Altgeld. In preparation for her visit, the group rehearsed as furiously as a theater troupe preparing the debut of a new play. As president, it was Augustine's job to chair the gathering. Hold Ms. Cerda's feet to the fire, Obama drilled her. Get a commitment to bring a center to Altgeld. A "floor team" was trained to keep audience members focused on the topic. Obama was the stage manager, carrying around a clipboard with a schedule of the meeting's events. On the big night, they pulled sliding doors across the Our Lady of the Gardens sanctuary to form a conference room. It was packed. OLG was the hub of community life in the Gardens, and an appearance by a city official was a big event.

Cerda arrived with two bodyguards, which made Lloyd snicker. She's afraid we're going to eat her up, he thought. And when Cerda got up to speak, she delivered a lecture about her résumé and her job at city hall.

"That's fine," Augustine said. "But the reason we're here is—"

"You don't even know what I do," Cerda retorted.

From the back of the room, a baritone voice broke the stalemate.

"Let Loretta speak!"

It was Obama, with his hand cupped over his mouth.

"We want to hear what Loretta has to say!"

The entire crowd took up the cry.

"Let Loretta speak!" they shouted.

Loretta spoke, and Cerda agreed to a series of meetings on bringing a center to the far South Side. It took six months of negotiations, and the MET decided to put the center in less-remote Roseland, but that was a victory because Roseland is only a fifteen-minute bus ride from Altgeld. It was a lot closer than South Chicago and a lot friendlier to blacks.

Even more exciting was the news that Mayor Washington would attend the ribbon cutting. A mayoral visit was a pageant that would fill South Michigan Avenue. Obama's phone blew up with calls from neighborhood politicians and pastors, begging for the chance to introduce Harold. It was his very first taste of power—for fifteen minutes, he would hold the most precious coin in Chicago politics, access to the mayor. Had Obama been more familiar with the Machine, he might have allowed the alderman or the state senator to speak before Washington, collecting chits he could cash in when he lobbied the city and state for money. Instead, he asked Loretta Augustine to introduce the mayor. That would promote the DCP, which had after all brought the intake center to Roseland. While Augustine had the mayor's attention, Obama instructed her, she should invite him to the organization's big rally that fall.

It was a raw spring day, with clouds the color of stone. Augustine dressed in a ruffled shirt and a belted trench coat, the nicest outfit she could afford on her salary as a teacher for the archdiocese. She waited nervously for the mayor on the windy street, which was blocked off with sawhorses for his arrival. When the limousine pulled up, the mayor popped out and waved to the crowd. A stout but nimble figure, he walked over to Augustine and gave her a hug.

"Ms. Augustine," said the bachelor mayor in the manner of a practiced ladies' man, "it's a pleasure to meet you."

"Do you mind if I take your arm?" Augustine asked. It was her job to stay close to the mayor. Plus, if she let him go, she'd be overwhelmed by the throng following him down the street. Everyone wanted to shake Harold's hand.

The pair strolled past the remnants of Roseland's commercial glory: Herman's Army Store, Old Fashioned Donuts, and the Ranch, a Western-themed steakhouse with photos of Roy Rogers and Tom Mix in its booths. Augustine pointed out the new facades on the Roaring Twenties storefronts.

When they reached the new intake center, Augustine gave a brief speech.

"This is the kind of success we can have when the community comes together," she said.

Reverend Alvin Love had walked the four blocks from his

church to watch the ribbon cutting. It was a big day in Roseland's history, he thought. Before, if you'd wanted anything from the city, you had to go through the alderman or a city hall bureaucrat who didn't know jack about the neighborhood. Before Obama walked into his study, Love had never heard of community organizing or Saul Alinsky. Now this little group of priests and preachers and housewives he'd joined was working in exactly the way Alinsky had intended, as Chicago's second party, a way for ordinary people to improve their neighborhoods without going begging to the Machine. It did help that the city had a mayor who'd beaten the Machine himself, with the help of just these sorts of church-basement groups. Community groups were welcome in the mayor's fifth-floor office. It hadn't been that way when Daley presided there. Organizers who worked in Chicago in the 1980s would recall the Washington years as a golden age, "a fantastic time to be a community person."

After Washington cut the ribbon, Augustine sighed with relief and headed for the punch bowl. Seeing her alone, Obama ran over in a panic.

"Where's the mayor?" he demanded. "You're supposed to be with him until he gets in his limo. You're supposed to ask about the rally."

Augustine gulped her punch and found the mayor, just in time to invite him to the DCP's fall rally. An assistant jotted down the information. Just as Obama had ordered, Augustine stayed by the mayor's side until the black car pulled up in front of the center. The MET did bring jobs to Altgeld. That summer, it hired teenagers to staff a program for children in the Our Lady of the Gardens gym. It also showed skeptical African-American pastors that Obama's Developing Communities Project could get city hall's attention.

"I think he really helped us to get organized in an effective way," Father Carmon would remember. "We had tried before to get the city's attention. When he came in, things really began to move."

The center stayed open only a few years, but that day on Michigan Avenue was historic nonetheless. It was the only time Barack Obama came face-to-face with Harold Washington. And if Harold Washington had never been mayor of Chicago, Barack Obama would not have become president of the United States.

Chapter 2

HAROLD

IN THE SOUTH SIDE precincts where he'd received a near-unanimous share of the vote in the last mayoral election, Harold Washington was simply "Harold," a beloved character whose official portrait grinned from the walls of beauty shops and four A.M. taverns, occupying the same position of reverence as St. Anthony of Padua in the homes of Italian Catholics. The black community was his family, because he had no family of his own. Long divorced, childless, he lived alone in a Hyde Park high-rise, his one-bedroom apartment barren except for piles of books and newspapers. He was not so much ascetic as indifferent to anything except politics. His ties were stained. His home-cooked meals were cans of Campbell's soup boiled in the can, because that didn't dirty a pot. As a young man, he had been a track star at DuSable High School, but as mayor, he ate so many deep-dish pizzas and Wendy's cheeseburgers that he snorted, "I can't run around a dime." A friend bought Washington an exercise bike, but it sat unpedaled in his living room. The mayor's idea of recreation was to leave city hall early on Thursday so he could spend the afternoon on political work.

Washington had begun his political career during the reign of Richard J. Daley, when most Chicagoans would have found a black mayor as horrifying as a black next-door neighbor or a black son-in-law. (A lot of them still felt that way even after he won. On the morning after Washington's victory in the Democratic primary, *Chicago Sun-Times* wiseass Mike Royko began his column, "So I told Uncle Chester—'don't worry. Harold Washington doesn't want to marry your sister.'")

Had it not been for Washington, Barack Obama might never have left New York. Obama wanted to live in a city with a strong African-American community, a community that controlled its own destiny. In the mid-1980s, that was Chicago.

"I originally moved to Chicago in part because of the inspiration of Mayor Washington's campaign," Obama would tell the Congressional Black Caucus Foundation in 2008 as he received its Harold Washington Award. "For those of you who recall that era, and recall Chicago at that time, it's hard to forget the sense of possibility that he sparked in people. I'll never forget how he reached out to everyone—black, brown, and white—to build a coalition for change."

Had it not been for Washington, who ruled for four and a half years without setting off a white-flight panic to the suburbs, black politicians would not have gained the confidence to run for the U.S. Senate, and whites wouldn't have had the confidence to vote for them. Blacks already had a long history of wielding political power in Chicago, but Washington was the linchpin figure who inspired them to expand their influence throughout the state of Illinois, and finally, across the nation.

"Everybody owes something to Harold Washington, because [his election] was something they never thought could happen," says Lou Ransom, editor of the *Chicago Defender*, the city's African-American newspaper. "If Harold can be mayor, what can't we do? Obama talks about the audacity of hope. That audacity grew into the notion that a black man can be president of the United States."

The black political culture that lifted Washington to city hall—and Obama to the White House—began developing even before Washington was born, in 1922. It had its roots in the First Great Migration from the South, which occurred during World War I, when blacks were needed in war industries to replace whites who had been drafted or gone home to Europe to fight for their native countries. Between 1916 and 1920, fifty thousand blacks moved to Chicago, riding north on the Illinois Central Railroad's "Fried Chicken Special," which traveled from the Mississippi Delta to the terminal at Twelfth and Michigan in fifteen hours, fast enough to get by on one box lunch. Many were lured by the promises of jobs and freedom in the *Defender*, which was left in train stations all over the South by Pullman porters.

"Have they stopped their Jim Crow cars?" the *Defender* asked its Southern readers. "Can you buy a Pullman sleeper when you wish? Will they give you a square deal in court yet? We'd like to oblige these unselfish souls and remain slaves in the South, but to their section of the country we have said, as the song goes, 'I hear you calling me, and have boarded the train singing "Goodbye, Dixie Land."'"

Mississippi bluesman Skip James sang about this land of promise in "Illinois Blues," letting his fellow blacks know that life in Chicago was better than chopping wood in a Delta lumber camp:

> *You know, I been in Texas and I been in Arkansas*
> *I been in Texas and I been in Arkansas*
> *But I never had a good time till I got to Illinois*

Timuel Black's parents came to Chicago in 1919 as part of that migration. Black's father was educated enough to read, write, and count, and self-confident enough to show up at the polling places on Election Day, always with a pistol in his pocket for protection. These qualities marked him as a troublemaker in Birmingham, Alabama—a "bad ass nigger," in the words of his son, who would become black Chicago's most prominent historian. The Black family was met at the Illinois Central station by relatives, who instructed them on how to behave in Chicago: Don't spit on the sidewalk; wear a suit, not a pair of overalls. If you're reading the *Defender*, put it behind a copy of the *Tribune*, so white folks can't see what you're up to.

Illinois was the Land of Lincoln, home of the man who had freed the slaves, so its race laws were extremely liberal for the era. Blacks had been granted the right to vote in 1870, and the first black was elected to the state legislature in 1876, just as post-Reconstruction politicians were stripping Southern blacks of their short-lived franchise. School segregation was illegal, and a civil rights law guaranteed political equality.

There was, however, a price for this freedom. It was distilled into this saying: "In the South, the white man doesn't care how close you get, as long as you don't get too high. In the North, he doesn't care how high you get, as long as you don't get too close." Chicago's blacks were confined to a long, narrow ghetto known as the Black Belt. It was bounded by Twenty-fourth Street on the north, Thirty-ninth Street on the south, the Rock Island Railroad tracks on the east, and Cottage Grove Avenue on the west. As the black population grew during and after World War I, the Black Belt stayed the same size. The whites made sure of that, both through genteel restrictive covenants among real estate agents and thuggish violence by Irish "athletic clubs," including the Hamburgs, who counted among their members a teenage Dick Daley. Between 1917 and 1921, fifty-eight homes were bombed by whites who resented the new migrants. In the summer of 1919, a lethal race riot broke out after a young black swimmer was stoned to death for drifting too close to a white beach. Fifteen whites and twenty-three blacks were killed, as young Irish toughs dragged blacks from streetcars and black snipers took potshots at hapless white deliverymen. Over a thousand homes were torched.

The riot taught blacks to stay on their side of the color line. By the end of the 1920s, more than three hundred thousand were corralled into the overcrowded, overpriced, rat-infested slum later portrayed in Richard Wright's *Native Son* and Gwendolyn Brooks's *A Street in Bronzeville*. Its population density and disease rates were four times that of the surrounding white neighborhoods.

It was this segregation, though, that allowed Chicago's blacks to achieve political power more rapidly than any community in the country. In that era, blacks still belonged to the Party of Lincoln. Their votes were welcomed by Republican mayor William Hale Thompson, who saw them as a bloc to counter the Irish, Italian, and Jewish immigrants who allied with the Democrats. By the late teens, blacks made up a majority in two of the city's fifty wards. They were fanatically loyal to Thompson, who led Chicago through most of the Roaring Twenties. In the 1919 mayoral election, the Black Belt gave Thompson 80 percent of its vote, as well as an admiring nickname: "the Little Lincoln." Following the great tradition of Chicago patronage, Thompson rewarded their loyalty with jobs, so many jobs that white Democrats derisively called city hall "Uncle Tom's Cabin." Edward H. Wright, boss of the all-black First Ward, became Thompson's assistant corporation counsel.

The election contributed to the tension that erupted in the

race riot. According to *Boss*, Mike Royko's biography of the first Mayor Daley, "Besides the threat they posed in housing and job competition, the blacks had antagonized the heavily Democratic white neighborhoods by voting Republican. They were given credit for Republican mayor William Thompson's slim victory that spring." During the campaign, Democrats had driven calliopes playing "Bye, Bye Blackbird" through white neighborhoods and passed out a leaflet depicting Thompson as the engineer of a trainload of Negroes. "This train will start for Chicago, April 6, if Thompson is elected," the leaflet promised.

More importantly, blacks had their own alderman. Oscar DePriest, first elected to the city council in 1915, would become America's most significant black politician between Reconstruction and World War II. Like many prominent blacks of that era, DePriest was of mixed race—a "quadroon," three-quarters white. His parents had been so active in Alabama's Reconstruction politics that they fled to Kansas after the Jim Crow laws were passed, fearing for their lives. DePriest arrived in Chicago in 1889, where he worked as a housepainter, sometimes passing for white to get jobs. Immediately, DePriest showed a talent for ward politics. A friend invited him to a meeting, where two candidates were vying for a precinct captain post. DePriest exploited the deadlock to win his first political office.

"The vote was twenty-twenty for rival candidates, and I saw right away that a deal could be made," DePriest would recall. "So I went to one of the candidates and said, 'Now you're the one who ought to be captain—I'll give you two additional votes if you make me secretary.' The man refused. I went to his rival and made the same proposition. He accepted. I was made secretary. I kept at it because it was recreation to me. I always like a good fight; the chance, the suspense, interest me. I never gambled nor played cards so it was fun to me."

DePriest was one of Chicago's great rogue politicians. Chicago's red-light district was in his ward, having migrated south following the Great Fire of 1871. After only two years on the city council, DePriest was indicted for taking money from brothels and gambling houses, and passing it on to the cops as protection. Defended by Clarence Darrow, he was acquitted but ordered not to run again by the Republican Machine.

DePriest kept his hand in politics by starting his own machine, the six-thousand-member People's Movement, which backed him when his next opportunity arose. He made it back to the city council in 1927, the same year Thompson was returned to city hall with the support of Al Capone. Thompson appointed DePriest committeeman—party chief—of the Third Ward. The following year, DePriest dutifully supported the incumbent white congressman Martin P. Madden against a primary challenge from an up-and-coming black Republican named William Dawson. Madden won but died before the November election. DePriest was in Indiana, taking the baths at a spa with a group of black politicians, when he heard the news. The next morning, he was in Thompson's office, demanding the nomination.

"You know, Oscar, I am with you," the mayor said.

One of DePriest's rival candidates, William H. Harrison, was an assistant attorney general of Illinois. In July, DePriest was indicted again, this time for allowing black racketeers to operate casinos. Harrison, a black independent who stood to gain by knocking DePriest off the ballot, offered to drop the charges if DePriest dropped his candidacy. DePriest told Harrison to "go to hell" and beat his white Democrat opponent by four thousand votes. Illinois's First Congressional District has had a black representative ever since, the longest run in the nation's history. The Voting Rights Act was decades away, but in Chicago, blacks were so concentrated on the South Side that whites couldn't gerrymander them out of a seat.

Washington, D.C., had not seen a black congressman since 1901, when North Carolina's George White gave a valediction declaring his defeat "the Negro's temporary farewell to the American Congress." DePriest wasn't just the South Side's representative. He stood for his entire race. In his maiden speech, favoring a bill to investigate American imperialism in Haiti, he scolded Democrats for caring more about West Indians than sharecroppers.

"I am very glad to see the gentlemen on the minority side of the House so very solicitous about the conditions of the black people in Haiti," DePriest said. "I wish to God they were equally solicitous about the black people in America."

DePriest appointed blacks to Annapolis and West Point. He fought to fund D.C.'s all-black Howard University. In the Capitol, an Alabama senator tried to prevent DePriest from using the Senate dining room. You're not big enough to stop a black congressman from sitting where he wants, DePriest told the senator.

In Chicago, pride in the only black congressman ran deep. DePriest was a hero when he walked down Forty-third Street, in the heart of the Black Belt (which had expanded since World War I), visiting speakeasies with his son, Oscar Jr. White Chicago may have had a Second City complex toward New York City, but black Chicago didn't. New York wouldn't achieve black representation until 1944, when Adam Clayton Powell Jr. was elected in Harlem. Harlem's population was more diverse, with blacks from the South Atlantic states, the West Indies, and Africa. It lacked the political unity of Chicago, where entire families and communities had migrated up from Alabama, Arkansas, and Mississippi. New York also lacked factories and the fat paychecks they provided. When South Siders drove to New York to see Joe Louis fight, they paraded their sedans through Harlem to envious whistles.

"The story of how the black migrants from the South gathered their strength to fulfill George White's prophecy is a story of machine politics—Chicago style," wrote St. Clair Drake and Horace R. Cayton in *Black Metropolis*, their study of the Black Belt.

So it took a shady politician from the Windy City to fulfill the promises of the Declaration of Independence and the Fourteenth Amendment. The beauty of a machine is that it offers a little something for everyone, even if it's only a free turkey for voting on Election Day.

DePriest liked to say, "I am a Negro before I am a Republican," but that wasn't enough to save his career when the New Deal converted blacks to the Democratic faith. DePriest had been a Herbert Hoover congressman. In 1934, he was defeated by a Democrat, after a black committeeman reminded his constituents that "Abraham Lincoln is dead."

The next boss of black Chicago was William Dawson, a ghetto grandee who strutted around Bronzeville on a wooden leg, which he stomped to give emphasis to his threats. Unlike his black power predecessor, Dawson didn't flaunt his race. If DePriest had been a Negro before he was a Republican, Dawson was a machine hack before he was a Negro.

Like most blacks who came of age before the New Deal, Dawson began his career a Republican. He changed parties only after seeing more opportunity on the other side of the ballot. After six years as alderman of the Second Ward, he lost his bid for reelection, so he accepted Mayor Edward Kelly's offer to become

Democratic committeeman. Soon, he was a congressman, sitting in DePriest's old seat.

Dawson's most generous political donors were the policy kings, the South Side numbers runners who sold poor blacks a chance at winning the rent money, at just ten cents a spin. They were a major force in the Black Belt's economy: The most successful owned vacation homes in Paris and Mexico.

"Now, if I were to run for a political office, I would have to raise campaign expenses," Dawson explained. "If I went to every professional man in the town, I would not be able to raise two hundred dollars. But if I went to the vice lords and policy kings, I would get two or three thousand from a couple of them."

At Dawson's urging, Mayor Kelly protected the policy kings. As Dawson put it, "If anybody is going to make money out of the frailties of my people, it's going to be my people."

But after Kelly went, so did the protection. As soon as Kelly was out of power, Chicago's organized crime mob, known as the Outfit, began knocking off policy wheel operators in a hostile takeover of the numbers game. Dawson appealed to Kelly's successor, Mayor Martin Kennelly, to defend his most important source of campaign funds. Kennelly, Chicago's postwar mayor, fancied himself a reformer (which made him completely out of place in city hall), and reformers don't stand up for gamblers. Dawson didn't forget the snub. When Kennelly tried to run for a third term in 1955, Dawson helped dump him in favor of Richard J. Daley. The Dawson-controlled black wards gave Daley over 70 percent of the vote.

Dawson was able to amass more power than DePriest because the Black Belt had changed since DePriest's day. In 1948, the Supreme Court outlawed restrictive housing covenants, and the well-to-do professionals who had provided the Black Belt with intellectual and political leadership immediately left for more prosperous neighborhoods. They were replaced by blacks of the Second Great Migration, many of them sharecroppers dispossessed from the Mississippi Delta by cotton-picking machines. Poor, barely literate, and country to the bone, these newcomers needed the jobs and welfare that only a machine could provide. Dawson could get you a nice apartment at one of the brand-new high-rise housing projects or a gig at the post office, sorting mail from midnight to eight.

Mayor Daley, who refused to allow anyone other than Mayor Daley to make decisions in Chicago, did not allow Dawson to choose his people's aldermen. Instead, he stocked the city council with a cast of docile South Side and West Side mediocrities known as the "Silent Six," who could be counted on to vote with the Machine, even when the Machine was blocking an open housing law that would have allowed poorer blacks to escape the ghetto. Dawson resisted Daley's power play, but as it turned out, the Silent Six helped solve a thorny problem for Daley's Machine and Dawson's sub-Machine.

"The blacks wanted out of their ghetto," wrote Bill and Lori Granger in *Lords of the Last Machine: The Story of Politics in Chicago*. "But how could the Machine encourage this without breaking up the old ethnic neighborhoods that gave it its strength? Nor did black Machine leaders have any interest in breaking up the tight black ghetto. Under Bill Dawson it was a powerful force as well as economically tied to the Dawson machine. Why let the chickens get out of the coop?"

DePriest, Dawson, and Powell all had one trait common to pioneering black politicians: light skin. Down unto Obama, mixed-race politicians have made advances that were later shared by the entire community. Virginia's Douglas Wilder, the first black governor since Reconstruction, was also light skinned. It's as though the color barrier can only be breached by someone whose ancestors have already lived on the other side.

"They were considered white," Timuel Black says of Chicago's first black congressmen. "They had to be smarter because they had white ancestors. That's part of the culture of America. That's true even today. Nobody speaks about it, but they can see it."

Black Chicago's fealty to the Machine began to fall apart during the civil rights movement of the 1960s. The poor black wards, controlled by Dawson, had provided the votes to put Daley in office and keep him there. One West Side ward, which was run by white precinct captains and white mobsters, voted for Daley 20,300 to 800. City hall rewarded its most loyal supporters with slights. Overcrowded black schools held classes in trailers, while white schools across the color line sat half-empty. The Robert Taylor Homes, the city's largest housing project, was separated by a highway from Daley's all-white Bridgeport—a highway placed there to maintain the color line. When black students moved onto Daley's street, he did nothing to stop the demonstration that drove them out.

Those insults could be borne—things were still worse down South—but when Daley's police began killing blacks, the community revolted. Daley, who had been seen as an antiwar liberal in the mid-1960s, changed his political persona to match the country's call for law and order. First, he publicly ordered police officers to "shoot to kill" arsonists during the West Side riots following Martin Luther King's assassination. The next year, police gunned down Mark Clark and Fred Hampton, the leaders of the local Black Panther Party. The men were shot to death in their beds during an early morning raid that the police and newspapers portrayed as a "wild gun battle." The killings galvanized Chicago's black political establishment. Ralph Metcalfe, the Olympic track star who had been a member of the Silent Six before succeeding Dawson in Congress, was transformed into a bitter critic of the mayor. Blacks couldn't take down Daley, but they did go after his hand-picked Cook County state attorney, Edward Hanrahan, who had plotted the Black Panther raid. Hanrahan was thrown out of office in 1972 by a coalition of inner-city blacks and suburban Republicans. It was the Machine's first big defeat, but a bigger one was coming. In the winter of 1979, Daley's successor, Michael Bilandic, dealt with the commuting woes created by a blizzard by ordering L trains to speed past stops in inner city neighborhoods. The snowfall was bad timing for Bilandic. The Democratic primary for mayor came around a few weeks later, too soon for the black community to forget the slight. Blacks voted overwhelmingly for Bilandic's opponent, Jane Byrne.

"Byrne's unprecedented showing accordingly provided black voters with a new sense of themselves, and the machine lost its aura of invincibility," wrote William J. Grimshaw in his book *Bitter Fruit: Black Politics and the Chicago Machine, 1931–1991.* "If black voters could elect a female mayor, why not a black mayor?"

Why not, especially when the female mayor turned out to be no better than the Machine mayor. Byrne dumped blacks from the school board, replacing them with whites. Desperate for a champion, black leaders pleaded with Harold Washington to run for mayor.

Washington had begun his political career as a minor operator in William Dawson's South Side Machine. In Chicago, every ambitious young politician needed a "Chinaman," a powerful patron who would secure him a government job and promote him for office when a spot on the ballot opened up. Washington's Chinaman was Ralph Metcalfe. Washington inherited a precinct captaincy from his father, and Metcalfe quickly put him on the city hall payroll as a lawyer in the corporation counsel's office. After Washington got into a shouting match with a white colleague, threatening to throw the man out the window, he stopped showing up for work, except on payday. That was okay, because he was still doing the important part of his job: getting out the vote for his Chinaman. In 1964, Metcalfe sent Washington to Springfield as a state representative, where he embarrassed the Machine by sponsoring an anti–police brutality law. He turned out to be a liberal, in tune with the movements of the 1960s and 1970s, campaigning for affordable housing, consumer protection, women's liberation, and abused children. After Metcalfe died, Washington beat the Machine loyalist chosen to take his old patron's place. He was congressman for the historic First Congressional District. In Chicago, that was as high as a black politician could go.

At first, Washington refused the calls to run for mayor. He had tried it in 1977, lost badly, and was enjoying his new job as a congressman. Then he offered a condition: He would run if one hundred thousand new black voters registered. Registrars hit the streets, urging blacks to "send Reagan a message" and "get Jane Byrne." They added 125,000 names to the rolls, expanding the black electorate by 30 percent.

Washington won the 1983 Democratic mayoral primary by defeating a pair of Irish politicians. Mayor Jane Byrne and Cook County state's attorney Richard M. Daley split the white vote, allowing Washington to squeak through with 36 percent. In a city that hadn't elected a Republican mayor since Big Bill Thompson, that should have been enough to ensure him victory. But Chicago had never elected a black mayor. The day after the primary, Irish, Poles, and Italians who had been baptized in the

Democratic Party began flocking to the Republican nominee, a Jewish attorney named Bernard Epton.

The election was entirely about race. When Washington campaigned at a church on the white northwest side, he was greeted by a jeering mob and the graffito DIE, NIGGER, DIE. On the South Side, a bus driver half-jokingly told his passengers, "Anyone here who's not going to vote for Harold Washington, get off my bus." In the black community, to be seen without a blue "Washington for Mayor" button was to be poorly dressed. Unfortunately, Washington's inattention to his personal and professional affairs had left him with a record of tax problems and attorney-client complaints, which allowed whites to insist their opposition had nothing to do with his blackness. He was so careless he'd neglected to file taxes for several years in the 1960s, which earned him a forty-day jail sentence. Epton ran an ad highlighting Washington's messy finances, ominously urging Chicagoans to stop him "before it's too late."

The city was so polarized that the chairman of the Cook County Democratic Party, Alderman Edward Vrdolyak, secretly urged white precinct captains to work for the Republican. He thought, at least, that he was doing it secretly. Two newspaper reporters had slipped into a meeting where Vrdolyak declared that the contest was "a racial thing." Their stories ran the weekend before the election. Washington won with 51 percent of the vote—all the blacks, most of the Latinos, and just enough white lakefront liberals who were reluctant to vote for a tax cheat but even more reluctant to support a candidate they thought was appealing to racism.

After Washington took office, Vrdolyak again tried to thwart him by forming "the Twenty-nine," a bloc of white aldermen who stonewalled every mayoral appointment and initiative. A local comedian dubbed the deadlock "Council Wars." *Time* magazine called Chicago "Beirut on the Lake." The black community was so politicized, so united in its support of Washington, that street-corner idlers discussed his school board appointments as avidly as they did the Bulls' first-round draft pick, a shooting guard from North Carolina.

Washington's election gave blacks a new sense of political confidence. To *Ebony* magazine, published in Chicago, the victory was as much an assertion of black power as Joe Louis's knockout of Max Schmeling. Chicago's blacks had knocked down the Irish Machine, which had ruled the city for half a century. Who was next?

The national Democratic Party was next. Jesse Jackson was inspired to run for president during the 1983 mayoral primary, after seeing former vice president Walter Mondale and Senator Edward Kennedy snub Washington. (Mondale endorsed Byrne, while Kennedy backed Daley, a fellow Irishman whose father had helped elect John F. Kennedy.) Jackson started a national voter registration drive and declared that blacks would no longer be taken for granted by the Democratic Party.

"Washington's win," he said, "is a particularly important victory, because it signifies to the world that a new inspiration is at work right here in Chicago."

The publicity-loving Jackson may have been eager to snatch back the title of America's leading black politician (with Washington as mayor, Jackson was no longer even number one in Chicago). Whatever the motivation, Jackson's run for president made an impression on Obama, who was still a twenty-two-year-old newsletter editor in New York. To a young black man with an interest in politics, seeing Jesse Jackson on the same stage as Mondale, Gary Hart, and John Glenn was a very big deal.

Chapter 3

THE ASBESTOS PIECE

THE WORKMEN BEGAN appearing at Chicago Housing Authority buildings in the spring of 1986. Linda Randle, an organizer at the Ida B. Wells Homes, a weary complex of cruciform apartment houses on the Near South Side, first noticed the men in white jumpsuits and breathing masks when she came to work one morning. A big white machine sat in the weed-scored concrete courtyard, and a yellow tarp hung from a seven-story-high roof. Cascading pebbles struck Randle in the face. She walked over to a man wearing a hazmat suit, knocked on his mask, and asked what he was doing.

"Removing asbestos," he told her. But he was removing it from only the first floor, where the tenant service office was located.

Every Tuesday, Randle met with her fellow organizers at the downtown offices of the Community Renewal Society, a nonprofit devoted to eliminating racism and poverty. At the next gathering, she began talking about the mysterious new project at Wells. Obama overheard the word "asbestos" and sat down next to Randle.

"We've got the same thing going on at Altgeld," he said. An Altgeld resident had discovered a newspaper ad soliciting bids to remove asbestos from a single building: the office.

When the Chicago Housing Authority began building its

vertical ghettoes in the 1950s, asbestos was considered the safest, most modern insulation available. Not until the 1970s did medical researchers discover that its fibers, if inhaled, clung to the lung, scarring tissue and impairing respiratory function. Asbestos exposure was the second leading cause of lung cancer, after cigarette smoking. CHA apartments were permeated with the material. Asbestos was wrapped around water pipes that ran along kitchen floors. It was in the floors themselves, as part of the tile.

Randle also shared the asbestos story with a friend named Martha Allen, who wrote for the *Chicago Reporter*, a muckraking urban affairs magazine. They peeled up a floor tile and took it to a laboratory, which found it contained between 30 and 50 percent chrysalite asbestos. Allen used that test as the basis for an exposé on asbestos in the CHA. Her story, which appeared in the *Reporter*'s June 1986 issue, included interviews with Ida B. Wells residents who told of constantly sweeping up white dust that drifted from decaying pipe insulation. One mother wrapped her pipes in plastic, because "that stuff was flying everywhere." "I was always cleaning it off the furniture and the floor, she said. "My kids were getting it on them, and they were itching."

Randle had lived in public housing and knew that CHA bureaucrats didn't give a good goddamn about residents' complaints. Their attitude was "Don't keep bothering us or we're going to find out what your kids are doing or what's going on in your apartment." But Allen's story was picked up by big media outlets. The *Chicago Tribune* ran a story, and Walter Jacobson, a bombastic local anchorman, started his own investigation. That gave the tenants some leverage.

At a Community Renewal Society meeting, Obama and Randle hatched a plan: They would bus Wells and Altgeld residents downtown to CHA headquarters, to demand a meeting with the agency's director, Zirl Smith.

This time, Obama would be dealing with a much larger, more obdurate bureaucracy than the Mayor's Office of Employment and Training. The CHA was far more than a landlord for poor black Chicagoans. It exercised a seigneurial power over its tenants. Terrified of eviction, they were reluctant to complain about even life-threatening problems. Many had waited years for an apartment. Losing it would mean moving back in with relatives or searching for a slumlord who would accept a public aid family. The projects were ruled by the Vice Lords or the Gangster Disciples, the elevators were broken, graffiti stained the stairwells, and steel mesh covered the balconies to prevent people from hurling objects into the courtyards. Still, the CHA was a step up from the cold-water flats in which many residents had been raised.

The bus trip would be pure Alinsky: the powerless using their moral authority to embarrass the powerful. Alinsky had done the same thing to Mayor Richard J. Daley in the 1960s, busing a caravan of blue-collar South Siders to city hall to force a compromise on the University of Chicago's plan to gentrify its surrounding neighborhoods.

"No one can negotiate without the power to compel negotiation," Alinsky wrote in *Rules for Radicals*, his manual for sticking it to the Man. "This is the function of the community organizer. Anything otherwise is wishful non-thinking. To attempt to operate on a good-will rather than on a power basis would be to attempt something that has not yet been experienced."

Obama sent out a press release and chartered a school bus from Altgeld to the Loop. Since it was an early morning trip, he even brought coffee, orange juice, and doughnuts. One of the passengers was Hazel Johnson, who had lived in Altgeld since the early 1960s. Johnson led a group of environmental activists that had battled the steel mills and a sewage treatment plant over dumping toxins in the Calumet River. She believed asbestos had contributed to her husband's death from lung cancer seventeen years before. The ride up the Dan Ryan Expressway took an hour and forty-five minutes in rush-hour traffic, so the residents were agitated by the time they got off. They were even more agitated when they were forced to wait in a hallway for two and a half hours.

"The director is busy," an assistant repeated, over and over.

Randle, whose Mississippi grandfather had taught her never to back down from a conflict, told Obama she wanted to bust through the doors and drag Smith out by his necktie.

"Linda, the only thing you're doing is getting up your blood pressure," Obama responded. "Calm down. We have to take the high road."

(While Obama taught Randle to keep a cool head around authority figures, Randle taught Obama how to behave in the ghetto, advising him not to wear his usual preppy attire when he knocked on doors in the projects. "Wear jeans," she advised. "No one's going to open the door if you look like a public aid caseworker.")

When the CHA staff realized reporters were waiting in the hallway, too, they invited the protestors inside for coffee and doughnuts.

"We want the director!" the residents shouted.

Smith never emerged, but through his aides, he agreed to attend meetings at Wells and Altgeld Gardens, where he would reveal the results of tests on pipe insulation.

The bus trip was a triumph, but Smith's visit to the Gardens turned out to be a fiasco. Obama reserved OLG's old, high-raftered gymnasium for the meeting and printed out leaflets, which were wedged into doors all over the housing project. More than seven hundred people crowded onto the pullout wooden bleachers, eager to hear just how bad their asbestos problem was. Obama assigned a young woman named Callie Smith to chair the meeting. Smith wasn't a DCP board member, but she did live in the Gardens, and it's a tenet of organizing that the powerful should be confronted by the people they're trying to screw over.

The CHA director was half an hour late. Then he was forty-five minutes late. Then an hour late. As the gymnasium grew restless, Obama walked around the room, urging people to stay in their seats.

"We need to keep this meeting together!" he lectured into the microphone.

Seventy-five minutes after the hour announced on the flyer, Zirl Smith finally arrived in his chauffeur-driven city car and took the stage before an angry, impatient crowd. The people of Altgeld Gardens felt they were getting the brush-off. Smith only magnified the insult with his first answer.

"Do you have a plan to remove the asbestos that's in our homes?" Callie Smith asked him.

Zirl Smith shrugged.

"I don't know," he replied. "We have not yet completed all the tests on the apartments. As soon as that is complete, we will start the abatement process."

The room erupted. "No," the residents shouted. "No! No!" The director tried to continue, but Callie Smith wrestled him for the microphone stand. Then someone in the gym suffered a seizure. The CHA director had been in the room less than fifteen minutes, but he used the medical emergency as an excuse to flee. Making a break for his car, he promised to call an ambulance on the two-way radio. But Altgeld Gardens wasn't ready to let Zirl Smith go. It hadn't gotten a straight answer about the asbestos in its floors and on its pipes. People leaped from the bleachers and surged out the door in pursuit, chanting "No more rent!" The crowd nearly surrounded Smith's car before the driver made an escape. The angry mob was completely beyond Obama's control, full of people he'd never trained to "calm down" or "stay focused."

After Smith rode away and the residents went home to their tiny apartments, a dispirited Obama asked the DCP members to stay behind and help him clean up. He blamed himself for the meeting's disintegration. Yvonne Lloyd convinced him that the ruckus hadn't been his fault.

"It wasn't us," she said. The DCP members had stayed true to Obama's training. They hadn't stood up and hollered when everyone else in the gym was acting the fool. "Sometimes, you can only control your own people. When you got a lot of other people throwing in, then you got a problem."

Even though the asbestos meeting ended in chaos, the asbestos piece was a success. The publicity from the *Reporter* article and the public meetings prompted the CHA to request an $8.9 million grant from the Department of Housing and Urban Development to clean up asbestos in Ida B. Wells, Altgeld, and three other housing projects. In the winter of 1988, a year and a half after the story broke, residents were shuffled into vacant units and motel rooms while the white-suited workers—some of them CHA residents— vacuumed asbestos particles from their furniture, stripped the insulation from the pipes, and retiled kitchen floors.

Even as a poorly paid organizer working in some of the city's most obscure neighborhoods, Obama was attracting the attention of powerful mentors—a skill that would later be essential to his political rise. First, he caught the eye of Al Raby, who had run Harold Washington's campaign for mayor and now headed the city's Human Rights Department. Raby was always on the look-out for young talent. After meeting Obama through a DCP proj-ect, he was inviting the young man out for beer and pool, and introducing him to fellow South Side liberals. Raby squired Obama into the office of Jacky Grimshaw, director of the city's Office of Intergovernmental Affairs, and dropped him off there for an hour.

"Al had this habit of finding young people who he thought might amount to something, and he would bring them into my office and introduce me and then leave," Grimshaw would recall. "I figured out my job was to talk to these folks and figure out if they were somebody of substance."

To Grimshaw, Obama was just another of Al's kids, "but you did get that you were talking to somebody who had a brain, who was easy to talk to. Nice sense of humor, that kind of thing, but I can't remember substantively what we talked about."

Raby also introduced Obama to his best friend, Stephen Per-kins, who worked for the Center for Neighborhood Technology, an urban environmental group. They ate breakfast at Mellow Yellow, a Hyde Park diner, where Obama impressed Perkins as "smart and committed and strategic." After that, they saw each other every six months or so.

Those meetings sound insignificant, but they were the begin-ning of one of this country's greatest social climbs, a climb that took Obama to the pinnacle of Chicago—and then American—politics. When Obama moved to the city, he knew no one except a great-uncle who worked at the University of Chicago library. So he set out to meet anyone who could help his career. Sometimes, he cultivated relationships for years before they paid off. Raby would write Obama a letter of recommendation for Harvard Law School. After Obama returned from Harvard, Perkins would ask him to sit on his organization's board. Jacky Grimshaw supported Obama's U.S. Senate campaign. After Obama won the election and signed a lucrative contract to write *The Audacity of Hope*, he bought the $1.7 million house next door to Grimshaw's.

As impressive as his ability to forge these friendships was the way he made influential people think *they* were cultivating *him*. John McKnight, a professor of urban studies at Northwestern University, was a cofounder of the Gamaliel Foundation, which trained community organizers. McKnight often attended the foundation's meetings, but in fifteen years, he'd never thought of getting to know an organizer socially. Then he met Obama. The young man stood out not just because of his inquisitiveness but because, unlike most Alinsky disciples, he was interested in understanding the motivations of powerful people. Most organizers saw the world in black and white. They equated compromise with selling out. Obama thought more like a lawyer, wanting to see "all the blacks and whites and grays." McKnight invited Obama to his house in Evanston and then his cottage in Wisconsin. In long talks, Obama told McKnight that he was beginning to think of Alinsky's methods as "limiting," because they focused on external institutions.

"You're organizing people in the neighborhood to confront institutions outside the neighborhood," Obama argued. "Shouldn't you also be training them to come together effectively to deal with problems in the neighborhood?"

That conversation was the beginning of Obama's decision to leave organizing for law and politics.

When Obama met Johnnie Owens, he was already thinking

about finding a successor at the DCP. At the time, Owens didn't realize that. He thought Obama just wanted to be pals. In 1987, Owens was working as a community planner for Friends of the Parks, and Obama was working to bring more facilities to Palmer Park, the grassy quadrangle across the street from Holy Rosary. Obama walked into Owens's office, looking to do some research, and they began to talk about Roseland's problems. Owens told Obama he'd grown up nearby, in Chatham, a neighborhood of middle-class bungalows closer to the lake. That seemed to pique Obama's interest.

"I'm pretty new to the area," Obama confessed.

Eager to establish a friendship, Obama suggested they continue the conversation another time. Not long after, the two men had lunch downtown. As they were walking up Michigan Avenue, Owens pointed at the Art Institute of Chicago, a block-long beaux arts museum with a pair of bronze lions flanking its stone facade. Its banners announced an exhibit by Henri Cartier-Bresson, one of Owens's favorite photographers.

"Yeah, you know, I'm gonna go check that out one of these days," Owens said.

"Well, let's go right now," Obama suggested.

They spent the afternoon in the gallery, looking at photos that Owens would always remember as astonishing.

Obama took this male courtship to the next step by inviting Owens over for Sunday dinner. It was a sign Obama was serious about the relationship; he rarely allowed anyone into his spare apartment. The walls were bare of posters, and Obama stored his James Baldwin, his Adam Smith, and his Martin Luther King biographies in an old ammunition box. Owens commented on a book that was critical of capitalism, figuring Obama agreed with the author.

"You see, Barack," he said, "this is one of the reasons we gotta change this system."

But as McKnight found, Obama's reading was motivated as much by intellectual curiosity as ideology.

"Yeah, but, John," he retorted, "if you want to be honest about it, where else can you find a system that allows you to do as much as you can do in this country?"

The whole scene—two guys sitting around after dinner, talking about ideas—was new to Owens. In his neighborhood, men drank together in taverns. They didn't hang out like this. But Obama lived in the academic enclave of Hyde Park, where even in the mid-1980s, the heyday of the Chicago Bears, Sundays were for brainy dinner parties, not football games. While Obama seemed secure in his identity as a black man, he rarely socialized outside Hyde Park, and Owens was one of his few black friends. Even his girlfriend was white.

Six months or so after they'd met, Obama invited Owens to Los Angeles for a two-week leadership training retreat put together by the Industrial Areas Foundation, the group Alinsky had founded. Owens was skeptical. In spite of his friendship with Obama, he thought of community organizers as impractical radicals standing on street corners and shouting, "Let's storm the Bastille!" Those two weeks changed his mind. He began to understand how an organized community, trained in the acquisition of power, could determine its own destiny. When they returned to Chicago, Obama asked Owens to come to work for the DCP, as his assistant. Owens accepted. This, he realized, was why Obama had cultivated him so avidly. The man always had an agenda, no question about it.

One of Owens's first DCP meetings was a training session at a hotel in the south suburbs. It was memorable not because of anything Obama said that weekend, but because of what he did. It was the only time any of the DCP's members saw their punctilious organizer cut loose.

"Barack, how did you even find this place?" Loretta Augustine asked when they pulled up in the Honda. "You musta worked really hard. This place is away from everything. Why are we here?"

"I wanted to eliminate all the distractions," he said.

That's Barack, Augustine thought. All business, all the time.

"However," he added, "at the end of training on Saturday night, we're going to have a party."

That was not the Barack she knew. Augustine couldn't wait to see Obama party. After the training session, Obama actually ate a full dinner, then set up a portable stereo and slotted in a tape of his beloved R&B. As soon as Obama began swaying to the bass, Owens tried to bust his chops.

"Barack, what you doin' out there on the floor?" he chided. "You know that ain't the place for you."

"What?" Obama shot back. "Who said I can't dance? I'll bust all y'all out."

Obama threw his hand over his head and spun it like he was twirling a lasso. Yeah, their director could write a funding grant and get a bureaucrat down to the Gardens. But he could *dance*, too.

As the leader of a church-based community group, Obama was attending a lot of Sunday services. Recruiting pastors was part of his job, and there's no better way to flatter a preacher than to sit through one of his sermons. Obama had arrived in Chicago unchurched, having been raised by a family whose attitudes toward religion ranged from indifferent to hostile. When his grandparents fled Kansas for the West Coast, they left behind the stringent prairie Methodism of their youth, exchanging it for Unitarianism, a less demanding and less judgmental brand of Protestantism. Once they reached Hawaii, they were far enough from their mainland origins to quit church altogether. Obama's mother, who married two men with Muslim backgrounds, would have fallen into the category of "spiritual, but not religious." A compassionate, nonacquisitive woman, she tolerated all faiths but embraced none. Her son would write that she was "skeptical of organized religion." Obama's father rejected Islam for atheism, making him the family member with the most conviction on religious matters.

Because he'd had no religious upbringing, and because he'd never lived before in an African-American community, Obama was only vaguely aware of the role the church played in black life. He knew, from his reading, that black Christianity had provided the spiritual underpinnings of the civil rights movement. But he didn't know that the typical black church also provided its parishioners with social services—food, clothing, and housing assistance—as well as political guidance. The pastors he met were African-American rabbis, as concerned with the temporal advancement of an oppressed people as they were with its salvation. Obama was put off by the political jealousies of some older preachers, but the more time he spent on the South Side, the more he began to see the importance of joining a church.

While Obama was determined to succeed as an organizer, it would be cynical to say he became a Christian to smooth his relations with the pastors. He was spending all his time working with religious people and seeing how churches could uplift a neighborhood. Every DCP meeting began and ended with a prayer. After a while, faith began to sink in.

Early on, Obama had several long talks about his spirituality with Reverend Alvin Love. Like his mother, he believed in God but wasn't sure he could fit into the mold of religion.

"I pray," he told Love, "but I haven't made the commitment I have to make as far as accepting Jesus Christ as my savior."

Love would have liked to have Obama as a parishioner but wasn't surprised to see him join Trinity United Church of Christ. Trinity was east of the Calumet Expressway, outside DCP territory. Joining a DCP church might have caused resentment among the other pastors. Also, Trinity's pastor, Jeremiah A. Wright Jr., was more cosmopolitan and intellectual than the Baptist and Church of God in Christ preachers Obama dealt with in his daily work. Their roots were in Southern gospel services. Wright was from Philadelphia, read Greek and Latin, and had studied at the University of Chicago Divinity School. His mother held a Ph.D. in mathematics. He planted a FREE SOUTH AFRICA sign on his lawn and welcomed gays and lesbians. That was common among white churches on the North Side, but most black churches were so traditional they still preached the epistle lesson "Wives, submit to your husbands."

Trinity's programs—it offered classes in financial management and counseled parishioners who were drinking too much or going through divorces—were a model of how a church could serve its community. The congregation appealed to both Obama's background and his aspirations. It was a magnet for well-educated strivers—the crowd W. E. B. DuBois had called the black community's "Talented Tenth." An offshoot of Congregationalism, the United Church of Christ had always occupied a high position on the social ladder. Trinity's members were seen as "very middle-class, stable" by other Chicago blacks. Obama was too cool and cerebral to feel at home in a storefront church with a name like True Vine of Holiness Church of God in Christ or Greater True Love Missionary Baptist. An Afrocentric minister, Wright dressed in a kente-trimmed robe and flattered his flock by preaching that Jesus was African. He appealed to its nostalgia for the down-home with such vernacular sermons as "Ain't Nobody Right but Us." But he also published a brochure called "A Disavowal of the Pursuit of Middleclassness." As so many pastors do, he preached against his flock's greatest weakness.

Wright's sermon "The Audacity to Hope" would inspire the title of Obama's second book. The biblical passage that was the sermon's subject, from 1 Samuel, was about Hannah, the barren wife of Elkanah, who continued to pray although God refused to bless her with children. But the message was about black America, which only advanced out of slavery, poverty, and ignorance because its people had hope.

"In order for a race despised because of its color to turn out a Martin Luther King and a Malcolm X, a Paul Giddings and a Pauli Murray, a James Baldwin and a Toni Morrison, and a preacher named Jesse, and in order to claim its lineage from a preacher named Jesus, somebody had to have the audacity to hope," Wright growled. "In order for Martin to hang in there when God gave him a vision of America that one day would take its people as seriously as it had taken its politics and its military power; in order for him to hang in and keep working and keep on preaching even when all the black leaders turned against him because he had the courage to call the sin of Vietnam exactly what it was—an abomination before God—he had to have the audacity to hope."

On the Sunday morning Wright delivered that sermon, Obama listened with tears streaming down his cheeks, never imagining that one day his name would have a place in that list of African-American pioneers.

By Obama's third year in Chicago, the DCP was thriving. With more than a dozen churches paying dues, Obama was earning $27,500 a year and employing Owens as a full-time assistant. So he decided to pursue a project that reached beyond Altgeld and Roseland: school reform. It fit perfectly into his mission of community empowerment. There was a move afoot in Springfield to establish local school councils—boards composed of parents who would have a say in hiring and firing the principals at their children's schools. The plan was adamantly opposed by Machine Democrats, who feared the councils would become training grounds for amateur politicians who might get the big idea of running for alderman. Obama organized a bus trip to the state capitol—another time-honored lobbying tactic—and conducted a teach-in on the three-hour ride down Interstate 55. The parents, who had grown up in Richard J. Daley's segregated Chicago, were skeptical that any politician would hear them out.

"They're not gonna listen to us," they told Obama. "They're elected officials."

"They'll listen to you," Obama assured them. Then he said, "This is what you do."

He split the parents into groups and gave each the name of a legislator. They were to write notes and hand them to the uniformed doorkeepers outside the house and senate chambers. It was intimidating just to walk into the capitol, past bronze statues of Abraham Lincoln, Ulysses S. Grant, and Mayor Daley, then climb three flights of marble stairs, past the two-story mural of George Rogers Clark parleying with the Indians, and stand in front of the ceiling-high wooden doors, among a crowd of professional lobbyists in suits and smart dresses. But the doorkeepers took the notes onto the floor. The legislators came out. To the parents' surprise, they listened and even asked questions. On the ride home, the parents, who had gone to Springfield glumly expecting to be ignored, were feeling sky-high—"energized, like we could do anything," one would later say. The school reform bill passed.

In the late 1980s, the Chicago schools were so decrepit, so indifferent to the task of guiding teenagers toward college, that Secretary of Education William Bennett condemned them as "the worst in the nation." No mayor in recent memory had sent a son or daughter to public school. Daley, Bilandic, and Byrne were Catholic, so their children were educated by the archdiocese, and Washington's brief marriage had been childless. At some inner-city schools, fewer than half the freshmen ended up graduating.

The Career Education Network, which aimed to prevent kids from dropping out of high school, was Obama's most ambitious piece yet. Obama wanted to recruit tutors for an after-school program at four South Side high schools. The tutors would help the kids study, but they'd also teach job skills and act as mentors. In a sign he was already maturing from organizer to politician, Obama wanted Mayor Washington to sign on.

"We can either partner with downtown or challenge downtown," he told Owens.

This time, he wanted to partner. It would fulfill his dream of working with Harold, and the mayor's endorsement would bring in other players. Obama got as far as a meeting with Joe Washington, the mayor's education adviser. It didn't go well.

Joe Washington (no relation to the mayor) was unimpressed with the young organizer from out of town. They got into a heated argument about the community's role in the schools. "He doesn't know shit about Roseland," Washington later told a friend. "Or Chicago."

Undeterred, Obama approached his state senator, Emil Jones Jr.

As president of the Illinois state senate, Jones would become Obama's political godfather. In the 1980s, though, Jones was just a backbencher. Obama wrote a proposal asking for half a million dollars in state aid. Jones could only deliver $150,000. That was enough to hire a director and four part-time tutors, and rent space in a Lutheran church. It wasn't enough, however, to spin off the Career Education Network into an independent organization that could eventually work in schools throughout the city, as Obama had envisioned.

Obama was frustrated. Owens thought he saw the wind go out of his boss's sails. After three years, he was beginning to see there was only so much he could accomplish from the outside, as an organizer going cup-in-hand to politicians. One weekend, he visited McKnight in Wisconsin, where he told the professor he wanted to quit organizing and go to law school.

"I've learned what I can from this, and I've seen its possibilities and its limits, and I want to go into public life," Obama said.

Obama asked McKnight to write him a letter of recommendation to Harvard. McKnight agreed but warned Obama that most organizers were unhappy in law and politics.

"The most important thing is what would you be satisfied with, because you have to do it every day," he told his twenty-six-year-old protégé. "To do something that's unsatisfying is a waste of life."

Lawyering, McKnight said, was nothing like organizing, "where you take the right position and fight for it to the end." And the essence of an elected official's job was compromise. That's why Alinsky had discouraged his pupils from getting involved in lawsuits or partisan causes.

"Most people I know who are organizers would not be satisfied with politics," McKnight concluded.

Obama understood, but he was still determined to follow his new course. McKnight wrote the letter, and Obama sent his application to Harvard.

After three years, Obama had not only learned all he could learn, he had also taught all he could teach. Thanks to Obama's training, the women of the DCP were starting to feel confident enough to undertake projects on their own. Waste Management Inc., America's largest trash hauler, operated the enormous landfill on 130th Street. The dump was a neighborhood blight. The tainted extract of sodden garbage leached into the groundwater through its porous clay lining. The gulls who perched on the Gardens' ziggurat rooflines were strays drawn away from the lake by the feast inside the dump. Word got out that Waste Management planned to expand into land abutting the O'Brien Lock, which allows river-going barges to enter Lake Michigan—the source of Chicago's drinking water. Alarmed, the DCP and the United Neighborhood Organization—a Latino group that goes by the acronym UNO— held a rally at Saints Peter and Paul Church in the South Chicago neighborhood. Two hundred people attended. That same night, Waste Management officials were meeting with community leaders in a conference room at South Chicago Bank, trying to win approval for the expansion. At seven o'clock, all two hundred demonstrators left the church and walked silently toward the bank. Once inside, they marched up the stairs and filed into the conference room without saying a word. The president of UNO read a statement about meeting behind closed doors to cut deals that would damage the far South Side. Then everyone left, as silently as they had entered.

Another rally, at the same church, was attended by the city's new mayor, Eugene Sawyer. Sawyer had been appointed to replace Harold Washington, who died of a heart attack on the day before Thanksgiving in 1987. DCP and UNO wanted a task force to debate the dump's expansion. Augustine prepared a speech. Since it was a bilingual crowd, she would have an interpreter. But she was asked to deliver one phrase in Spanish: *vamos a decide*. We will decide. Obama walked her through the presentation, including the pronunciation of those three words. When Augustine recited "*vamos a decide*" the room burst into cheers and chants of "We will decide!" For that performance, Augustine was appointed to cochair the task force, which succeeded in blocking Waste Management's plans. Obama, she believed, had given her the confidence to speak before a crowd.

"I wanted to follow him," Augustine would say years later. "I wanted to be part of the things that I felt he could make happen, and I really wanted to learn. He brought out something in me. I was never that outgoing before. I would feel like something needed to be said but I was afraid to say it. He changed that dynamic to the [point] that when I would be at these meetings, and I knew something needed to be said, it was something inside of me that overcame that fear of speaking up and out that went from 'Needs to be said, but I'm afraid' to 'It needs to be said, and if I don't say it, even though I'm afraid, I'm gonna die. I have to say it.'"

Johnnie Owens was surprised to hear Obama was quitting the DCP, even more surprised to hear he was quitting for Harvard Law School. Obama gave his assistant the news in a roundabout way that emphasized it would be a change for Owens, too.

"Are you ready to lead?" Obama asked Owens one day at the rectory.

"Lead?" Owens responded. "What are you talking about?"

"I've been accepted at Harvard."

"What?"

Owens was thrilled for his boss. On the other hand, he wasn't sure he was ready to take over a community organization. He was going to have to run the fledgling Career Education Network and deal with two dozen pastors. And he'd be succeeding a leader who, in three years, had become beloved by his followers. Loretta Augustine, Yvonne Lloyd, and Margaret Bagby were as loyal to Obama as they were to the DCP.

To make the change easier, Obama took Owens around to all the DCP churches.

"I'm leaving," he told his priests, bishops, and reverends. "John's gonna take over. I have complete confidence in him. If you like what I did, you'll like what he does even better."

Some did. Owens ended up serving six years as the DCP's director, twice as long as Obama. Alvin Love, who eventually became president of the group, thought Owens was the best community organizer he'd ever met. But, he always added, Obama had trained him.

It was different for the women of the DCP. None of them had expected Obama to stay forever—he was too smart, too talented, to spend his life driving them to church-basement meetings in a decaying Honda. They wanted to see Obama go to Harvard, but when they lost him, they also lost some of their devotion to community organizing.

"We continued working, but I guess, I don't know, I dwindled away," Margaret Bagby would say. "I just got tired, I guess."

Eventually, all three women left Chicago. Bagby found a house in the suburbs, Augustine moved to Mississippi with her second husband, and Lloyd, by then widowed, went home to Nashville.

Just before Obama left for Harvard, he wrote an article about organizing for *Illinois Issues*, a statewide political journal. Entitled "Why Organize? Problems and Promise in the Inner City," it was later reprinted in the anthology *After Alinsky*.

Despite the success of the civil rights movement, the election of black mayors, and the Buy Black campaign, the inner city still suffered, Obama argued. In some ways, it was worse off, because middle-class blacks, who had once been bound there by restrictive covenants, were now free to leave, taking their money and education with them. Politicians and businesses couldn't transform the ghetto "unless undergirded by a systematic approach to community organizing."

"Organizing begins with the premise that (1) the problems facing inner-city communities do not result from a lack of effective solutions, but from a lack of power to implement those solutions; (2) that the only way for communities to build long-term power is by organizing people and money around a common vision; and (3) that a viable organization can only be achieved if a broadly based indigenous leadership—and not one or two charismatic leaders—can knit together the diverse interests of their local institutions," Obama wrote.

Alinsky's disciples still believed an organizer's task was to wrest money and resources from powers outside the neighborhood. Why not, Obama suggested, build power within the neighborhood?

"Few are thinking of harnessing the internal productive capacities, both in terms of money and people, that already exist in communities."

That could have been a manifesto for Obama's next Chicago endeavor, which he undertook the year after he came back from Harvard.

Chapter 4

PROJECT VOTE!

IN HIS THIRD YEAR of law school, Obama was named president of the *Harvard Law Review*, the first African-American to win that position. His election scored him a profile in the *New York Times* and even more job offers than most *Law Review* presidents have to fend off.

Obama was getting calls from judges and law firms all over the country. Abner Mikva, a former Chicago congressman then serving on the District of Columbia court of appeals, invited him to interview for a clerkship. The old gray judge had heard about Obama from one of his current clerks, a fellow Harvard law student. Most of Mikva's young assistants were Ivy League WASPs, so he was interested in diversifying his staff. At least an Ivy League black would be different. Mikva asked his clerk to approach Obama on her next trip back to Cambridge. She did but came back with bad news: "He doesn't want to interview with you."

"Oh," Mikva replied. "He's one of those uppity blacks who just wants to clerk for a black judge."

"No," the clerk said. "If he were going to clerk, he certainly would interview with you, but he's going back to Chicago and run for public office."

Mikva was both floored and impressed. He himself had arrived in Chicago as an outsider, a Jew from Milwaukee who attended the University of Chicago Law School and decided to make his career in the city. On his first attempt to get into politics, he walked into a ward office and announced that he wanted to volunteer for Adlai Stevenson's campaign for governor. "Who sent you?" the man behind the desk demanded. Nobody, Mikva admitted. He was a volunteer. The ward heeler brushed him off with a phrase that became part of Chicago's political lore: "We don't want nobody nobody sent."

That is one brash kid, thought Mikva, who didn't know that Obama had already spent three years on the South Side. You just didn't come to Chicago and say, "Here I am. Elect me."

Obama could have gone to work at Sidley and Austin, the white-shoe Chicago law firm where he had interned over a summer and met his fiancé, Michelle Robinson, a fellow Harvard Law student who served as his mentor. But in spite of the money, Obama wasn't interested in becoming one of dozens of first-year associates in a corporate shop. Instead, he was responding to the courtship of Davis, Miner and Barnhill, a small firm specializing in civil rights litigation. One of its founders, Allison Davis Jr., was the son of the first black professor to win tenure at the University of Chicago. Another, Judson Miner, had been Harold Washington's corporate counsel. Miner called Obama after reading about his *Law Review* presidency in the *Chicago Sun-Times*. The piece mentioned that Obama was interested in civil rights and planned to come back to Chicago. Miner figured everyone in the country would be trying to hire this guy, but Davis, Miner *was* the leading civil rights firm in Chicago. He had nothing to lose by throwing his hat in the ring. Thinking, What the hell? he dialed the *Law Review* office and asked for Obama.

"Is this a recruiting call?" the secretary asked.

"Well, I really don't know the fella, so I guess it's a recruiting call," Miner said. "It's a curiosity call."

"All right," she said with a sigh. "I'll put you on the list. You're number six hundred forty-three."

"Okay. Great. Here's the deal. I'll let you use my name if you promise to call me as I percolate to the top, so I can prepare for this phone call."

The secretary never called back. Obama did—that same day. When Miner returned home from an evening bike ride, his daughter told him that "a man with a very funny name" had left a message. Obama knew about Miner's work in the Washington administration. They agreed to have lunch the next time Obama came to Chicago for a job interview.

"You won't be offended if I fly there on another law firm's dime, will you?" Obama asked.

Miner ran a twelve-lawyer office, so he said no, he wouldn't.

They met at a Thai takeout joint and talked for three hours. Obama was impressed to learn that Davis, Miner gave legal advice to not-for-profits in the black and Latino community, helping them set up government partnerships. That offered the possibilty of continuing his work as an organizer.

"How satisfying is it dealing with these problems as a lawyer?" Obama asked Miner. "Have you ever thought you could have been more effective addressing those issues in some way other than being a lawyer?"

Miner went back to his office, called his wife, and told her he'd just had lunch with the most impressive law student he'd ever met. Like so many powerful, accomplished men before and after him, he had succumbed to Obama's talent for charming potential mentors.

"Gosh, I don't know that I've ever met a young man who was more comfortable with himself," Miner gushed. "He's just enormously comfortable with his own intellectual capacity, and not in an offensive way at all, in an enormously positive way. He never once reminded me who he was. This kid has powerful credentials, but he didn't brag about that or say 'I can do whatever I want.' He was just a curious kid who had a lot of questions. There was an even keel to him."

After another half-dozen lunches, Obama agreed to join Davis, Miner. But, he said, he was going to need a year off first. He was working on a book, which would be published as *Dreams from My Father*. He didn't want to start full-time until he was sure the writing wouldn't be a distraction. And he'd agreed to head up a voter registration drive that summer. Miner knew that nearly every other law firm in Chicago was pursuing Obama, offering to pay for his bar exam and let him do whatever he wanted until he was ready to start. The first black president of the *Harvard Law Review* was the class of '91's most coveted rookie. So Miner said, "Fine, Barack. See you next year."

Project Vote! was the brainchild of Sandy Newman, a Washington, D.C., lawyer and civil rights activist looking to register minority voters. Newman focused his efforts on D.C. and had only been tangentially involved with Chicago, donating money to the registration drive that helped elect Harold Washington. He'd avoided the city because in Chicago, voter registration was closely controlled by ward organizations, which typically paid street beaters a buck for every voter they signed up.

In the early 1990s, Chicago's black political community was in a funk. Washington had been dead for four years, and the new mayor, Richard M. Daley, had beaten black candidates two elections in a row. Blacks created the Harold Washington Party in an attempt to keep control of city hall, but the movement foundered without its namesake political genius. Washington had drawn in Latinos and white liberals with a message of inclusion; his would-be successors drove them away by shouting about black empowerment. Worn-out and discouraged by their loss of power, by 1991 Chicago blacks were voting at their lowest rate ever. As a transient community with a high proportion of renters, blacks needed continual reminders to register. It had been nearly a decade since anyone had given them a good reason. Newman thought a Project Vote! chapter might reverse that trend.

In search of a director, Newman called his community organizing contacts in the city. They kept mentioning this ex-organizer who'd just returned to town from Harvard Law School. So Newman hired Barack Obama.

Even before Obama registered a voter, Project Vote! got a huge break. Carol Moseley Braun was the Cook County recorder of deeds, an obscure clerical office, but she decided to seek the Democratic nomination for U.S. Senate out of anger toward the incumbent, Alan Dixon, who had voted to confirm Clarence Thomas to the Supreme Court. A wealthy trial lawyer also ran, making it a three-way race. When the two white guys eviscerated each other, Moseley Braun slipped between them to win the March primary. Blacks were thrilled by the prospect of electing a sister to the all-white Senate.

As a grassroots campaign, Project Vote! was a bridge between Obama's past as a community organizer and his future as a politician. It was also a chance to duplicate the effort that had brought his idol Harold Washington to power.

Still a rube about the mechanics of Chicago politics, Obama

went to see a West Side alderman who had worked on Washington's registration drive. He walked into Sam Burrell's office carrying a book bag, looking like a law student.

"You've been successful at this," Obama said to Burrell.

Burrell gave Obama an explanation he probably didn't want to hear.

"The reason I'm so successful is that I reimburse them for expenses," he explained. "I pay a dollar a vote."

Burrell offered Obama the services of his office manager, Carol Anne Harwell. They set up headquarters on Michigan Avenue with a five-person staff. Officially, Harwell was a secretary, taking care of "the female things" around the office, but she became one of Obama's first guides to black Chicago politics. As a West Sider, she taught him that her part of town was different from the South Side he'd gotten to know. West Side blacks were even poorer than South Side blacks, she explained. Closer to their Southern roots. South Siders looked down on West Siders as "country," while West Siders thought South Siders were stuck-up, "bourgeois." That was all new to Obama.

"He didn't know anything," Harwell would recall. "He was so naive. I gave him the address of a meeting on the West Side. We didn't have cell phones or pagers. Barack is very punctual. He was a couple of minutes late. He has this Kansas City twang. He said, 'Y'all didn't think I was ever gonna get there. I had no idea Chicago is that big.' "

It may have been the most intense summer of Obama's life, a test of the discipline and organization he had already shown as a community organizer and a law student. Not only was he running a voter registration drive, he was writing his memoir, studying for the bar exam, and preparing for his wedding to Michelle that fall. In exchange for $200,000 in seed money, Obama had promised Newman 150,000 new voters. In spite of Burrell's advice, he was adamant that he wasn't going to buy those names, Chicago-style. But Obama needed Burrell's operation, the United Voter Registration League, to sign up voters on the West Side. So he worked out an accounting trick that allowed him to look honest while still acknowledging the realities of inner-city politics. Burrell's workers were paid "expenses" for car fare and lunch. Inevitably, those expenses worked out to a dollar a voter.

On the South Side, with its older, more prosperous black community and better-established civic groups, Obama had an easier time finding volunteers. He started at his own church. Once Obama got Reverend Wright behind the campaign, he could count on forty or fifty bodies every weekend. (Trinity was the largest church in the Twenty-first Ward, so that was one alderman Obama didn't have to ask for help.) The NAACP and Operation PUSH contributed volunteers. So did ACORN, beginning Obama's long involvement with that activist group. They stood outside L stations, supermarkets, and welfare offices. They trolled Taste of Chicago, a civic eating festival that draws six-figure crowds to Grant Park, the great lakefront commons. Obama signed up voters at the Bud Billiken Parade, which marches through the South Side's black neighborhoods each July.

But not everyone embraced Project Vote! Obama got the brush-off from Lu Palmer, a militant journalist and radio host who ran the Black Independent Political Organization, a group that considered itself the torchbearer of Harold Washington's legacy. Palmer, who was practically a separatist, was suspicious of the half-white, half-Kenyan guy with the Harvard degree and the Hyde Park apartment.

"When Obama first hit town, my recollection is that he came here running some voter registration drive," Palmer would say a few years later. "He came to our office and tried to get us involved, and we were turned off then. We sent him running. We didn't like his arrogance, his air."

As a former organizer, Obama's instinct was to bypass politicians and work with community groups. Moseley Braun made that power-to-the-people ideal easy to achieve. Her primary campaign had been an insurgency against a regular Democrat: Alan Dixon, a former Illinois secretary of state, was a genial, undistinguished solon who went by the nickname "Al the Pal." The ward bosses would have pushed harder for Dixon in the general election. But the NAACP chairmen and the church ladies in white gloves and feathered hats were thrilled to sign up voters for Moseley Braun. There had only been one black senator since Reconstruction. And there had never been a black woman. Project Vote! was officially nonpartisan, but it practically became an arm of the Moseley Braun campaign. "We have got to get Carol elected" was in the mind of every volunteer. All over town, blacks were telling registrars, "I want to register. Carol Moseley Braun is running for Senate." Bill Clinton was also on the ballot that year, but in black Chicago, he hardly figured as a selling point.

Black pride was running high all over the country in 1992. It was the summer of Spike Lee's *Malcolm X*. Young people wore silver X baseball caps and black power T-shirts. One shirt bore the in-your-face motto IT'S A BLACK THING, YOU WOULDN'T UNDERSTAND. Another featured a triptych of three black idols, Martin Luther King, Malcolm X, and Nelson Mandela (who had just been released from prison and would soon be elected president of South Africa), with the legend MARTIN, MALCOLM, MANDELA AND ME.

Obama wanted to tap into that spirit, so he asked his staff for a slogan that would connect Project Vote! to the legacy of Malcolm X.

Someone came up with "Register and Vote by Any Means Necessary."

"It's kind of harsh," said Obama, showing an ear for what would sound too militant to whites.

"How about 'It's a Power Thing'?" suggested a staffer named Bruce Dixon, who'd been hired to organize the North Side.

Obama loved it. He added "Register and Vote" and had the slogan framed in a red, yellow, and green kente border. It was a coveted T-shirt and poster that summer.

Project Vote! made Obama a small-time celebrity in the black community. He spoke from the pulpits of churches, addressed a rally in Jesse Jackson's Rainbow PUSH headquarters, and was interviewed on WVON (originally Voice of the Negro, now Voice of the Nation), Chicago's black talk radio station. Since Obama was responsible for raising money to supplement Newman's contribution, he was introduced, for the first time, to the wealthy Chicagoans who would one day fund his campaigns for the U.S. Senate and the presidency. Ed Gardner, founder of Soft Sheen Products, an African-American hair care manufacturer, donated thousands of dollars. John Rogers, an investment banker who is now one of Obama's closest friends, was the fund-raising cochair. The chair, John Schmidt, was a Harvard-educated lawyer who had served as Mayor Richard M. Daley's first chief of staff. Schmidt organized events at the University Club, where Obama met big-time Democratic donors Lewis Manilow and Bettylu Saltzman, who eagerly wrote him checks. Chicago's liberal elite was enchanted by the articulate young black man with the Harvard Law degree.

"In front of that kind of audience, he was as good as he was going to get," Schmidt would recall. "He learned how effective he could be in a room full of lawyers."

At Project Vote! headquarters, Obama was an intense, disciplined, but low-key boss. He would sit in his tiny office, chain-smoking Pall Malls and studying tallies, always with one figure in mind: the 150,000 voters he'd promised Newman.

"How many registrations to get to where we need?" he'd ask his field organizers at their weekly meetings. "In order to get this funding, we gotta have these registrations."

Brian Banks, a Harvard grad and Altgeld Gardens native, was in charge of the South Side. When Banks tried to hire his live-in girlfriend to work on a freelance project for the campaign, he got a reminder that his boss wasn't from Chicago.

"Look, you can't do this," Obama told him quietly but firmly.

Banks responded with a "you're crazy" look, but Obama continued.

"We're not going to run this with people from your family getting paid," he said.

Obama was also learning to use his sex appeal as a political tool. With his baritone voice; tall, lean figure; brilliant smile; and Ivy League intellect, Obama was enormously attractive to females. To the middle-aged women of the DCP, he had presented himself as a surrogate son. But now he was a thirty-year-old man, running a citywide program with a six-figure budget. The head of Project Vote! was going to have to suggest a deeper relationship with his female followers, and Obama did. In politics, 1992 was the Year of the Woman. Most Project Vote! volunteers were women, as excited about Moseley Braun's gender as her race. They were also motivated by Obama's magnetism. One loyal registrar came back to the office with over a thousand sheets that summer.

Banks had played basketball in high school and college, so he knew about groupies, and he also knew when guys were exploiting their female admirers. Obama was aware of his charisma, but he was too focused on voter registration to fool around.

"One of the reasons this project was so successful is there were a lot of women who wanted to spend time with him," Banks would say. "He'd walk into a room, and there'd be people swooning. I've seen a lot of guys who used that to have sex, but he just wanted to use that to do something."

Project Vote! added more than 150,000 new voters to the rolls—a record for a Chicago registration drive. For the first time, voters in black-majority wards outnumbered voters in white-majority wards. And they came out in November, thanks to get-out-the-vote phone calls made from Teamsters headquarters. Over half a million blacks voted, the highest turnout since Harold Washington's first election. Carol Moseley Braun defeated her Republican opponent 53 percent to 47 percent, and Bill Clinton became the first Democrat to carry Illinois since Lyndon Johnson in 1964. Illinois became a blue state that year. It has not changed colors since.

Moseley Braun not only inherited Harold Washington's movement, she expanded on his achievements. Before Harold, a black Chicago pol's highest aspiration was U.S. representative. After Harold, it became senator, and ultimately president. Plenty of other cities have had black mayors—Detroit, Atlanta, Dallas, Houston, New York, Los Angeles, Philadelphia, Baltimore—but in none of those places have blacks achieved so much statewide political success. (Moseley Braun was actually the second black politician to win a statewide election in Illinois. In 1978, Roland Burris, a product of the South Side Machine, was elected to the first of three terms in the minor office of comptroller. Burris later served as attorney general, then became notorious when Governor

Rod Blagojevich appointed him to complete Obama's term in the U.S. Senate.)

Chicago has two unique advantages. First, it's in Cook County, which contains nearly half of Illinois's voters. Second, the local Democratic Party is a countywide organization. After Moseley Braun won the primary, precinct captains in white Chicago neighborhoods *and* the suburbs whipped up votes for her in the general election.

"They had to go out and sell the black person to demonstrate that the party was still open," political consultant Don Rose would explain. "It was a hard-fought thing. If you use Harold Washington's election as the pivot point, what you begin to see is black politicians making challenges to the regular organizations, and then the organizations having to support them."

Obama's success won him his first notice in the *Chicago Tribune*. In a special Black History Month section, he was named one of "25 Chicagoans on the road to making a difference."

"Barack Obama, 31, Attorney," the agate-type profile read. "A community activist who headed Project Vote!, a voter registration effort responsible for signing up many of the 150,000 new African-American voters added to the rolls for last November's historic election. In 1990, he was the first black editor of the *Harvard Law Review*."

Obama's wedding took place at Trinity United Church of Christ, with a reception at the South Shore Country Club, a once-segregated institution on the lakefront, just south of Hyde Park. By marrying Michelle, he was binding himself to black Chicago, where he'd chosen to make his home and career. The Obamas would eventually become members of the city's black elite, a community of entrepreneurs, doctors, publishers, attorneys, and politicians. Their Harvard degrees would help them conquer that world, but they hadn't conquered it just yet. Michelle had grown up middle-class, in the Highlands, an enclave of South Shore: Her father worked at the city's water filtration plant, and she attended Whitney Young, a public high school for overachievers.

Obama had two best men: his Kenyan half brother, Malik, and Johnnie Owens. The guest list represented both the life he was leaving behind and the one he was about to enter: Jerry Kellman was at the wedding. So were Loretta Augustine, Yvonne Lloyd, and Margaret Bagby. The only elected officials present were Sam Burrell and Toni Preckwinkle, a pair of aldermen who'd worked on Project Vote! Jesse Jackson Jr. attended because his wife, Sandi, was a childhood friend of Michelle's.

The DCP women were thrilled to see Obama marry Michelle. They'd been worried that their promising young man would be prey for "some jezebel or some bimbo." But Michelle was clearly as brilliant as Barack. When the couple made the rounds at the reception, Bagby told Michelle that her new husband was destined for the White House.

"Ahh, yeah, right," Obama laughed, the same as he'd always done when Margaret insisted he'd be president someday. Then he moved on to the next table. As a law student, he'd visited Roseland whenever he returned to Chicago, and as head of Project Vote!, he'd enlisted DCP members as volunteers. But after the wedding, those three women would rarely see him again.

Chapter 5

THE YOUNG LAWYER

IN EARLY 1993, Obama went to work full-time at Davis, Miner. He was given a narrow office at the head of the stairwell on the second floor, right next to Judd Miner's. He hung up a photo of Harold Washington—the same tinted studio portrait seen in so many South Side parlors—and set about doing the late mayor's unfinished business.

Davis, Miner carried the banner for Chicago's white liberals and black nationalists. A decade before they had united to put Washington in office. Now, they were out of power. In 1989, Richard M. Daley had been elected to complete Washington's unfinished term, defeating Alderman Timothy Evans, who skipped the Democratic primary to run as the candidate of the Harold Washington Party. It was another racially divisive election. Unable to hold Washington's multiethnic coalition together, Evans got only 7 percent of the white vote, a third of what his party's namesake had received. With the Daleys restored to the mayor's office, battles once won in the city council had to be argued in court.

"Judd Miner basically made his living by suing the city," said a man who served as an expert witness in one of his cases.

That's exactly what Miner was doing when Obama joined his firm. One of Obama's first cases was *Barnett v. Daley*, which alleged that the city's 1991 ward map was racially biased and should be re-drawn to ensure the election of more black aldermen. This was essentially a continuation of "Council Wars": Harold Washington had won his council majority in a special election, after a federal judge ordered that the 1980s ward map be reconfigured for ra-cial balance. The plaintiffs were members of Washington's old council bloc, the defendants mostly white ethnic aldermen who had sided with Edward Vrdolyak.

The 1990 census was the first in which blacks outnumbered whites in Chicago. Yet the city council had twenty-three whites, twenty African-Americans, and seven Latinos. The new Daley administration had maintained a white majority by creating wards where blacks made up more than 90 percent of the population, the suit argued. The Southwest Side—one of the city's most bitter ra-cial battlegrounds—was 68 percent African-American. Yet it had two white wards and two wards that were 98 and 99 percent black, respectively.

"To this day, electoral politics in Chicago is infected by racial bias and racial appeals, and it has touched on the right of African-Americans to participate in the electoral process and to elect can-didates of their choice unless they have voting control of a ward," argued Miner's brief, which charged that the redistricting vio-lated the Fourteenth Amendment, the Fifteenth Amendment, and the Voting Rights Act.

On *Barnett v. Daley*, Obama did associate work: he prepared discovery documents, joined Miner in taking depositions, and wrote memos. The case dragged on through the federal courts until 1998, long after Obama had left the firm for the state sen-ate. The plaintiffs won—sort of. The U.S. District Court of Ap-peals ordered one Southwest Side ward redrawn to add more black voters. The Irish incumbent won the special election.

Most of Obama's work at Davis, Miner had a racial or social-justice angle. He won an out-of-court settlement for a black medical equipment salesman who accused his employer of racial harassment. He sued a bank for redlining in black neighborhoods. Obama was deeply involved in a voting rights case, *ACORN v. Edgar*, in which he sued Illinois's Republican governor Jim Edgar for refusing to implement the federal National Voter Registration Act. The act, better known as Motor Voter, required states to register voters at the library, the Public Aid Department, and the secretary of state's office. It forbade purging voters who skipped an election. Given his leadership of Project Vote!, the case was a natural for Obama—a bridge between law and politics, as Project Vote! had been a bridge between community organizing and politics. Having worked with ACORN on Project Vote! Obama saw that registering poor folks would be that much harder if the state refused to obey Motor Voter.

Obama authored *ACORN v. Edgar*'s final brief, filing it on January 19, 1995, less than a month after Motor Voter took effect.

"ACORN as an organization is aggrieved by the State of Illinois' failure to comply with the mandatory provisions of the NVRA by January 1, 1995, because such failure significantly impedes ACORN's ability to effectively promote voter registration which would be much enhanced by the NVRA's streamlined procedures for mail-in registration and agency-based registration at motor vehicle, public assistance, disability, and other designated offices," Obama wrote.

"A significant number of ACORN members are registered to vote, but have not voted in the last two preceding calendar years because of a lack of candidates addressing their needs or for other reasons. These members wish to remain registered to vote and would be significantly harmed by being purged from the voting registration rolls, including being deprived of their rights to serve as jurors in federal cases. A significant number of ACORN members are not registered to vote, are not registered at their current residence addresses, or are likely to change their addresses in the foreseeable future. A significant number of ACORN members go to motor vehicle departments to obtain or renew drivers' licenses, or go to state offices to receive public assistance or disability services. These members would likely register to vote or have their addresses upgraded on their current voter registration if the registration procedures were implemented at these offices in the manner required by the NVRA."

The Republican-controlled state senate and the state board of elections countered that allowing people to register just anywhere would lead to vote fraud in Chicago—a timeless bugaboo for Illinois Republicans.

While drafting the brief, Obama organized meetings and traded faxes with a half-dozen other civil rights attorneys, soliciting opinions. But he was still a cub lawyer, and this was a hot case. Right after he filed, the League of Women Voters and the Justice Department jumped in. Obama stepped aside, allowing their lawyers to make oral arguments. In fact, he only spoke once during the entire proceedings, when he asked the governor's attorney whether the state planned to comply with Motor Voter by setting up a two-tier system that would only allow people to register for federal elections at the secretary of state's.

"Other people really took the lead in court," Steve Melton, an attorney for the Cook County clerk's office, would recall. "He was younger. Some of us were older than him. Other attorneys were from large firms, so it was natural to defer to them. Once the suit was filed, and it got some momentum, he still attended court hearings. It became evident early on that the judge was on our side. Others took more of a role in pushing the case forward."

A federal judge ordered Illinois to implement Motor Voter. The victory won Obama some attention from a good-government group that would later support his political career: the Independent Voters of Illinois Independent Precinct Organization. As its doubly independent title suggests, IVI-IPO represents the anti-Daley strain in Chicago politics. The group is especially influential in Hyde Park, where it was founded. For his work on *ACORN v. Edgar*, Obama won the IVI-IPO's Legal Eagle Award. During a dinner at the Blackstone Hotel, he was handed the plaque by Senator Paul Simon, every do-gooder's favorite political Boy Scout and a man who would one day play a big role in making Obama a United States senator.

Winning the *Harvard Law Review* presidency may have been the most important election of Obama's life. It provided him with a golden ticket to Chicago's upper class, preparing the way for all his later achievements. Had Obama simply been a black Harvard Law grad—or a white *Law Review* president—he wouldn't have been offered so much publicity, so much money, and so many jobs, from journalists, publishers, law firms, and political donors. But as the first black man to hold the world's most prestigious law school post, Obama was a blue-chip prospect, especially in Chicago, which is used to losing its brightest law students to New York and Washington. The *Law Review* presidency scored him a fellowship at the University of Chicago, where he taught until his election to the U.S. Senate and where he finally met Judge Abner Mikva, who became his first political mentor.

Obama's great-uncle Charles Payne was a librarian at the U of

C. Payne, the brother of Obama's grandmother Madelyn Dunham, boasted to a law librarian that his nephew was the first African-American president of the *Law Review*. The law librarian passed the intelligence on to Douglas Baird, chairman of the law school's Appointment Committee. Baird was perplexed, because Payne was a WASP.

"Sorry, you must be mistaken," he told the librarian. "I know Charles Payne, and he may have a nephew who's the president of the *Harvard Law Review*, but he doesn't have a nephew who is the first *black* to hold that position."

Shortly after, Baird received a visit from Michael McConnell, a colleague who would one day be named a federal judge by George W. Bush. McConnell had just published an article in the *Harvard Law Review* and raved about this kid named Obama who'd done a brilliant job editing it.

"He should be on our radar screen," McConnell suggested. "He might be interested in teaching law."

Baird dialed the same Cambridge phone number that so many other lawyers were calling that spring and got Obama on the line.

"I'm not interested in teaching law," Obama told Baird. "I've got a contract to write a book on voting rights. That's going to occupy most of my first year after law school."

(After the *New York Times* published an article about Obama's *Law Review* presidency, a literary agent landed him a $125,000 contract with Simon and Schuster. Due to the demands of law school, Obama was unable to finish the project. He later took a more modest advance from Times Books, for the book that became *Dreams from My Father*.)

"Why don't you write the book here?" Baird suggested. "We'll make you a law and government fellow. We can pay you a token salary and give you an office with a word processor."

If Obama did decide to teach law, Baird calculated, he'd already be on the U of C campus. And as every attorney knows, possession is nine-tenths of the law.

Obama accepted Baird's offer and hunkered down to work inside the law school, a six-story glass building with an inch-deep fountain in the courtyard. Its boxy frame and dark reflective windows rhyme not at all with the Oxonian courtyards on the main campus, built in the early twentieth century with John D. Rockefeller's fortune. After Obama had been at the school about a month, he returned to Baird's office and told him the book had taken an unexpected turn.

"It's really less a book about voting rights than it is my autobiography," he reported.

Baird was a little surprised—Obama seemed awfully young to be writing an autobiography—but he wanted to indulge his prize catch.

"That's not a problem," Baird said. "You should write the book you're going to write."

In the fall of 1992, as Obama was winding up Project Vote! and typing away on *Dreams from My Father*, Baird prevailed on him to teach a seminar called "Current Issues in Racism and the Law." The assignment came with a new title, lecturer in law, which Baird hoped would be the first step toward a professorship.

U of C is one of American academia's most expensive gigs. It's not quite the Ivy League, but your bank account can't tell the difference. At that time, both the faculty and the student body were 90 percent white. Obama's fifteen-student seminar drew a disproportionate number of African-Americans and Latinos. Not only were they excited about a class on minority rights, they were inspired to see a black teacher. Baird told a Latino student named Jesse Ruiz to go see Obama. Ruiz found the new lecturer sitting in his office, working on his autobiography. Taking time out to talk, Obama told Ruiz he had worked as an organizer in Roseland.

"I grew up in Roseland," Ruiz said, astonished.

Obama mentioned his *Law Review* presidency—he mentioned it often in those days, before he entered political circles where the *Law Review* presidency wasn't enough to get him what he wanted and where bragging about it actually turned people off. Ruiz realized he'd heard of the guy before. Prior to law school, Ruiz had worked at a steel mill in Indiana. He was sitting at his desk one day when he read about the first black *Law Review* president. I'm not going to be in the steel industry forever, Ruiz had thought, and if this African-American guy who worked in Chicago could be head of the *Law Review*, I could go to law school. Soon after, he enrolled at U of C.

Although his students might have welcomed it, Obama didn't use the seminar to preach liberal remedies for racial ills. That has never been his political style, and it wasn't his teaching style, either. He covered Supreme Court decisions from *Plessy v. Ferguson* to *Brown v. Board of Education* to *Plyler v. Doe*, a Texas case that granted rights to all schoolchildren, regardless of immigrant status. He asked his students to see whites' side of the issues— "Sometimes people have an inherent belief in some things," he explained, perhaps thinking back to his grandmother's suspicion of black men. And he warned the minority students not to carry their grievances into the courtroom.

"Just don't go with your gut," he told them. "As a Latino or African-American or an Asian lawyer, you're going to have issues, but you're going to have to keep that out of thinking like a lawyer."

Later, when he became a senior lecturer, Obama taught constitutional law. Jim Madigan, a student who later became a law school lecturer himself, took Obama's class in the late 1990s. Madigan was worried that a black professor teaching a roomful of white kids about slavery would make for some uncomfortable mornings. Obama flashed his liberal leanings by approaching cases from the point of view of the aggrieved party, whether it was Dred Scott, the slave suing for his freedom, or Michael Hardwick, a homosexual convicted of sodomy in Georgia in 1982. But even in the Dred Scott case, Obama was able to credit the concerns of slave owners, who expected to see their property rights respected, and of the Supreme Court, which worried that ruling in favor of a black man would incite the Southern states to secede. Overall, though, he believed that courts should play an active role in righting injustices.

As a gay man, Madigan was interested in how Obama would approach *Bowers v. Hardwick*, the sodomy case. Obama was not just a straight, married man. He was a smooth, handsome guy. Women crushed on Obama. That set him apart from the gray, abstracted professors who made up most of the law faculty.

"I remember myself, as a gay guy, when the *Bowers* case was on the horizon, I was a little interested in how it would be taken up, because he just had the vibe of a ladies' guy," Madigan would remember. "I guess I was surprised at how well he handled it. It was pretty consistent that he approached that case the same way that he approached the Dred Scott case, taking the perspective of this African-American guy, taking the perspective of this gay guy. I think there was a model of consistency there that I always found pretty impressive, because the thing that was very personal for me, but was pretty alien for him, he handled in the same way that something that seemed very personal to him but was pretty alien to me, like a race-based law."

Obama's preoccupation with the human consequences of a case, rather than simply legal doctrine, was just one way he cut against the grain of the law school's culture. U of C professors are sharply intellectual: At lunch in the faculty lounge, they enjoy a bloodthirsty debate on the merits of a Supreme Court decision far more than a discussion of how the case will affect a poor South Side family living a few miles from campus. In the classroom, the give-and-take is equally aggressive: One professor, who is now a federal judge, once reduced a student to tears. (Obama's lectures were more conversational. He was less interested in pontificating than in drawing students into the discussion. Unlike judges, politicians want to be liked.) U of C is a citadel of legal thought, known especially for its conservative thinkers. Richard Posner, the school's most prominent scholar, was appointed to the Seventh Circuit Court of Appeals by Ronald Reagan. Richard Epstein, a corporate law expert, became an Obama critic who took the negative in a debate titled "Should Conservatives Vote for Obama?" Still, U of C is an urban, intellectual, cosmopolitan institution, so its professors tend to be libertarians rather than social conservatives. They are more devoted to free markets than traditional values. (The economics school, whose many Nobel Prize winners share the same viewpoint, has a research institute named for Milton Friedman, a former faculty member.)

"The idea of being fervent about personal liberties is not really that out of sync with a lot of civil rights issues, at least civil rights issues as they emerged in the sixties and seventies" is Baird's explanation of how the faculty squares its philosophic conservatism with the personal liberalism that prevails in Hyde Park. "Everyone in the law school would be absolutely committed to not tolerating racial discrimination at all, not tolerating gender discrimination, or discrimination on grounds of sexual orientation, or anything like that."

Conservative liberalism sounds like an academic affectation, but "if you try to use the word 'conservative liberal,' you're missing the point," Baird would say. "They're against big government, but that's not the same as being against voting rights."

As a teacher, Obama was well liked, but he wasn't a star, even after he was elected to the state senate. Most students were more excited about taking classes from federal judges or full-time professors. A legislator just wasn't as glamorous. When Obama auctioned off a day in Springfield for a law school charity auction, it went for a few hundred dollars. Obama didn't spend a lot of time in the faculty lounge, either. Lecturers weren't expected to join in the law school's intense repartee. They had day jobs. Obama could be spotted early in the mornings drinking coffee in the downstairs Green Lounge, or playing basketball in the gym after work.

"Conservative liberalism" had no appeal to a lecturer who'd learned his politics in Altgeld Gardens. But Obama did find like-minded allies at the law school. Cass Sunstein, a constitutional law expert who became the most-cited legal expert in America, was Obama's closest friend there. (Obama would appoint Sunstein to his administration as "regulatory czar.") Both were progressive Democrats, but they were pragmatists, too. Sunstein hardened Obama's practical streak, testing his ideas with exacting debates and nudging him in the direction of judicial minimalism, the idea that judges should decide cases as narrowly as possible, rather than boldly remaking the law. At the University of Chicago, no answer is ever deemed definitive, and every answer begets further questions. That intellectual rigor could later be seen in the way Obama approached his work as a legislator, trying to find common ground by bringing together parties with conflicting views.

Obama also met Elena Kagan at U of C. She went on to serve as dean of Harvard Law School, until he appointed her U.S. solicitor general then Supreme Court justice.

If you walk through the main lobby of the law school today, the first room to the left has this plaque outside the door:

BARACK OBAMA

SENIOR LECTURER 1996–2004

LECTURER IN LAW 1992–1996

FELLOW IN LAW AND GOVERNMENT 1991–1992

FORTY-FOURTH PRESIDENT OF THE UNITED STATES

UNITED STATES SENATOR 2005–2008

ILLINOIS STATE SENATOR 1997–2004

DURING HIS TWELVE YEARS AT THE UNIVERSITY OF
CHICAGO LAW SCHOOL, MR. OBAMA TAUGHT
CONSTITUTIONAL LAW III, CURRENT ISSUES IN RACISM
AND THE LAW, AND VOTING RIGHTS AND THE
DEMOCRATIC PROCESS. CLASSROOM V WAS HIS
FAVORITE ROOM IN WHICH TO TEACH.

Classroom V, a tiered amphitheater seating eighty students, is also where Obama developed the eloquence that, when seasoned with the call-and-response rhythms of the black church, made him the greatest political speaker of his generation. As a constitutional law professor, his job was to encourage open conversation among students of vastly differing political views.

"Where in the Constitution do we find justification for *Roe v. Wade*?" he would ask. "How do we reconcile this understanding of the Fourteenth Amendment as it applies to sexual orientation?"

No other presidential candidate ever spent so much time think-ing deeply about the fundamental doctrines of American legal thought or the nuances of the American Constitution. His public voice, the soaring rhetoric of the 2004 convention speech or Elec-tion Night 2008, grew naturally out of the legal discussions in that classroom. Obama taught the Emancipation Proclamation there, speaking the words of Lincoln. The oratory of an earlier era of American thinkers was familiar to him, as to no other politi-cian, but he would use those antique cadences to express a world-view more modern than any other politician's. Lincoln had done the same, freeing the slaves with a document that could have been composed by Cicero. It's an advantage of being a lawyer-president, but it was only part of Obama's education as a public speaker. As he would learn, in a later campaign for office, a politician can't simply talk like a professor. A speech and a lecture are not the same thing.

Chapter 6

HYDE PARK

AS A HARVARD LAW STUDENT, Obama had rebuffed Abner Mikva's offer of a job interview. As a U of C lecturer and an aspiring politician, he was much more interested in putting his networking skills to work on the judge. In the years since their non-encounter, Mikva had resigned from the bench, served two years as Bill Clinton's White House counsel, and returned to Hyde Park. Now semiretired, he lived in a lakefront penthouse, where the doorman addressed him as "Judge Mikva," and lectured part-time at his alma mater.

One day, as Mikva was arriving to teach his class on the legislative process, Obama spotted him walking in the door and introduced himself.

"We've met before," Obama said. "At a reception."

Mikva had ribbed Obama about turning down the job interview. Obama, afraid he'd offended the judge, had assured him it was because he was so eager to get back to Chicago.

"Of course I remember you," Mikva said. Obama was easy to spot on the law faculty.

This time, Obama suggested they meet for breakfast. They did, and before long he was calling the older man "Ab." Obama could not have chosen a more reliable friend or a better model for his political career. Mikva was an avatar of the independent liberalism that defines politics in Hyde Park. Like Obama, he was an outsider to Chicago, having grown up in Milwaukee. In most neighborhoods, where the path to office is a degree from a local high school and years of ringing doorbells for the Democratic ward organization, that would have been a handicap. Not in Hyde Park. The University of Chicago welcomes outsiders—especially if they come from the Ivy League.

"We've got a lot of people who came from Harvard," as one political veteran puts it.

In a city notorious for segregation, Hyde Park was the first white neighborhood to welcome blacks—and to vote for them. In the 1950s, after the Supreme Court struck down restrictive covenants in *Shelley v. Kraemer*, middle-class professionals began moving from the Black Belt down to Hyde Park. They encountered no resistance, partly because the neighborhood was dominated by racially tolerant Jews and liberal professors, and partly because the new residents had college degrees. Hyde Parkers may be snobs, but they're not bigots. As the saying goes, they don't judge a man by the color of his skin, they judge him by how many books he's read. The newcomers—sophisticated First Migration blacks who listened to Ella Fitzgerald and Billie Holiday—found Hyde Park more congenial than their old neighborhoods, which were filling up with cotton pickers who loved that raunchy country blues played by Muddy Waters and Howlin' Wolf.

Hyde Park may be on the South Side, but it is not of the South Side. Crowded with expensive high-rises overlooking Lake Michigan, Hyde Park resembles the tony North Side neighborhoods at the other end of Lake Shore Drive far more than the weary ghettos a few miles inland, with their threadbare corners occupied by liquor stores and chicken shacks. The neighborhood is defined by the U of C, which sees itself as an island of culture surrounded by water on the east and slums in the other three directions. Students have long been warned not to stray beyond certain barrier boulevards. In the 1950s, the university became so alarmed by the impinging urban rot that it first threatened to move out of Hyde Park, then began an aggressive urban renewal project on its borders. Resentful South Siders called the project "Negro removal," and comedian Mike Nichols cracked that "Hyde Park is where the black middle class and the white middle class stand arm in arm against the lower class." (Saul Alinsky—not surprisingly a Hyde Parker—founded the Woodlawn Organization to fight the university's efforts.)

Blacks and whites also stood arm in arm against the Machine. Hyde Park maintained its independence because Mayor Daley had nothing to offer its doctors and professors. On Election Day, winos got muscatel, poor blacks got a turkey, and white ethnics got a patronage job as a bridge tender or a sewer inspector. The best Daley could offer a surgeon was a post in the Health Department, which wouldn't pay half what he made at the U of C hospital. Paul Douglas, the economics professor who became a United States senator, was Hyde Park's most celebrated officeholder. But Douglas was backed by the Machine, which needed a liberal reformer on the ticket as a loss leader to distract attention from its grubby regulars. Hyde Park's most beloved politician, the man who set the template for all the independents who followed, was Alderman Leon Despres. An old acquaintance of Leon Trotsky's (he had spent time at the Communist's Mexican villa), Despres was elected to the city council on the same day Daley was elected mayor and spent the next twenty years as a pain in the Boss's ass, the lone dissenter on countless 49–1 votes. Despres spoke out for civil rights and introduced an open housing bill, which only he voted for.

"We've got the only black alderman on the city council," Hyde Parkers boasted, "and he's white."

Normally, Daley punished rebellious aldermen by cutting off their patronage. But Hyde Parkers didn't want patronage. They wanted potholes filled, water mains repaired, and police on the street—which were actually easier to get if their alderman didn't have to beg the mayor for jobs, too. So Daley just cut off Despres's microphone whenever the alderman launched into an anti-Machine rant on the council floor. In the eyes of Hyde Parkers, who couldn't stand Daley's racism and election fraud, that merited a medal in the crusade for good government.

In 1966, Hyde Park elected its first black state senator, Richard Newhouse. He was a U of C Law grad, which made him good people. That was also the year Martin Luther King Jr. protested segregation in Chicago—the year before the suit-and-tie civil rights movement was succeeded by urban riots—and Hyde Park was full of whites who belonged to the Urban League and got a warm, self-satisfied feeling when they voted for a black man.

Mikva was already in the legislature by then. When a state representative seat had opened up a few years earlier, the Independent Voters of Illinois had gone looking for a candidate. The IVI, a group founded to smite the Machine, was influential in Hyde Park and a few North Side wards full of young professionals and folk music devotees. (It later merged with the Independent Precinct Organization to form the IVI-IPO.) The white Protestants had fled to the suburbs, taking their Republican votes with them, so independents were the only opposition to Daley's rule of Chicago.

The Boss's men dubbed them "goo-goos," a derisive term for good-government types.

Mikva didn't let his sponsors down. He joined a liberal bloc in Springfield that fought for open housing. When he voted with Republicans on an antipatronage measure, regular Democrats rolled their eyes. Patronage was the source of the Machine's power, providing an army of political appointees to get out the vote.

"He has to vote crazy like that," complained a Southwest Sider. "He comes from that crazy Hyde Park."

Mikva was elected to Congress in 1968. When Illinois lost a congressional seat in the next census, Machine legislators decided that Hyde Park belonged in Ralph Metcalfe's historically black First Congressional District. Mikva wasn't chased out of Washington that easily. He moved to the North Shore, whose liberal suburbanites were not so different from Hyde Parkers: They would vote for a Democrat as long as he wasn't allied with the mayor. Soon he was back in Congress, where he remained until Jimmy Carter made him a federal judge.

One of Mikva's successors in the state legislature was Carol Moseley Braun. It's no coincidence that two of the first three black senators since Reconstruction had their political beginnings in Hyde Park. There's no better place in America for a black politician to learn how to represent white constituents. The Voting Rights Act created more opportunities for blacks to win high office, but it also ghettoized Americans in segregated districts. Hyde Park is such a checkerboard that it can't be labeled black turf or white turf.

Moseley Braun "wasn't afraid of white people," said a white supporter. "She could be comfortable speaking to them and not having it in her head all the time that 'They're looking at me as a black.' She operated on the level that, 'Well, I'm the same as you are, and I have the same training and abilities that you have.' The one thing about communities like Hyde Park is everybody takes that as, 'Well, okay, that's the way it is.' The fact that you happen to be black doesn't undercut that."

By the time Obama arrived in Hyde Park, its biracial character could be seen at Valois Cafeteria ("See Your Food," their neon sign tells customers invitingly), where the short ribs special was priced for the budgets of winos and grad students alike. Valois was the subject of the book *Slim's Table*, which examined the wary relationship between the campus and the ghetto. (Obama ate breakfast there often. After he became president, the owners began setting out a placard each morning listing his favorite meal: eggs, sausage, and pancakes.) But Obama's favorite Hyde Park restaurant was the Cajun-themed Dixie Kitchen & Bait Shop. As a state senator, he would sing its praises for a local TV show called *Check, Please*. (The episode never aired because Obama didn't let anyone else on the panel get a word in.) On the chess tables in Harper Court, black hustlers played aggressive five-minute blitz games against nerdy math majors. The hustlers brought street slang into the chess vernacular, hooting, "Gimme them panties! I want them panties off!" after capturing a rook or a bishop. The tables were torn up after the chess scene got too rowdy. The Hyde Park Hair Salon, Obama's barbershop, laid out *Ebony* and *Jet* for waiting customers, but the owner, Zariff, could cut straight or kinky.

Barack and Michelle bought a two-bedroom condo on East View Park, a fenced-off block of identical three-flats a few hundred yards from Lake Michigan. Obama was often seen at the Hyde Park Co-op with his wife's grocery list—an errand that gave him a chance to sneak a cigarette—or on the basketball courts near Promontory Point, where high-flying ballers look as though they're soaring into the empty sky over the lake.

Obama was also building his visibility in Hyde Park's political and intellectual circles. In hip North Side neighborhoods, lampposts and kiosks are covered with flyers for indie rock concerts. In Hyde Park, they're papered with lecture notices. The life of the mind is big-time entertainment. The Democratic Socialists of America invited Obama to appear on a panel called "Employment and Survival in Urban America"—a coup for a law lecturer. The headliner was sociologist William Julius Wilson, a U of C idol who always drew a big crowd on campus. (In the mid-1990s, the *Princeton Review* named U of C America's worst party school, inspiring this joke: "Q: How many University of Chicago students does it take to screw in a light bulb? A: Quiet! I'm trying to study in the dark." They do cut loose once a year, around Hanukkah, when the university sponsors a debate on the tastiness of latkes vs. hamantaschen.)

Obama also appeared on a panel with fellow Hyde Parker William Ayers, to discuss the question "Should a child ever be called a 'super predator'?"

Bill Ayers and his wife Bernardine Dohrn were the sixties' most glamorous radical couple: The Bonnie and Clyde of the Weather Underground, they spent eleven years in hiding after an accidental bombing that destroyed a Greenwich Village town house, killing three of their comrades. Ayers came from an upper-class background—his father, Thomas Ayers, was CEO of Commonwealth Edison, Chicago's biggest utility—so when the couple came in from the cold, they didn't do time, the way some biker toolbox bomber and his old lady would have. Their case was dropped, due to FBI misconduct, and Ayers père used all his social clout to restore Bill to respectability. Dad's campaign was successful. Ayers became a highly regarded professor of education at the University of Illinois–Chicago, while his wife joined the faculty at Northwestern University Law School. As a professor, Ayers advocated "social justice teaching," a philosophy that gives students more control over their curriculum and parents more control over schools. Like Obama, he lobbied for the creation of local school councils in the late 1980s, although the two men never worked together on that effort.

Ayers and Dohrn settled in Hyde Park, where they were embraced in liberal circles. They became generous contributors to left-wing causes and sent their children to the University of Chicago Laboratory Schools, a private academy that educates the offspring of Ph.D.s, J.D.s, M.D.s, and even a few successful B.A.s. Its old boys and girls, who include Supreme Court Justice John Paul Stevens and thrill killer Richard Loeb, are known as "Labbies." (Besides their own sons, Malik and Zayd, the Ayerses also raised Chesa Boudin, the son of Kathy Boudin, a fellow bomb-thrower imprisoned for her role in a bank robbery that killed two police officers.)

"Bill and Bernardine are respected members of the community," says a friend of the couple who edits a radical magazine.

Another acquaintance, though, dismisses Ayers as a "narcissist" because he promoted his memoir, *Fugitive Days*, by saying, "I don't regret setting bombs. I feel we didn't do enough." On the book's publicity tour, Ayers posed for *Chicago* magazine with an American flag wadded at his feet.

Obama wrote a brief review of Ayers's book *A Kind and Just Parent: The Children of Juvenile Court* for the *Tribune*, calling it "A searing and timely account of the juvenile court system and the courageous individuals who rescue hope from despair." Ayers spent five years teaching in Cook County's juvenile court system, which was founded by Jane Addams, Chicago's proto-do-gooder, a pioneer in both education reform and community organizing.

Obama and Ayers both served on the board of the Woods Fund, a foundation that had supported Obama's work as a community organizer. But their biggest project together was the Chicago Annenberg Challenge. In 1993, Walter Annenberg, the Daddy Warbucks publisher of *TV Guide* and former ambassador to the United Kingdom, announced that he planned to spend $500 million to reform urban schools across America. Ayers co-wrote a grant proposal for Chicago, remarking on the overlap between the Challenge and school reform efforts that had begun with the local school council law.

"Chicago is five years into the most far-reaching attempt to restructure a major urban school system ever attempted," Ayers wrote in the proposal. "The Chicago reform law unleashed enormous amounts of civic energy around education. Since 1989, a strong and growing infrastructure of resources, created by community groups, civic associations, the business community, universities, social service agencies, and neighborhood organizations working with one or a cluster of schools, has been developed to support schools. Foundation and corporate grants to groups working on public education have quadrupled."

Annenberg gave Chicago $49.2 million, with the understanding that the local chapter would raise double that amount over the next five years. Obama was nominated for the Chicago Annenberg Challenge's board by Deborah Leff, president of the Joyce Foundation, which had funded the Developing Communities Project and had named Obama to its own board the year before. (The Joyce Foundation became a major contributor to the Annenberg Challenge.) As a thirty-three-year-old associate of a small law firm, Obama was the least-distinguished member of the group, which included the vice president and general counsel of Ameritech and the president of the University of Illinois. But at the first meeting, at the Spencer Foundation, an educational research fund with offices in a posh Michigan Avenue office tower, Obama was elected president.

From his new position inside the establishment, Obama reached back to help the neighborhoods where he'd worked as a community organizer. This was why he'd gone to Harvard. Instead of begging his state senator for five hundred grand to help a few South Side high schools, Obama now controlled millions, which could be spread out over an entire school district. The Challenge gave $100,000 to a DCP-sponsored group that aimed to increase family involvement in Roseland schools. It wasn't much different from the tutoring project he'd started with Johnnie Owens.

In its five years of existence, the Annenberg Challenge handed out 210 grants, almost all to elementary schools. The idea was to fund projects that gave teachers time for professional development, reduced class sizes, and connected schools. Schools were grouped into "networks," so several could participate in each program. The New Schools Multicultural Network, in a Latino neighborhood on the Southwest Side, got $650,000 to encourage English proficiency among parents and Spanish proficiency among students. The South Side African Village Collaborative received $27,500 to place six "village elders" in each of ten South Side schools. (Among them Bryn Mawr Elementary, Michelle Obama's alma mater.) The Challenge also funneled $264,000 to the Small Schools Workshop, which was chaired by Ayers. That money came directly from the Joyce Foundation, which meant Obama was involved in approving it twice.

A few schools claimed big successes. Galileo Scholastic Academy hired a full-time literacy coordinator who put teachers through Great Books training and started a young authors contest. In five years, Galileo nearly doubled the percentage of students reading above the national norm.

Chicago is an enormous school district—at the time, it had 410,000 students—so even $150 million was spread thinly. Each Challenge school got an average of $47,000—just 1.2 percent of a typical annual budget. After the Challenge ended, a study by the University of Illinois at Chicago found that the money hadn't made much difference.

"Our research indicates that student outcomes in Annenberg schools were much like those in non-Annenberg schools and across the Chicago school system as a whole, indicating that among the schools it supported, the Challenge had little impact on student outcomes," the study concluded.

Student academic engagement was "slightly greater" in the Annenberg schools. Classroom behaviors, sense of self-efficacy, and social competence were all "weaker."

Do-gooder money distributed from a downtown office building could not alter the demographics of the Chicago Public Schools: 85 percent of the students were black or Latino. An equal number came from low-income families. When Walter Annenberg conceived the Challenge, he wondered why the whole world wanted to attend America's colleges but not its public schools. His half billion dollars didn't change that. Obama's first daughter, Malia, was born while he headed the Challenge. Like most well-to-do Hyde Parkers, he ended up sending her to the Lab School.

The Annenberg Challenge undoubtedly helped Obama. It put him at the head of a major civic undertaking and placed him alongside the city's wealthiest philanthropists. The board met monthly for the first six months and quarterly after that. Obama's duties included meetings with Vartan Gregorian, president of Brown University. When Obama and Gregorian lunched at the Metropolitan Club, they were joined by Maggie Daley, the mayor's wife; Scott Smith, publisher of the *Chicago Tribune*; and Penny Pritzker, a member of the family that has used its multibillion-dollar Hyatt Hotels fortune to stick its name on theaters, libraries, parks, and the University of Chicago's medical school. Five years after that luncheon, Pritzker would become the first big-money donor to support Obama's U.S. Senate campaign. As a candidate for the state senate, he listed the Annenberg Challenge on his campaign literature alongside his civil rights work.

Bill Ayers wasn't Obama's "terrorist pal," as right-wingers would one day claim. But he was more than just a "guy who lives in my neighborhood," Obama's attempt to brush off the relationship. They were colleagues, members of overlapping social and professional circles, but they weren't close friends.

Obama *was* friends with Rashid Khalidi, the controversial Arab-American scholar. He had much more in common with Khalidi than with Ayers. Both were outsiders to Chicago, both had Muslim fathers, both had distinguished themselves at influential universities. Khalidi was born in New York City, the son of a Lebanese Christian mother and a Palestinian father who worked at the United Nations. An Oxford Ph.D., he headed the U of C's Center for International Studies. Author of *Palestinian Identity*, Khalidi supported a Palestinian state and harshly condemned America's unwavering support for Israel. The campus newspaper, the *Chicago Maroon*, called him "a University personality both revered and reviled for his heavy criticism of the State of Israel and American policy." Obama and Khalidi shared the sort of friendship that world-class universities foster. Even though Obama had settled in Chicago and married into a Chicago family, he was still the son of Honolulu, Jakarta, and New York. His outlook was as much global as it was local. He would be far more engaged by a discussion of Middle Eastern policy in the dining room of International House than an argument about the White Sox's pitching staff at Jimmy's Woodlawn Tap. Like Obama, Khalidi would go back east to realize his ambitions. In 2003, he was named the Edward Said Professor of Middle Eastern Studies at Columbia University. During a farewell party, Obama toasted him warmly, recalling conversations that had given him "consistent reminders of my own blind spots and my own biases."

Dreams from My Father was finally published in 1995. Obama gave a reading for two dozen friends in the back room of 57th Street Books and managed to cause a small stir in Hyde Park. *Dreams* was reviewed in the *New York Times* ("persuasively describes the phenomenon of belonging to two different worlds, and thus belonging to neither") and the *Washington Post*. Just as impressively, it scored Obama a feature story in the *Hyde Park Herald*, the neighborhood weekly. A lot of Hyde Parkers write books. It's the local industry. To really impress someone with your intellectual achievements, you have to win a Nobel Prize, and even those are a bit commonplace in Hyde Park. Chicago has had more laureates than any city in the world—most of them connected to the U of C. Obama charmed the *Herald*'s reporter. She noted his "dark brown eyes" and quoted him as saying that working as a community organizer in Chicago had helped him resolve his racial identity crisis.

"I came home to Chicago," Obama said. "I began to see my identity and my individual struggles were one with the struggles that folks face in Chicago. My identity problems began to mesh once I started working on behalf of something larger than my-self. Through this work, I could be angry about the plight of African-Americans without being angry at all white folks."

Obama tried to get his book reviewed by N'DIGO, a maga-zine for Chicago's upscale blacks. He made weekly phone calls to the publisher, Hermene Hartman, but she turned him down. Obama was a bright, ambitious guy but awfully young to be writing an autobiography, Hartman thought. And the story, with its scenes from Hawaii and Kenya, seemed too exotic for her au-dience. N'DIGO's rejection foreshadowed Obama's later diffi-culty in convincing Chicago blacks that he was one of their own.

Dreams from My Father was a modest success, selling around ten thousand copies between the hardcover and a Kodansha Interna-tional paperback edition that came out a year later. The book did little for Obama's political career. He never mentioned it in his campaign literature, although it did come up in newspaper pro-files as a helpful biographical source for reporters. Quite a few people who met Obama after 1995 had no idea he was an author and were surprised when they saw his name on a bookshelf. Dreams was available in Chicago bookstores for several years, but it eventually lapsed out of print, until 2004, when the publisher rushed out a new edition to take advantage of Obama's star-making speech at the Democratic National Convention. After that, it sold enough copies to make Obama a millionaire. For a writer, there's no better publicity tour than a presidential campaign.

While Obama struck out with N'DIGO, his networking was paying off elsewhere. A guy as skinny as Obama doesn't eat out all the time because he's hungry. In Chicago, he was establishing himself as the city champion of networking, a critical skill when you arrive as a twenty-three-year-old stranger in a place where everyone else started building friendships in grade school.

During his community organizer days, Obama often break-
fasted at Mellow Yellow with Stephen Perkins, vice president of
the Center for Neighborhood Technology. When Obama went
off to Harvard, Perkins thought the social change movement was
losing a promising leader. Now that he was back in Chicago,
Perkins asked him to join the center's board. The center needed
someone with Obama's interest in inner-city economic development. Like any aspiring politician, Obama wanted to build a
long résumé of civic involvement. Unfortunately, he didn't stay
long enough to make a contribution. Perkins had always admired Obama for being "strategic." Almost as soon as he joined
the board, he was running for the state senate.

Chapter 7

THE FIRST CAMPAIGN

A SEX SCANDAL created the opening Barack Obama needed to get into politics.

Chicagoans are used to seeing their politicians misbehave, but usually the transgressions involve a lust for money. A secretary of state is found dead in his Springfield hotel room, alone except for $900,000 in kickbacks stuffed into shoeboxes. A congressman uses official funds to buy gift ashtrays and trades in postage for cash, as though he's redeeming green stamps at the supermarket. An alderman shakes down a liquor license applicant for a bribe. The list of hinky officeholders is endless, repetitive, and forgettable.

Representative Mel Reynolds caused such a sensation because his sins were carnal, not financial. Reynolds, a second-term congressman from the South Side, was accused of having sex with a sixteen-year-old girl he'd met during his 1992 run for office. Reynolds had spotted the jail bait while driving around his district and pulled over to chat, even though he was supposed to be politicking and she was too young to vote. Soon after, she joined his campaign as volunteer and mistress. Two years later, the girl confessed to the affair to her next-door neighbor, who happened to be a Chicago police officer. The state's attorney set up a phone-sex sting. While sitting in a prosecutor's office, the girl called

Reynolds and told him she couldn't make their tryst because she
had to babysit.

"What you gonna wear?" Reynolds asked.

"Well, my peach underwear, like you told me to. I was hop-
ing we could do something really special but I see that's not
going to happen, I guess."

"I was definitely gonna fuck," Reynolds said.

"Really?"

"Right in my office. I was gonna masturbate too."

At the panting congressman's urging, the girl spun a story of sex
with a lesbian lover. When Reynolds asked if the other woman
would be willing to do a threesome, the girl said no—but she
knew a fifteen-year-old girl who might. A fifteen-year-old Catholic schoolgirl.

"Did I win the lotto?" Reynolds exclaimed.

There was no fifteen-year-old schoolgirl. But Reynolds's declaration of his lust for teenagers turned into a catchphrase. Jay
Leno joked about it on *The Tonight Show.* The case was so sala-
cious it made headlines in Chicago for more than a year.
Reynolds won reelection in his heavily Democratic district, but
by 1995, he was facing a trial that threatened to cost him his seat
in Congress.

Reynolds's downfall was so distressing because he wasn't supposed to be another Chicago pol. His election had represented
the same sort of postracial promise and generational change that
Obama's would a dozen years later. Born in Mississippi, raised in
a housing project, Reynolds had attended Harvard and won a
Rhodes Scholarship. After two failed primary runs, he finally
unseated Representative Gus Savage, a crude black nationalist
who campaigned by reading aloud lists of Reynolds's contributors, lingering over the names of Jews.

Reynolds protested that he was only guilty of phone sex and erotic fantasies, but as his trial approached, a challenger stepped forward. State Senator Alice Palmer announced she would run against Reynolds in the Democratic primary the following March. Palmer's seat was up for reelection in 1996, so, win or lose, she would be leaving the legislature. As a middle-aged woman, Palmer figured to be an appealing candidate against a congressman caught in a sex scandal. She immediately won the support of EMILY's List, which donates to female politicians around the country.

Palmer's state senate district included Hyde Park, so this was Obama's chance.

"If Alice decides she wants to run, I want to run for her state senate seat," he told his alderman, Toni Preckwinkle.

Obama also discussed his ambitions with Jesse Ruiz, his old law school student. The two were now friends, sharing an annual summer luncheon. In 1995, Ruiz brought a copy of *Dreams from My Father* for Obama to sign.

"You're the only guy I know who wrote a book," Ruiz said. "Who knows? You might make something of yourself someday."

That day was now, Obama told Ruiz. He laid out a plan for a political career that would begin in the state senate and culminate with his election to Harold Washington's old job.

"I'm going to need help from you," Obama said earnestly.

"Barack, Mayor Daley is going to be there forever," Ruiz said, scoffing. But he agreed to work on Obama's senate campaign. A state senate seat seemed achievable. Ruiz held a small fund-raiser in the apartment of his then-girlfriend (now his wife), raising $1,000.

Around this time, Obama had dinner with Douglas Baird. Now dean of the law school, Baird took Obama to the Park Avenue Café, a fancy downtown restaurant. The dean had woo on his mind. He wanted Obama to become a full-time assistant professor and dedicate himself to law teaching and academic writing.

During the meal, Baird asked Obama about his law school grades. Obama, who took his intellectual image seriously, shot Baird an irritated look. Wasn't a Harvard degree proof enough that he knew the law?

"Douglas," he said, "I graduated magna."

So Baird offered him a job.

"Barack, I'd like you to become a full-time academic," Baird said, "but you have to understand, if you become a full-time academic, you have to seriously commit yourself to academic scholarship. There's no sense getting into something if you don't have relatively clear expectations."

"Douglas, that's not me," Obama said.

Obama enjoyed teaching, but he didn't see himself as someone who wrote academic papers or attended conferences where scholars critiqued the works of Richard Posner. It was too far removed from real life. He was going into politics, he told Baird. He was running for the state senate. Obama even asked Baird for a donation. Baird wrote him a check but found it amusing that at one point during the dinner, Obama leaned over and revealed he was wearing an Armani tie. A guy in an Armani tie, Baird thought, asking me for money.

Obama wanted to run for the legislature with Alice Palmer's blessing. But despite his political involvement, Obama had never met his state senator. He had an in, though: Brian Banks, his old colleague from Project Vote!, was managing Palmer's campaign. Obama called him.

"I want to run," he told Banks. "I want to talk to Alice."

Banks arranged a meeting at the North Side home of Hal Baron. Baron, who had been Harold Washington's policy director, was chairing Palmer's campaign. At the meeting, Obama told Palmer of his plans.

"Do you have any problem with that?" he asked, wanting assurance, "and will you come back if you lose?"

The second question was especially important to Obama. By the time he met Palmer, Mel Reynolds had been convicted, been imprisoned, and resigned his seat in Congress. That meant Palmer was no longer running in the March 1996 primary. She was running in a special election, scheduled for November 28, 1995, which would give her enough time to refile for the state senate if she lost. And defeat was a real possibility because two better-known challengers had entered the race: Emil Jones Jr., minority leader of the state senate, and Jesse Jackson Jr., the thirty-year-old son and namesake of the civil rights leader. Palmer assured Obama she was all in. It was going to be Congress or bust.

Alice Palmer wasn't a Hyde Parker—she lived in nearby South Shore—but she was perfectly attuned to the neighborhood's character. She had begun her career as an academic, earning a Ph.D. from Northwestern and serving as that university's director of African-American student affairs. Although she was politically active—she founded the Chicago Free South Africa Committee— Palmer didn't get into electoral politics until she was forty-nine, joining in a rebellion against the remnants of the Machine. Her committeeman had supported Jane Byrne for mayor against Harold Washington. After Washington's death, progressives all over the city set out to defeat black and Latino politicians who hadn't had Harold's back. In 1984, Palmer was swept into office as part of the New Ward Committeeman Coalition, a gang of liberals who held regular meetings at a Mexican restaurant and supported pro-Washington candidates for city council.

Seven years later, Palmer was running a nonprofit called Cities in Schools, which brought mentors and money to inner-city students. Richard Newhouse, the long-serving state senator from the Thirteenth District, fell ill and resigned from his seat. It was up to the committeemen to appoint a replacement. They wanted Palmer.

"I'm writing a grant," she protested. "I'm busy."

But she was drafted anyway and went to Springfield, where she served as an independent Democrat, helping to ensure that lottery money funded education and holding hearings on universal health care.

Palmer did more than give Obama her blessing and promise to get out of the way. She introduced him as her successor. On September 19, 1995, Obama announced his candidacy before two hundred supporters at the Ramada Inn Lakeshore. Palmer preceded him to the microphone, where she anointed him as a scion of the lakefront liberal movement.

"In this room," she declared, "Harold Washington announced for mayor. It looks different, but the spirit is still in this room. Barack Obama carries on the tradition of independence in this district, a tradition that continued with me and most recently with Senator Newhouse. His candidacy is a passing of the torch because he's the person that people have embraced and have lifted up as the person they want to represent this district."

It wasn't just Palmer who signaled that Obama was the independent movement's choice. In attendance were both Hyde Park aldermen, Barbara Holt and Toni Preckwinkle. Also in the crowd was Cook County clerk David Orr, who as an alderman had been one of Washington's few white allies on the city council.

Obama began his first run for office with a lawyer joke. "Politicians are not held to highest esteem these days—they fall somewhere lower than lawyers," he said, before delivering the message Hyde Parkers wanted to hear: "I want to inspire a renewal of morality in politics. I will work as hard as I can, as long as I can, on your behalf."

Obama opened a campaign office on Seventy-first Street, far from Hyde Park but close to the center of the district, which reached south into South Shore and west into Englewood, one of the city's poorest, most barren neighborhoods. As his campaign manager, he hired another Project Vote! veteran, Carol Anne Harwell, who had run races for Alderman Sam Burrell, County Clerk David Orr, and Danny Davis, a county commissioner who would later go to Congress. Harwell had been baffled by Obama's interest in the seat.

"Why do you want to do that?" she'd said when Obama told her he planned to run.

"We can make some changes," he responded. Then he added, "Alice asked me."

Harwell's job was to transform Obama from a law lecturer to a Chicago politician. Despite Palmer's endorsement, his election was not a sure thing. There were two other candidates: Marc Ewell, the son of a former state representative, and Gha-is Askia, who had the support of Senator Emil Jones and a name as exotic as Obama's. Outside of Hyde Park, Obama was unknown in the district. Not only did he have to get known, he had to overcome the rest of the South Side's suspicion toward uppity U of C types. He decided to spend most of his time campaigning in Englewood. Starting every evening around suppertime, he'd doff his suit coat so he could roll up his sleeves and don the leather jacket he'd worn as a law student.

"Where are you going?" Harwell would ask.

"We're going to circulate some petitions."

"It's cold, Barack."

Undaunted, Obama would drive his Saab into the hood. He didn't bother to wear a hat or gloves, even as Chicago sank into winter. That was something else he needed to learn about local politics. After he caught a cold, Harwell scolded him.

"Barack, this is Chicago," she said. "You have to learn how to dress."

Obama was a big hit with the little old ladies who answered the doors of Englewood's worn two-flats and decaying houses. They were just as eager as the women of the DCP to mother this skinny young man. He was offered fried chicken sizzling in stovetop pans and invited to sit down and explain where he'd gotten that funny name.

"My father was from Africa," he explained, and that led to even more conversation, until Obama had spent fifteen minutes to get a single name on his petition. Door-knocking hours were six P.M. to eight P.M., and sometimes Obama would leave an apartment house with only three signatures.

"Barack, you can't sit and talk to them," Harwell lectured. "I'm gonna give you a goal. We're gonna do two sheets."

As with everything else he'd ever attempted, Obama proved a quick learner. His forays into Englewood also reawakened street smarts he hadn't needed in Hyde Park or at Harvard. One Saturday, as he was walking a precinct with Jesse Ruiz, a group of campaign volunteers ran up to Obama with serious news.

"There's a bunch of thugs coming over and asking us who gave us permission to walk in their neighborhood, and one of them flashed a gun," a volunteer reported.

Ordinarily, Obama didn't hesitate to approach gangbangers

on street corners. But these were his volunteers. And there was a gun involved.

"It's time to go," he snapped.

Obama got a boost from another old colleague when Bill Ayers and Bernardine Dohrn hosted a Sunday brunch for a dozen Hyde Parkers at their house. Again, Palmer was there and introduced Obama as her chosen successor, touting his bona fides as a community organizer, a Harvard graduate, and a law school teacher.

During the campaign, Obama found time to attend the Million Man March in Washington, D.C. And he was the subject of his first feature-length profile, a flattering, 4,300-word cover story in the *Chicago Reader*, an alternative weekly that served as a house organ for the city's independent movement. Obama told writer Hank DeZutter that he was running for office to empower ordinary citizens, just as he'd done as a community organizer.

"What if a politician were to see his job as that of an organizer," he wondered, "as part teacher and part advocate, one who does not sell voters short but who educates them about the real choices before them? As an elected public official, for instance, I could bring church and community leaders together easier than I could as a community organizer or lawyer. We would come together to form concrete economic development strategies, take advantage of existing laws and structures, and create bridges and bonds within all sectors of the community. We must form grassroot structures that would hold me and other elected officials more accountable for their actions."

The quote hearkened back to that long-ago conversation with John McKnight in the Wisconsin cabin. Obama had quit community organizing not because he disagreed with its goals, but because he wanted to be on the inside, making decisions. As a community organizer, he had protested decision makers. As a lawyer, he had sued them. As a state senator, he would finally be one of them.

As payback for Palmer's support, Obama acted as an adviser to her congressional campaign. He attended strategy meetings and helped develop a position paper on building a freight-handling airport in the south suburbs. Still, Obama felt conflicted about supporting Palmer, for both personal and political reasons. He wanted to help a mentor, but Michelle was an old schoolmate of Jesse Jackson Jr.'s wife, Sandi. Harwell had advised him not to take sides in the congressional race, to avoid making enemies of the Jacksons, or of Mayor Richard M. Daley, who was supporting Emil Jones.

Against those powerful Chicago dynasties, Palmer's campaign was floundering. By nature, she was an academic, not a politician, driven more by the need to change public policy than by the ego gratification of winning elections. This shared wonkiness was one reason she and Obama had hit it off, but it made her ill-suited for a congressional race. As a committeeman, Palmer had done little to build her ward organization. As a result, she was unknown even to some of her own constituents.

Jesse Jackson Jr. had no problems with name recognition. His father was one of the most famous black men in Chicago, and he used that connection astutely, collecting money from Rainbow PUSH donors and spending it on expensive mailers and phone banks. Most of his money came from out of state. Bill Cosby and Johnnie Cochran wrote checks. Jones, a son of the Machine, was depending on ward organizations. True to her background in community groups, Palmer ran a grassroots campaign. She tried to dismiss Jackson as a young upstart trading on his family name.

"Politics, like good cooking, needs some seasoning," she said, following up with a jibe against Jackson's father. "I came out of a tradition of taking people seriously, that not everything can be reduced to a sound bite that rhymes."

"Junior," as he was called then, and still is, had inherited his father's gift for oratory, although he came off as more disciplined, less passionate, enunciating each word as though he'd been trained in elocution. Yes, he conceded, he was half the age of his rivals, but that was an asset. A congressman needed years to build seniority, and he had those years. His goal was to become chairman of the House Ways and Means Committee, like Chicago's own Dan Rostenkowski, who was also elected to Congress at age thirty. Why elect an old man like Emil Jones, who was more valuable in his current job as leader of the state senate Democrats? In a flourish that no doubt made his father proud, Junior took a swipe at Jones while working in Chicago's biggest sports stories of 1995: Bulls forward B. J. Armstrong's expansion draft loss to the Toronto Raptors and Michael Jordan's retirement from basketball.

"I'm not running against Emil Jones," he insisted. "I am trying to build a stronger team. B. J. should never have been traded, M. J. should have stayed in basketball, E. J. should stay in Springfield, and J. J. should be sent to Congress."

Jones didn't have much of an answer for that. He was an ineffective public speaker who talked in a deep mumble best suited for giving orders in the back room of a ward office.

"If he was named Jesse Smith, he wouldn't even be on the radar screen," Jones groused, ignoring the fact that nepotism had never bothered Chicago voters. (When Jones himself retired from the senate, he was succeeded by Emil Jones III.)

A week before the election, a *Chicago Tribune* poll found that

Jackson had 97 percent name recognition in the district, compared with 69 percent for Jones and 61 percent for Palmer. Palmer was leading among white voters, who had a strongly negative view of the Jackson family. She tried to take advantage of that by locating her campaign headquarters in the suburbs. Whites had helped Mel Reynolds overthrow Gus Savage, but they could make a difference only in a close race. And this race wasn't close at all.

On November 28, the night of the special election, Palmer and her supporters gathered at a hotel in the suburb of Harvey. Her defeat was obvious as soon as the first returns came in, and it only looked worse as the numbers piled up. Jackson got 50,600 votes; Jones, 38,865; and Palmer 9,260. She lost her own ward, even her own precinct.

Obama and Harwell followed the returns from Obama's campaign office. To Harwell, Palmer's loss meant nothing for the state senate race.

"We need to move forward," she told Obama.

Obama, however, was genuinely conflicted. Palmer had endorsed him, and he wasn't going to make a decision without talking to her first.

"We need to call Alice," he said. "She's still the senator, and if she wants the senate seat, she should have it back."

Obama drove to the hotel where Palmer was making her concession speech.

"I wanted to build a coalition that bridges city and suburbs, young and old, men and women and ethnic groups in order to forge a new social contract," Palmer told her small crowd. Of the fact that not many people had voted, she said, "I'm not disappointed for myself, but for the missed opportunities people had to say change was needed."

Once she left the podium, Palmer repeated to Obama and Hal Baron that she did not plan to reenter the race for state senate. That satisfied Obama.

"If she's not running, then I'm still running," he told Baron.

It did not, however, satisfy Palmer's husband, Edward "Buzz" Palmer, a politically active Chicago police officer who had helped found the African-American Patrolman's Union.

"What the shit is she saying?" Buzz Palmer exploded to Baron. "Go up there and tell her to take it back!"

The filing deadline for the March primary was on December 18. That was three weeks away, plenty of time for a politician with her own ward organization to gather the 757 signatures necessary to appear on the ballot. The next morning, the *Tribune* reported that Palmer was "undecided" about reclaiming her seat.

Palmer's husband was not alone in wanting to keep his wife in Springfield. State Representative Lou Jones, an influential member of the Legislative Black Caucus, thought Palmer was too valuable to lose. The easiest way to avoid a fight, they figured, was to talk this young upstart Obama into stepping aside. Without Alice Palmer's knowledge, Obama was summoned to a meeting at Jones's house. Buzz Palmer was there, as were historian Timuel Black and Adolph Reed, who taught political science at Northwestern. These were elders of Chicago's black community. They told Obama that he was a promising young man, but it was not yet his turn. The senate seat belonged to Alice. In Chicago, you get ahead by working your way up through an organization. If Obama stepped aside now, they would support him for another office down the road.

Obama shook his head.

"I'm not gonna do that," he said.

He had made a deal with Palmer, he said, and she had told

him on Election Night that she wasn't running. He'd opened a campaign office and collected thousands of dollars from supporters.

If anything, the sit-down made Obama more determined to stay in the race. He left Jones's house livid at the condescending, bullying tone of the lectures he'd just heard. By the time he caught up with Harwell, he was still angry. It was one of the few times she'd ever seen him vent his emotions.

"They talked to me like I was a kid," Obama sputtered. "They said, 'You don't know what you're doing.' It was 'Alice said this, Alice said that.'"

Since Obama refused to yield, the Draft Alice Palmer Committee was formed. Headed by Black, it also included state Senator Donne Trotter and one of Obama's old supporters, Alderman Barbara Holt. The unexpected primary fight put many Hyde Park independents in a quandary. Obama and Palmer were both progressives. Both had been endorsed by the IVI-IPO in their races. The voters had to ask themselves which was more important: Palmer's pledge to Obama or her experience in Springfield.

"Like many, I supported Obama as a successor to Alice," former IVI-IPO chairman Sam Ackerman told the *Hyde Park Herald*. "But now we don't need a successor."

A week after losing the congressional election, Palmer decided she would attempt to reclaim her state senate seat, and asked her supporters to begin collecting signatures. Suddenly forced to play hardball politician, Obama found a way to call Palmer an Indian giver without actually using that politically incorrect term. The primary, he predicted to the *Herald*, would be determined by how voters felt about his message.

"I'm not going to win because people feel Palmer went back

on her word," he said, using his rival's last name, in case anyone thought they were still friends.

Privately, though, Obama was uncomfortable with the aggressive political maneuvers his locally born and bred supporters told him were necessary to defeat Alice Palmer. On December 18, Palmer filed her petitions. The next day, an old Hyde Park politico named Alan Dobry went downtown to the board of elections and began paging through the sheets. Dobry was a longtime supporter of Palmer's. As Fifth Ward committeeman, he had encouraged Palmer to take the state senate seat, assuring her she could do more for education as a politician than as a non-profit executive. Dobry had even knocked on doors for Palmer during her congressional run. But he had also pledged to support Obama's state senate campaign and he wasn't going back on his word just because Palmer had lost her race for Congress. Hyde Parkers respected Dobry's political judgment, so he'd look like a fool if he went around the neighborhood telling people, "Oh, we made a bad mistake. We're going to do it differently and we're not going to run Barack. We're going to run Alice again."

As an Obama supporter, Dobry felt obligated to do whatever he could to help his candidate win. In Chicago, challenging petitions is a tactic that goes back to the days when voters signed their names with fountain pens. Politicians pay good money to election lawyers who specialize in disqualifying signatures. As a member of an independent organization, Dobry had fought the Machine's efforts to knock his candidates off the ballot. By answering their challenges, he had learned to raise his own. Now, he and his wife, Lois, were examining Palmer's petitions, looking for mistakes. Right away, he found errors that suggested a hurried, slapdash effort. One sheet was filled with signatures from an adjacent district. On some petitions, entire households had signed, even though not everyone at the address was registered to vote. Dobry suspected Palmer's campaign had enlisted students from South Shore High School, who had then gone out and signed up their friends. Palmer's petitions contained 1,580 signatures, more than twice the number required to place her name on the ballot, but if these first sheets were any indication, there were enough duds to knock that figure below the minimum.

State Senator Rickey Hendon was also at the board of elections that day, looking to knock off challengers for his own West Side seat. He wasn't surprised to see the Dobrys—they were well-known political operatives—but he thought they were acting funny. When they left the room, he sidled over to peek at their papers and couldn't believe what he saw.

Oh, Lord, Hendon thought. Alice Palmer.

Hendon and Palmer were friends and allies in Springfield. They shared similar inner-city backgrounds and progressive politics. Hendon loved the fact that Palmer still behaved more like a schoolteacher than a politician—some days, she brought cookies onto the senate floor. So he found a phone and called her at home.

"Alice," he told her, "the Dobrys are down here going through your petitions."

"But they circulated for me," Palmer protested, recalling the couple's support in her run for Congress.

"They are knocking you off the ballot."

Palmer realized then that she had blundered. She had ignored that old Chicago maxim "We don't want nobody nobody sent." Nobody had sent her Barack Obama. He'd been introduced by Brian Banks—a fellow Harvard man. As for the Dobrys, they were part of the Hyde Park political cabal. Like Harvard grads, Hyde Parkers always stuck together.

The next meeting of the IVI-IPO was scheduled for January 6. The Draft Alice Palmer Committee decided to make an appearance to insist the organization switch its endorsement. The meeting, held in the basement of a Lutheran church, was so acrimonious that a fistfight nearly broke out between Palmer's supporters and allies of Toni Preckwinkle, who was still backing Obama. But the organization stuck by its original endorsement. This was far more important for Obama than for Palmer. He needed all the support he could get. If both candidates appeared on the ballot, Obama would be the underdog: a political novice with an exotic handle running against an incumbent. "Barack Obama" sounded like a name adopted by one of those self-converted Muslims who ran their own storefront mosques and appeared on the public access TV show *Muhammad and Friends* in robes, beards, and kufis. Would voters see any difference between Obama and Gha-is Askia, the actual black Muslim running for state senate? Realistically, eliminating Palmer was the only way to win.

At first, Obama was reluctant to challenge Palmer's petitions. Harwell had spent the week between Christmas and New Year's down at the board of elections and came to the same conclusion as Dobry: Palmer's sheets were full of errors and nonvoters. But to Obama, knocking his patroness off the ballot seemed so crude, so brass knuckled, so . . . Chicago. He had learned his politics from the great anti-Machine movements: Saul Alinsky's community organizing, the Hyde Park independents, and the Harold Washington crusade, represented by his boss, Judd Miner. Now he was being asked to bump aside a fifty-seven-year-old schoolmarm and win his first political office with a tactic that any thick-fingered hack might chortle about at the ward's annual smoker. A Chicagoan wouldn't have thought twice, but Obama was from Hawaii, a state that didn't even get politics until two years before he was born. He was finally persuaded by Harwell, and field coordinator Ron Davis, who cut through Obama's agonizing by growling, "The hell with this. The petitions are garbage."

Obama went after all three of his rivals: Palmer, Ewell, and Askia. The board of elections agreed that none had collected enough valid signatures to qualify for the ballot. Palmer had one last chance: If her supporters could collect two hundred affidavits from challenged voters, affirming they had signed her petitions, the board might approve her candidacy. Her campaign made an effort, but there wasn't enough time to track down all those people before a January 17 hearing. Palmer withdrew from the race. Six months earlier, she'd been first in line to challenge a kinky congressman. Now she'd lost her job to a thirty-four-year-old rookie.

Years later, asked about his challenge to Palmer, Obama would say glibly, "I think the district got a pretty good state senator." Palmer disagreed. She never forgave Barack Obama for taking her seat. She cursed out Brian Banks for introducing him to her.

"This was all a plot," she insisted.

"Look," Banks said. "You sat down with him and you gave whatever support you gave to him."

Still, Palmer felt Obama had stabbed her in the back. Her onetime protégé was "a betraying ingrate," she told friends. After leaving the senate, Palmer resumed her academic career, going to work for the University of Illinois–Chicago, where she taught public affairs and was a special assistant in the office of the president.

Palmer stayed out of politics until 2008, when she let the world know what she thought of Obama by campaigning for Hillary Clinton. She even went to the Democratic National Convention in Denver as a Clinton delegate. When the delegates were asked to nominate Obama by acclamation, Palmer didn't raise her voice.

Chapter 8

STATE SENATOR OBAMA

OBAMA WAS ELECTED to the state senate with no opposition—he knocked his Republican opponent off the ballot, too—but once he arrived in Springfield, he had to answer for his treatment of Alice Palmer. Palmer had been a beloved member of the Legislative Black Caucus, so some of its members held a grudge toward her replacement.

When a new senator introduces his first bill, it's traditional for senior members to haze the sponsor by asking ridiculous questions. On March 13, 1997, two months after he was sworn in, Obama stood up in the senate chamber to speak in favor of an innocuous measure: allowing community colleges to distribute a directory of graduating students to local businesses.

"Mr. President, ladies and gentlemen of the senate, I come humbly before you on this extremely humble bill"—those were Obama's first recorded words as an elected official.

After Obama described his humble bill, Senator Rickey Hendon asked to be recognized. He had a question for the freshman senator. Hendon was a flashy, theatrical politician, nicknamed "Hollywood" for his love of TV cameras and his background as the producer of an independent comedy called *Butterscotch and Chocolate*. He seemed like a natural to begin the fun.

"Senator, could you pronounce your name for me?" he asked Obama. "I'm having a little trouble with it."

Obama pronounced his name.

"Is that Irish?" Hendon asked.

"It will be when I run county-wide," Obama cracked.

"That was a good joke, but this bill's still going to die. This directory, would that have those one-eight-hundred sex line numbers in this directory?"

"I apologize," Obama said. "I wasn't paying Senator Hendon any attention."

"Well, clearly, as poorly as this legislation is drafted, you didn't pay it much attention, either. My question was, are the one-eight-hundred sex line numbers going to be in this directory?"

Obama seemed flustered by Hendon's crude line of questioning. He answered with a jibe at his colleague's district.

"Not—not—basically this idea came out of the South Side community colleges. I don't know what you're doing on the West Side community colleges. But we probably won't be including that in our directory for the students."

Then Hendon reminded the body how this Hyde Park senator with the unpronounceable name had come to join them.

"I seem to remember a very lovely senator by the name of Palmer—much easier to pronounce than 'Obama'—and she always had cookies and nice things to say, and you don't have anything to give us around your desk. How do you expect to get votes? And—and you don't even wear nice perfume like Senator Palmer did . . . I'm missing Senator Palmer because of these weak replacements with these tired bills that make absolutely no sense. I—I definitely urge a no vote. Whatever your name is."

By the standards of freshman hazing, this was incredibly

hostile. Other senators asked silly, good-natured questions. "In the bill, you talk about fostering employment," joshed Denny Jacobs, a Democrat from Rock Island. "How does this relate to a foster child, or whatever the case may be? What is a foster employment?" Carl Hawkinson of Galesburg, the only other Harvard Law graduate in the chamber, asked, "How do the quality of these questions compare to those you received from Professors Dershowitz, Tribe, or Nessen?"

"I must say they compare favorably," Obama assured him. "In—in fact, that is the—this is the toughest grilling that I've ever received. If I survive this event, I will be eternally grateful and consider this a highlight of my legal and legislative career."

In the end, the bill passed unanimously. Even Rickey Hendon voted aye.

But Obama's friction with Hendon—and other black legislators—went far deeper than a tough primary against a popular incumbent. Politics is a business, and politicians learn to work with the newcomers, just as a ballplayer learns to play alongside the rookie who replaced his best friend in the lineup. Hendon, who had just begun his second term, was aiming for a spot in the senate leadership, and he saw this obviously intelligent, talented newcomer as a threat. Hendon was also a much more traditional politician—and a more traditional black man—than Obama. He had come up on Chicago's West Side, which has the city's most violent chapters of the Gangster Disciples, its earthiest blues taverns, its loudest bid whist games, and its busiest heroin street corners. Hendon had been a teenager during the 1968 riots that burned out storefronts on Madison Street. He earned his first office—alderman—by producing TV shows and plays for big-shot politicians who then slated him as a candidate. Unlike Obama, he had paid his dues. Wherever he went, he carried the West Side attitude, that the bourgeois blacks on the South Side take eight or nine slices of pie while the West Side gets the crust. That South Siders look down on West Siders, and that nowhere do they look down from a greater height than Hyde Park. That no self-respecting West Sider can ever let a South Sider punk him.

After that hazing, Hendon began needling Obama in the black caucus. When Obama brought up a proposal, Hendon would dismiss it with, "You think you're so smart, you went to Harvard." After-hours, Hendon sat in his office, smoking cigars with Senator Donne Trotter, who represented the far South Side of Chicago. Together, they'd malign Obama as "arrogant" and "Harvard." Behind his back they called him "Senator Yo Mama." They even bought a copy of *Dreams from My Father* to mine for embarrassing tidbits. Paying Obama a royalty was worth it for the extra ammunition.

Obama tried to brush off the criticism. "Ah, Hendon, you've always got something to say." In caucus meetings, Emil Jones tried to keep peace between the senators.

"Focus on the issues," he'd order them.

But even that increased the tension. Jones was minority leader. As the most powerful Democrat in the chamber, he was essential to any senator's advancement. And, from Obama's first year in Springfield, it was obvious that Jones saw him as a comer.

Obama's black colleagues may have been jealous, but Obama's behavior, and his overall demeanor, didn't help the relationships. He enjoyed telling people he'd gone to Harvard, as if the whole capitol didn't know already. And he had a habit of listening to a debate with his chin cocked in the air, like a setter catching a far-off scent. Put together with his education and his neighborhood, the pose made him seem haughty. He sometimes gave the impression that he was slumming, killing time in the legislature until he could occupy an office better suited to his intelligence and education. Alderman Sam Burrell took a bus down to Springfield on a lobbying trip and saw an Obama far different from the young law school graduate who'd toted a backpack into his office a few years before to ask for advice on Project Vote! As Burrell stepped off his bus, Obama strode loosely across the capitol lawn, waving and calling out, "Hey, Sam." That easy walk, that self-assured greeting. It's like he's white, Burrell thought. Every black man in America had a little voice in the back of his head that said, "You can't." It was just part of growing up as part of a race that had been barred from the best schools, the best jobs, the best neighborhoods. Obama had never heard that voice. His white mother, his white grandmother, and his white grandfather had never told him, "You can't. The white man won't let you." And now look at him. He was acting as though he owned everything under the capitol's pewter-colored dome.

In Springfield, Obama developed closer relationships with his white colleagues than his black colleagues, both on the senate floor and after hours. The Springfield of state government is a community entirely separate from the prairie city of the same name. Nicknamed "Springpatch," or just "the Patch," it is a temporary carnival of politicians, lobbyists, journalists, tourists, and legislative aides who swarm into town for a few days each week between January and May. Most are from the Chicago area, 180 miles away. That's too far to commute, so they kill their evenings at the Sangamo Club or the bar of the Abraham Lincoln Hotel. Others work late or drink with lobbyists in their hideaway offices. Obama played poker. A pair of lobbyists put the word out that they were organizing a game at the Panther Creek Country Club. Obama had learned to play cards in college, so he showed up at the club and, after dinner, sat down in an upstairs room with three small-town Democrats: Denny Jacobs of Rock Island, Terry Link of Vernon Hills, and Larry Walsh of Elwood. While a Bulls game flashed on TVs in the background, they played three-dollar-limit games of Omaha and seven-card stud. Obama was a different breed of politician than his partners: urban, a reformer, more intellectual than glad-hander. He was an ambitious thirty-five-year-old, while they were middle-aged men who'd peaked as state legislators. But Obama worked hard to fit in. The game, which came to be called the Committee Meeting, eventually moved over to Link's house. Obama brought beer, even though he wasn't much of a drinker, and chipped in for pizza.

In the 1990s, Senate Democrats were in the minority, so their members had a lot of free time. (Link, elected at the same time as Obama, couldn't even get a bill out of committee his first two years.) Through months and months of Tuesday nights, Obama built friendships with his poker buddies. Jacobs, whose best-known achievement was bringing riverboat gambling to Illinois, boasted to his wife that he'd met a future president of the United States.

"You better get your ass out of here," he told Obama. "You're too smart for this place."

Walsh, a corn and soybean farmer from Will County, south of Chicago, discovered that Obama was also a passionate White Sox fan. (Walsh admired Obama for the same reason black legislators disdained him: He wasn't a race man. When Obama considered a bill, his first question wasn't "How is this good for African-Americans?" but "How is this good for Illinois?") Link and Obama became golf buddies, sneaking away from the capitol for a round at Panther Creek. Basketball was still Obama's game—he played every morning at the Springfield YMCA—but he saw that legislative deals were cut on Panther Creek's fairways, so he signed up for lessons, determined to be something more than a duffer. Even with the instruction, he had trouble breaking 90.

The four men didn't always agree politically. Obama was a big-government liberal. His poker pals were fiscal conservatives. At the beginning of every session, Obama introduced a constitutional amendment guaranteeing health care to everyone in Illinois.

"You think universal health care is the best thing since sliced bread," Jacobs chided.

The amendment always failed, but it got the attention of Emil Jones, who named Obama the Democrats' spokesman on health care.

During his first year in Springfield, Obama also became the party's point man on welfare reform, which affected thousands of families in his inner-city district. In Washington, the Republican Revolution was still a powerful movement. Congress had passed a bill requiring every state to rewrite its welfare laws, with the aim of forcing public aid recipients to find jobs. It was the biggest change in welfare since the program began during the Great Depression. Liberals were determined to ensure that the poor received job training and child care while they looked for work. The Illinois senate Republicans were led by a pale, comfortably overweight suburbanite named James "Pate" Philip, who had publicly denigrated the black race's work ethic. They introduced a hard-line bill that placed a five-year limit on benefits, with little provision for training and education. The bottom line was look for a job or lose your check. As a freshman from the minority party, Obama had no say in writing the proposal. But any welfare bill also had to pass the state house of representatives, which was controlled by Chicago Democrats. Obama did have a role in drafting the compromise that reached the governor's desk.

Working with Representative Barbara Flynn Currie, another Hyde Park liberal, and staffers from the National Center on Poverty Law, he produced amendments that gave poor people a chance to study for better jobs. Anyone working more than thirty hours a week was exempt from the five-year time limit, essentially qualifying for a perpetual earnings supplement. Only one-third of wages counted toward reducing welfare payments. And high-school students, or college students carrying at least a C average, were exempt from the time limit.

Even liberal welfare activists thought the new system was better than Aid to Families with Dependent Children. The caseload dropped dramatically, from 250,000 families to 30,000. Obama worked hard to ensure that the savings were spent on subsidies to child care centers. If the state was forcing mothers to go to work, it was only fair to give their children a place to go, too.

The welfare bill excluded immigrants. Obama wasn't happy about that, but he voted "aye" because the Republicans had refused to budge on the issue. (Latino senators voted "no" in protest.) It was a necessary compromise, but in a floor speech before the bill passed, Obama implored the senate to make sure no needy Illinoisan was left out of welfare reform. In its acknowledgment of liberal and conservative views and its use of anecdote, the speech showed that Obama was already developing the political rhetoric he would use in *The Audacity of Hope* and as a presidential candidate.

"This may be as important a bill as we pass in this session," he began. "It will affect a huge number of people. I am not a defender of the status quo with respect to welfare. Having said that, I probably would not have supported the federal legislation because I think it had some problems."

Obama, the foreign student's son, asked the senate to revisit the ban on immigrants—"Everyone in this chamber, at some point, comes from an immigrant family. And I don't like the notion that those people who are here legally, contributing to our society, paying taxes, are not subject to the same benefits, the same social safety net that the rest of us are."

Welfare reform needed a legislative oversight program, because how else would welfare families be heard? They couldn't hire lobbyists; they didn't buy tickets to fund-raisers. The lower class and the political class only met by accident. It had happened to him the weekend before. He'd been out in the alley behind his condo, smoking a cigar, when he'd seen a family searching for cans to recycle. The father was pushing a shopping cart; the mother, a stroller.

"This was their visible means of support," Obama said. "This is the job that awaited them if they weren't on welfare. We have an obligation to that family. We have an obligation to that child. I strongly urge that—although we've taken a good step on this bill—that we look at this carefully and continue to make a commitment to ensuring that all Illinois children and all Illinois families have an opportunity to succeed in this economy."

The Gift Ban Act was another bill that put Obama on the wrong side of poker pal Jacobs, the carnivorous Mississippi River pol. Jacobs reveled in expensive dinners with lobbyists, while Obama was one of the few legislators who always paid his half of the check. In 1997, Paul Simon, who had just retired from the U.S. Senate, asked the legislature to form a blue-ribbon panel on ethics reform. Ordinarily, requests like that were filed away with proposals to create a unicameral legislature or move the state capital to Metropolis. Illinois hadn't changed its ethics law since the mid-1970s, when it enacted a campaign disclosure system in response to Watergate. It was one of the few states with no limits on campaign contributions or gifts to politicians. One promiscuous lobbyist stood in the capitol rotunda with a stack of checks, which he dealt out to departing senators. Some legislators began their day by trying to figure out who would take them to lunch.

But 1997 was different. The state's most powerful officeholders had been caught in scandals. Governor Jim Edgar's largest campaign contributor, Management Services of Illinois, had received several no-bid contracts from the state and then bilked taxpayers out of $7 million. In Secretary of State George Ryan's office, clerks were selling trucker's licenses in exchange for bribes, which ended up in Ryan's campaign fund. One of the illegal truckers caused an accident that killed six children. Illinois politicians reform themselves as often as a mountain man bathes: only when the stench becomes unbearable. This was one of those times.

Also, Paul Simon was asking. Illinois's most popular politician, and its most honest, he hadn't inspired the term "simonpure," but it certainly applied to him. In the 1950s, Simon had made his name as a muckraking small-town newspaper editor, exposing gambling and prostitution in small towns across the river from St. Louis. After winning a seat in the legislature, he furthered his goody-goody image by writing an expose on his colleagues for *Harper's*. In the U.S. Senate, he reported every gift, right down to a five-dollar box of cookies. Simon's scrupulous accounting won him the "Straight Arrow Award" in a poll of congressional staffers. Upon leaving the Senate in 1997, his retirement project was a public policy institute at Southern Illinois University. The ethics bill was its first undertaking.

Illinois's sleazy political culture was largely a product of the Chicago Machine, which lived on long after Tammany Hall and other big-city boss operations were put out of business. But even

Illinoisans grow tired of kickbacks and insider contracts, which means that the state also provides a unique platform for reformers. You can't have Eliot Ness without Al Capone. Goo-goos and grafters, as a popular book about Chicago politics put it. Paul Simon was a goo-goo. So was Abner Mikva. Both recommended Obama to Emil Jones, who eagerly appointed him to the reform panel. Let a freshman from Hyde Park tell the guys they can't have dinner at the Sangamo Club anymore. Denny Jacobs sure wouldn't do it. As Jacobs liked to put it, "The public doesn't care about ethics. I think ethics comes next to athlete's feet when it comes to tripping the public's trigger. What it does trigger is the media."

Working with Simon and his institute, the panel came up with a bill that prohibited lobbyists from handing out donations on state property and banned fund-raisers within fifty miles of Springfield. If a lobbyist took a legislator or a state employee out to eat, he couldn't spend more than $75. Legislators could no longer accept sports tickets or vacations. Obama wanted to limit campaign contributions, too, but that would have struck at the power of the house and senate leaders. They collected huge sums of money from lobbyists, then doled it out to grateful members. Finally, the bill required that contributions be posted on the Internet, which in 1997 was still a novelty to most politicians.

The Gift Ban Act passed the Republican-controlled senate with no trouble. George Ryan was running for governor, and he didn't want the newspapers harping on ethics. (Ryan won the election and served four years as governor, followed by six years in a federal prison for corruption.) It was a sensitive subject for the secretary of state, who had vacationed in Jamaica on a lobbyist's dime. In the house, members worried that they'd be fined or jailed for niggling violations. One representative complained about the ban on using campaign funds for personal use. Would he be breaking the law by buying a patriotic shirt for a Fourth of July parade, then wearing it to a family picnic? Another wanted to know whether a contribution was "face-to-face" if he turned his back to receive it.

The bill impressed editorial boards and made Obama a go-to guy for ethical reform groups, but inside the capitol, it reinforced his image as a self-righteous goo-goo.

"Carrying the mantle of ethics in Springfield makes you a bit of an outsider," says Cynthia Canary of the Illinois Campaign for Political Reform, a group whose cause is as idealistic, and as hopeless, as temperance in Ireland. In the immortal words of Alderman Paddy Bauler, "Chicago ain't ready for reform!" (He later expanded on this with a quote that Obama's detractors would have found amusing: "Christ! Who the hell would want to live here if it was? This is the big city, boy! This ain't Honolulu!")

Denny Jacobs was the first to flout the new law. He held a fund-raiser at Norb Andy's, a restaurant famous for serving that Springfield delicacy, the horseshoe: a hamburger patty on an open bun, smothered in French fries and gooey cheese. No idealist, Jacobs was always friendly to his political enemies: He took time out from his donors to offer soft drinks to the protesters on the sidewalk.

The Gift Ban Act was declared unconstitutional by a friendly judge in Will County, but the Illinois Supreme Court upheld the law on appeal. Its most important legacy was electronic filing. Before the Internet, journalists and other busybodies had to fill out forms in triplicate to inspect campaign contributions. Afterward, anyone with a computer could learn that, say, the chairman of the Senate Transportation Committee was taking money from a paving contractor. Lobbyists are still paying off legislators, but at least now everyone can watch it happen.

In Chicago, a state senator is not a big wheel. Downstate, in rustic Central and Southern Illinois, legislators are local heroes. A Decatur housewife who sees her senator in the grocery store has a dinnertime story. Most Chicagoans can't even name their state legislators. Obama could shop at the Hyde Park Co-op or browse at 57th Street Books without anyone whispering "*There's Senator Obama.*" Aldermen don't suffer the same anonymity. The city council—now *that's* a big deal in Chicago. Both Mayors Daley began their political careers in the state senate, only to leave for more glamorous local offices.

Why is the legislature such an ignoble political backwater? First of all, it meets in faraway Springfield. Chicagoans also assume that their legislators are sprockets in their local machines, puppets of the ward bosses who put them in office. (Rod Blagojevich got his start in politics because his father-in-law, a powerful alderman, wanted to demonstrate his clout by electing a state representative.) Once these half-bright hacks get to Springfield, most of the decisions are made by the "Four Tops"—the house and senate party leaders who control all the campaign funds.

Hyde Parkers are less cynical about their politicians than most Chicagoans, but they're also less starstruck. After all, a U of C English professor earns twice as much money as a state senator. And fawning over petty elected officials is not Hyde Park's idea of sophistication. Obama worked hard to get attention. He served spaghetti at the IVI-IPO's annual fund-raiser at the United Church of Hyde Park. He was a "celebrity judge" for the Harper Court Art Council's Second Annual Creative Writing Contest. He flipped pancakes at the Hyde Park Neighborhood Club's annual fund-raiser and marched in colonial attire during the Fourth of July parade on Fifty-third Street.

Obama also had a column in the *Hyde Park Herald*, "Springfield Report." Every local pol got one. In an early "Springfield Report," he attacked Republicans for refusing to pass limits on campaign contributions—"I, for one, continue to be a strong advocate of contribution limits and public financing of campaigns; without such limits and public investment, it's hard to see how we can fully eliminate the influence of big money over the process." It was not a surprising viewpoint for a junior member of the minority party representing a goo-goo district. Later on in the column, Obama added a rare personal note to his bureaucratic missive: "Some of you may have noticed my absence at this year's Fourth of July parade. I had a good excuse: that was the day that my wife, Michelle, gave birth to our first child, Malia Ann Obama (8 pounds, 15 ounces). Both mother and daughter are doing great, and we wish to thank all of you who sent cards and called to wish us the best. Hopefully, Malia will be joining us at next year's parade/birthday celebration!"

For a freshman, Obama ran up an impressive record of bringing public works to his district. In 1998, for example, the state set aside $44.6 million to rebuild the eroding Lake Michigan shoreline south of Fifty-fifth Street. In reality, Obama wasn't responsible for bringing home that big money. It was his state representative, Barbara Flynn Currie, who became house majority leader the year Obama joined the senate. Currie was a more effective state legislator, and as someone who'd represented Hyde Park since Obama was a high school senior in Hawaii, she was more in touch with neighborhood issues.

Obama didn't have a lot of power or influence in the capitol.

He occupied a one-room office in a crowded suite on the mezzanine, a half floor where junior senators are hidden away. He wasn't earning much money, either, especially for a young father with a mortgage and student loans from Harvard. The senate gig, which was part-time, paid $48,403 a year. Most legislators had a law practice, a family business, or a farm. At first, Obama thought he could continue as an associate at his law firm, but after a few weeks in Springfield, he called Judd Miner and told him the legislature was too much work.

"Judd, this is unfair to you guys," he said. "This is going to be much more time-consuming than I thought, and rather than get paid regularly while I'm here, I'd rather just keep track of my time. Let's talk when I come back in May and see what a fair arrangement is."

Obama was turning down a salary he could have collected with very little effort. That was a testament to his honesty, Miner thought. Obama hung on to his corner office and the title of "counsel," but his brief career as a practicing attorney was over.

That meant he needed a job, though. There was an offer on the table from U of C. Obama went back to Douglas Baird with a proposal that would make him less than a full-time professor but more than a part-time lecturer: a two-thirds teaching load, no expectation of academic writing, and full benefits, which would include health insurance, and Lab School tuition for his children. He'd teach Mondays and Fridays, the days the senate wasn't in session. It was an unusual request, but Obama was starting to get a sense of his own exceptionalism. Most schools, most law firms, would jump through hoops to keep the first black president of the *Harvard Law Review* around. U of C said yes. Baird had to clear it with the provost, whose only reservation was giving Obama the title "senior lecturer," which was usually reserved for federal judges and other eminences. But Obama got the title, too. Baird thought it was a great deal. The school was getting more work out of a popular lecturer, and when Obama grew bored with the lowly position of state senator—as a man of his gifts was bound to do—he might consider teaching law full-time.

Most Chicagoans look on any part of Illinois south of Interstate 80 as an underpopulated, uncultured rural appendage, good for growing corn and soybeans but not worth visiting. Obama, the hip urban senator who knew more about Kenyan village life than he did about small-town America, wanted to see the rest of the state. Through his work with Paul Simon, he got a chance. Simon lived in the southern marches of Illinois, a region known as Little Egypt. In the middle of 1997, his public policy institute held a fund-raising dinner in Chicago. Obama attended with John Schmidt, his chief money man from Project Vote! They sat with Steve Scates, a farmer from Shawneetown, across the Ohio River from Kentucky. A heavyset man with a bashful drawl, Scates had been appointed state director of the Farm Service Agency by his old friend Simon. Obama had never been to Little Egypt, which lies far below the Mason-Dixon Line, nearer to Nashville than Chicago. If he was ever going to run for statewide office, though, he'd have to make his Muslim name and his dark face known in all corners of the state. Best to start with Scates, who was an important Democratic donor in his region.

"Even though I'm a state senator from Chicago, I want to know the rest of the state," he told Scates at that dinner. "I'd like to visit you guys at your farm."

Scates invited him down. When Obama got back to Springfield, he proposed a trip to his legislative director, Dan Shomon. After session was over, he said, they should drive down south, hitting some of his colleagues' golf outings. Shomon thought it was a grand idea. A former newspaper reporter who had worked eight years in the capitol, he wanted to expose his urbane, over-educated boss to rural life, and, frankly, he also wanted to teach Obama to behave like a commoner. Obama already had a reputation for haughtiness around the capitol. If voters saw him the same way, he'd never get ahead in politics. Obama and Shomon made an unusual-looking pair—Obama was tall and lean, while Shomon was squat and bushy haired, with squinty eyes behind thick glasses. But their partnership, which would last until Obama ran for the U.S. Senate, fit into a long tradition of smooth, charismatic politicians and brilliant, untidy sidekicks, each contributing a necessary element for political success. Think of Louis Howe and Franklin D. Roosevelt, Theodore Sorensen and John F. Kennedy, or Karl Rove and George W. Bush. That's who Shomon was to Obama early in his career.

In its four-hundred-mile run from Lake Michigan to the Ohio River, Illinois encompasses three American regions, each cultur-ally and linguistically distinct from the others. The northern third of the state was settled by Yankees from New England and west-ern New York. Highly educated, utopian, they built small reli-gious colleges and supported abolition, prohibition, and women's suffrage. After these settlers came millions of immigrants from Ireland, Italy, Poland, and Russia: Peasant stock, Catholic and Jewish, they were less idealistic about politics, allowing ward bosses to substitute themselves for old-world lairds and dukes. The prairies of Central Illinois are corn and soybean country, where people still say "warsh" for "wash," go to evangelical churches on Wednesday night and Sunday morning, and hunt pheasant in the fall. Lincoln lived there, and his memory is revered with statues and plaques in every town where he practiced law. (Springfield has restored his entire block to its 1850s glory; in Charleston, where he debated Stephen A. Douglas, visitors can view a chip from a rail he split, displayed like a sliver of the true cross.) And then there is Little Egypt. The oldest part of the state, it was settled by migrants who arrived from Kentucky, Tennessee, and Virginia in the age of Andrew Jackson. It is a landscape of deep coal mines, forests, and shadowed hollows. The name's origin is uncertain: Some say it comes from the meeting of the Ohio and the Mississippi, similar to the Nile Delta, others from a hard winter when northern farmers were, like the sons of Jacob, forced to go down to Egypt to get corn. Wherever the term came from, it is reflected in the town names—Cairo, Karnak, Thebes—and the SIU mascot, the Saluki. Paul M. Angle, the author of *Bloody Williamson*—which details the region's family feuds, Ku Klux Klan activity, and a massacre of twenty-two scabs by striking miners—compared it to Appalachia in its "family hatreds, labor strife, religious bigotry, atavistic narrowness."

True to its Southern roots, Little Egypt has a history of racial conflict—a 1967 riot in Cairo resulted in a years-long black boycott that drove white businesses out of town. Also true to its Southern roots, it is poor—the poorest part of Illinois—and ancestrally Democratic. Black Democrats had won there before. Roland Burris, a native of Centralia, carried Little Egypt in his races for comptroller and attorney general. Carol Moseley Braun swept the region in 1992, running on a ticket with Bill Clinton and Al Gore, two Southern Democrats whose famous bus tour stopped in Vandalia. Obama's task wasn't as difficult as it seemed.

Shomon had worked as the Downstate coordinator on several statewide campaigns, so he tried to get Obama to go native—as much as that was possible for a black Harvard lawyer in coal country. As Obama would recount in *The Audacity of Hope*, Shomon, the perfect political mate, even nagged him about his clothes and his condiments.

> Four times he reminded me we have to pack—just khakis and polo shirts, he said; no fancy linen trousers or silk shirts. I told him I didn't own any linens or silks. On the drive down, we stopped at a TGI Fridays and I ordered a cheeseburger. When the waitress brought the food I asked her if she had any Dijon mustard. Dan shook his head.
>
> "He doesn't want Dijon," he insisted, waving the waitress off. "Here," he shoved a yellow bottle of French's mustard in my direction—"here's some mustard right here."
>
> The waitress looked confused. "We got Dijon if you want it," she said to me.

In Shawneetown, Obama and Shomon toured Scates's fifteen thousand acres of corn, soybeans, and wheat, which were spread across two counties. As far as Scates could tell, Obama had never been on a farm. He asked questions about the operation and wanted to learn what people who weren't farmers did for a living in that country. Scates took him to the Greek-revival bank in Old Shawneetown—the oldest bank in Illinois—where he snapped a keepsake photo.

"This young man has a fabulous future," said Scates's wife, Kappy, who worked in Senator Dick Durbin's Marion office. Kappy bought a copy of *Dreams from My Father*, which she eventually lent to Paul Simon, who enjoyed it so much he ordered his own copy. Steve Scates thought their guest was "down-to-earth," which spoke to Obama's talent for adjusting his persona to that of a listener—common to all politicians but essential for a biracial legislator who represented a college campus and a housing project. Scates was just happy to see a Chicagoan in his part of the state. Little Egypt, which sits on the northernmost salient of the Ozarks, has the most dramatic scenery in Illinois, including the Garden of the Gods, a preserve of rock spires and waterfalls. But few city dwellers are willing to drive six hours through flat farm country to see it. They'd rather vacation in nearby Michigan or Wisconsin, both of which share Lake Michigan and don't have locals with Dixie accents or GOD SAID IT. I BELIEVE IT. THAT'S THAT bumper stickers. (Obama went into culture shock when he passed a store offering "Good Deals on Guns and Swords.") Downstaters like to complain that Chicago is a drain on the rest of the state, even though it provides the criminals who fill the prisons that offer the only good jobs in tapped-out coal counties. Scates, who had an office in Springfield, was always trying to organize legislative junkets to his hometown. In the house and senate, debates over hunting, guns, and animal rights often split along regional lines, not party lines, with Downstate Democrats and Republicans uniting against their urban and suburban colleagues.

Obama repaid Scates by speaking at the Farm Service Agency's Diversity Days. It's not easy to get blacks and Latinos interested in working with farmers, but Scates was trying, and he thought a black state senator could help.

Obama's tour of Little Egypt helped him see that his adopted home state was America in miniature, a fact he would repeat over and over again when he ran for higher office. As the Census Bureau will tell you, Illinois's demographics match the nation's more closely than any other state's.

"North, south, east, west, black, white, urban, rural, Southern, Northern," he would say later. "For someone who cares deeply about the country and the struggles that this country's going through, I can't think of a better laboratory to work on the pressing issues we confront."

Obama faced no opposition when he ran for reelection in 1998. Nonetheless, he raised $46,000, most of it from small donors. He was going to need the campaign funds. After only two years in the state senate, he was already getting restless. Guys like Larry Walsh and Denny Jacobs were comfortable in Springfield, knowing their folksy acts would not play outside their hometowns. Walsh didn't even mind being in the minority party. Without "the high pressure of legislation and all that" he had time to pal around, build friendships with other legislators, and meet with his constituents. Obama was frustrated. Walsh saw him as a guy who could never take a big enough bite of the apple. As a powerless Democrat, he was barely getting to nibble. His universal health care bill, which he now called the Bernardin Amendment, after the late Archbishop of Chicago, was again defeated. So were bills on fair pricing of prescription drugs, higher pay for nursing home aides, and domestic violence training for state employees. He did achieve one of his pet goals as a legislator: lowering taxes on the poor. It was easier to appeal to the Republicans on that one. Tax cuts are the GOP's raison d'être.

Originally, Obama wanted to create a progressive state income tax. That was impossible, because the Illinois constitution requires a flat tax. Everyone from the chicken cook to the banker pays the same 3 percent. So Obama proposed an earned income tax credit for Illinois. At first, he asked for 20 percent, since the state income tax was a fifth of the 15 percent that low-income workers pay the federal government. He got 5 percent. Obama also proposed increasing the personal exemption, which was only $1,000 when he joined the legislature. He wanted to stagger it, with the poor getting a bigger exemption, but that probably would have been unconstitutional, too. Instead, the Republicans raised the exemption to $2,000 on everyone. That meant a family of four living at the poverty level didn't have to pay state taxes on half its income.

Obama also lobbied hard for a bill to increase the amount of money welfare parents received from child support payments. The old law gave 25 percent to the custodial parent, with the rest going to the state and federal government as a reimbursement for welfare payments. The Democrats wanted that increased to two-thirds as long as the parent was working. They saw it as a way to reward people for getting off welfare. The bill passed the house, but Governor George Ryan was a stone wall of opposition. Working with Senator David Sullivan, a Republican from the Chicago suburbs, Obama lobbied the other members of the Public Health and Welfare Committee. The committee chairman opposed the measure, but Obama and Sullivan flipped enough senators to move it to the floor, where it passed. It was a yeoman's job of legislating, especially for a senator with a reputation for disdaining the dirty work of cloakroom deal making.

Governor Ryan vetoed the bill. When it came back to the senate, the override failed by one vote—that of a Democratic senator stuck in traffic. Several Republicans voted "present." Seeing his chamber's support for the bill, the senate president struck a deal with the governor: Single parents could keep half the money.

Throughout his time in Springfield, Obama had called on Abner Mikva for advice on how to get along in the legislature. Now he called with another question: What would Mikva think of his running against Bobby Rush, the First District's congressman? He's getting restless already, Mikva thought. It wasn't a surprise.

Springfield can be a narrow, parochial place for someone who has great ideas, wants to do great things. Mikva had spent ten years there before seizing his chance to move up to Washington. Obama was trying to do it in four. The kid had obviously made up his mind. He wasn't asking for an opinion. He was asking for help.

Rush had made a serious blunder that year by running for mayor of Chicago against Richard M. Daley, who enjoyed a monarchical popularity in the city. Coming out of that election with 28 percent of the vote, Rush looked like a weakened politician. Even so, he would be hard to beat—any incumbent is. But Mikva had lost races before. Sometimes, losing taught you more about your friends, your enemies, and yourself than winning did. Mikva wanted to do whatever he could to advance his protégé's career. So he agreed to help Obama against Bobby Rush.

Obama got a different reaction from his poker buddies. Don't do it, they warned him. You'll be breaking a cardinal rule of politics: Never run against an incumbent of your own party.

Chapter 9

DEFEAT

WHILE OBAMA'S PATH TO POWER had gone through Columbia and Harvard, Bobby Lee Rush learned politics on the streets. Rush's entire life had been a series of escapes from the fates that destroyed so many black men of his generation. He was born in rural Georgia to parents who were too proud to endure segregation. They moved the family to Chicago when Rush was a young boy. At seventeen, he dropped out of his inner-city high school to join the army but went AWOL during the Vietnam War to help found the Illinois Black Panther Party.

As the Black Panthers' deputy minister of defense, Rush was the sole survivor of the party's ruling triumvirate. His compatriots, Mark Clark and Fred Hampton, were gunned down by the police in the 1969 raid that catalyzed the black political rebellion against the Machine. A photo of Rush wearing a fur hat and wielding a long-barreled pistol became one of the best-known images of 1960s militance in Chicago.

Rush left his radical past behind to earn two masters' degrees, become an ordained Baptist minister, and win election as an alderman, standing with Harold Washington against the Twenty-nine, who tried to maintain white control of the city council. All along, he saw himself as an underdog, bent on self-improvement. Describing Rush as a boy, his father told him, "You wanted to read so bad and study so much that you said you wanted to die in a classroom." As a man, he was a disciple of motivational guru Tony Robbins, who urged his listeners to "awaken the giant within." Rush was a hero of the civil rights movement, the black power movement, and the Washington years, and he was proof that a black man could succeed. You couldn't out-ghetto Bobby Rush in Chicago.

Obama didn't intend to try. He didn't think he'd have to. In that disastrous run for mayor, Rush even lost his own ward, which hadn't voted for a white candidate since before Harold Washington. To many, the election was a sign that Daley had finally brought an end to "Beirut on the Lake"—the city's black vs. white political wars—and that Rush's style of racial confrontation had had its day.

The First District is a bellwether of black politics, not only in Chicago, but in the nation. Rush had won the seat by unhorsing Representative Charles Hayes, an elderly veteran of Martin Luther King's voter registration drives. Obama thought the district was ready for another generational change, to a postracial politician who could reach out to whites.

Plus, for an old firebrand, Rush was a surprisingly bland figure. He had worked hard to overcome a childhood stutter, and while he spoke fluidly, he rarely raised his voice on the stump. To Obama, Rush was an uninspiring, ineffectual congressman who had ridden to Washington, D.C., on his public image and was now doing little for his district. But fighting on his home turf—the South Side—Rush turned out to be wilier and more potent than Obama expected.

On a Sunday in late September 1999, after attending a children's book fair in Hyde Park, Obama held a press conference announcing his candidacy for Congress. He promised to focus on issues he thought Rush had neglected: crime, education, health care, and economic development. Then he basically called Rush a washed-up revolutionary whose addiction to identity politics prevented him from passing meaningful bills.

"Rush represents a politics that is rooted in the past, a reactive politics that isn't very good at coming up with concrete solutions," Obama argued.

Rush was passionate about one issue: gun control. The Black Panthers romanticized weapons, but Rush had renounced his old pistol-toting image to cosponsor thirty-one gun control bills in Congress, including the Brady Bill and the assault weapons ban.

That fall, Rush was given a personal reason to loathe guns. On October 18, 1999, his twenty-nine-year-old son, Huey, was shot by two men who believed he was holding money for a drug dealer. He died four days later.

After Huey's death, Rush went on a media tour to condemn the "glorification" of firearms. His was an irresistible story: the ex–Black Panther who had once served six months on a weapons charge but now understood firsthand the evil that guns do. Rush was in *Newsweek* and *People*, on National Public Radio, *Queen Latifah*, and *Today*.

Huey's murder brought enormous sympathy to Rush. Plenty of South Siders had lost sons, grandsons, nephews, or cousins to street violence. Obama heard the news on the radio, while he was driving to a meeting at which he hoped to win the support of one of the few South Side politicians who hadn't endorsed Rush. Afterward, he got a phone call from Jesse Jackson, who told him, "You realize, Barack, the dynamics of this race have changed." Obama got the message and suspended his campaign for a month.

Obama had another, more tangible problem. At the beginning of the campaign, he had spent a small amount of his four-figure war chest to commission a poll. The result: Rush had 90 percent name recognition in the district. Obama had 11 percent.

Obama had some dirt on Rush's relationship with Huey, who was born out of wedlock to a fellow Black Panther and raised by an aunt. Now he couldn't use that. So he tried attacking Rush politically. From the beginning, though, Obama's campaign was off-key and out of touch with the South Side.

I got my first sight of Obama early that winter, at a church in the Bronzeville neighborhood. I was writing about the race for the *Chicago Reader*. It was a Saturday afternoon—as a greenhorn challenger, Obama wasn't getting the Sunday pulpit invitations—and maybe a dozen people were scattered in the worn pews. Weak December sunlight strained through the stained glass. Obama wore a suit and tie—he had not yet pioneered open-necked campaign casual. Posing uncomfortably before the baptismal, he tried to relax the crowd with self-deprecating wit.

"The first thing people ask me is, 'How did you get that name, "Obama,"'" although they don't always pronounce it right," he said lightly. "Some people say 'Alabama,' some people say 'Yo Mama.' I got my name from Kenya, which is where my father's from, and I got my accent from Kansas, which is where my mother's from."

Obama's standard gag came off as just the sort of awkward, beginning-of-the-semester joke you'd expect from a law professor trying too hard to prove he has a sense of humor. If anyone caught that Obama was trying to connect himself to both the birthplace of civil rights and a time-honored party joke, they didn't laugh or nod.

Obama went on to deliver this not-so-devastating dig at his

opponent: "Congressman Rush exemplifies a politics that is reactive, that waits for crises to happen then holds a press conference, and hasn't been particularly effective at building broad-based coalitions."

He even *talked* like a law professor.

Obama criticized Rush for not reaching outside the black community in his campaign for mayor. It was time for blacks to stop cursing whites and Latinos and figure out what the races had in common. I've been a community organizer, Obama argued, so I can walk into a housing project. And I've been to Harvard Law, so I can walk into a corporate boardroom, too.

"I'm more likely to be able to build the kinds of coalitions and craft the sort of message that appeals to a broad range of people, and that's how you get things accomplished in Congress," he said.

But the Democratic primary wouldn't be decided by a broad range of people. It would be decided by South Side blacks—mainly older blacks who had grown up in the Jim Crow South or in a Chicago of restrictive covenants and color lines. Among those voters, Obama's connections to rich white colleges aroused suspicion.

Rush and his allies fed that suspicion, portraying Obama as a lackey of elite whites. They didn't just attack Obama's credentials. They attacked his education, his neighborhood, and his political allies. They even questioned his blackness. Any opposition research must have begun with *Dreams from My Father*, so Rush knew that black identity was a sensitive spot for the young man who had grown up in a white family. To Rush, a night-school graduate of Roosevelt University and the University of Illinois–Chicago Circle, Obama's Ivy League degrees divorced him from the community he was trying to represent.

"He went to Harvard and became an educated fool!" Rush ranted during an interview in his campaign office, which was decorated with a photo of John Coltrane. "We're not impressed with these folks with these Eastern elite degrees."

During a debate on WVON, Chicago's black radio station, Rush, the old street fighter, talked about leading marches to urge punishment of an off-duty cop who had killed a homeless man.

"It's not enough for us just to protest police misconduct without thinking systematically about how we're going to change practice," Obama responded in measured, mellow tones.

Rush jumped on him.

"We have never been able to progress as a people based on relying solely on the legislative process, and I think that we would be in real critical shape when we start in any way diminishing the role of protest," Rush argued. "Protest has got us where we are today."

After the debate, Rush was still rankled by Obama's suggestion that the black community's marching days were past.

"Barack is a person who read about the civil rights protests and thinks he knows all about it," he said. "I helped make that history, by blood, sweat, and tears."

The black nationalist community, the old bulls who had demonstrated against the Black Panther killings and registered voters for Harold Washington, also resented Obama for his association with another white institution of higher learning: the University of Chicago. Black activists still harbored hard feelings about the university's slum clearance in the 1950s and 1960s. It had been a campaign to drive poor blacks from Hyde Park's academic island, they believed.

There were whispers that a "Hyde Park mafia" was bankrolling an "Obama project" to push the young man up the political ladder. Mikva, whose old North Shore congressional district was the wealthiest in the Midwest, tried to connect Obama with the lawyers and Jewish donors essential to the success of any liberal Democrat, black or white. Mikva wrote Obama a $250 check and held a party in Hyde Park, inviting friends and old law partners from outside the neighborhood. ("It didn't raise much money," Mikva would recall.) Obama was getting money from some of Chicago's most prominent white political givers: $1,000 from former Federal Communications Commission chairman Newton Minow; $1,000 from Tony Rezko. Authors Scott Turow and Sara Paretsky chipped in money. So did some of Obama's Harvard professors. Rashid Khalidi hosted a coffee for Obama at his apartment, serving Lebanese delicacies prepared by his wife, Mona. Obama hired his Springfield sidekick Dan Shomon to manage the campaign.

But Obama also used his run for Congress to build the network of young, rich blacks who would support his Senate campaign a few years later. More than half the members of his finance committee were black entrepreneurs under fifty. They included John Rogers Jr., the millionaire founder of Ariel Investments. Rogers had grown up in Kenwood, just north of Hyde Park, as a Republican—his mother, Jewel LaFontant, was a deputy solicitor general in the Nixon administration and later testified before Congress for the Supreme Court nomination of her old boss Robert Bork. But, as an ambitious Chicagoan, Rogers had drifted toward the Democratic Party. He was finance chairman of Carol Moseley Braun's campaign for Cook County recorder of deeds. When Clarence Thomas was nominated to the Supreme Court in 1991, Rogers officially switched teams.

Rogers had played basketball at Princeton with Obama's brother-in-law, Craig Robinson. He had served on the finance committee of Project Vote! and was at the Ramada Inn when Obama announced his campaign for state senate. That's when he decided Obama was a "magical talent." Rogers was excited to see someone his own age sacrifice a lucrative law career for public service.

Of course, the other half of Obama's finance committee was made up of whites like John Schmidt, who had also raised funds for Project Vote! The more Obama tried to reach outside the black community, the more he was attacked from inside. Because of his academic success, he was even compared to imprisoned ex-congressman Mel Reynolds.

Lu Palmer, an outspoken black journalist, had dismissed Obama as "arrogant" when the young man was organizing Project Vote! and later tried to dissuade him from running against Alice Palmer.

"I said, 'Man, you sound like Mel Reynolds,'" Palmer told me in an interview for the *Reader*. "There are similarities. If you get hung into these elite institutions, and if you so impress white folks at these elite institutions, and if they name you head of these elite institutions, the *Harvard Law Review*, that makes one suspect."

Nobody played the Oreo card more aggressively than State Senator Donne Trotter, the third candidate in the Democratic primary. Trotter, who promoted himself as "Chicago's Native Son," sprang from a more elite strain of the city's black community than Rush. The Trotters had arrived in Chicago around 1900 and were pillars of the South Side's middle class. Trotter's grandfather had been one of the city's most prominent ministers, leading a congregation in Hyde Park. Trotter upheld the family image with tailored suits, bow ties, soul food lunches, and smooth jazz oozing from the speakers of his Jeep.

When it came to racial innuendo, though, Trotter was anything but smooth. He had already developed a disdain for Obama in Springfield, dubbing him "Senator Yo Mama." In an interview at a juice bar on Forty-third Street, in the heart of Bronzeville, Trotter let fly with the campaign's most infamous slur.

"Barack is viewed in part to be the white man in blackface in our community," Trotter said. "You just have to look at his supporters. Who pushed him to get where he is so fast? It's these individuals in Hyde Park, who don't always have the best interests of the community in mind."

(Making those nasty remarks was Trotter's job. He wasn't trying to win. He was a hatchet man. Emil Jones had put him in the race to split the anti-Rush vote.)

Alderman Toni Preckwinkle tried to help Obama connect to the streets. Preckwinkle held a grudge against Rush, because he had run several candidates against her in the last aldermanic elections. When Obama came to Preckwinkle's office to talk about running for Congress, she told him, "Look, I've tried to stay out of Bobby's way. I don't do him any harm. He sent all these people after me this time. I'll be happy to help you, but you've got to decide right away what to do and get going."

Obama didn't make up his mind until the summer. Preckwinkle thought that was awfully late, but she still loaned him her chief of staff, Al Kindle, a veteran fixer who had begun his career organizing wards for Harold Washington. Kindle had actually met Obama back in 1985, when he was working for a gang prevention project that started an after-school program in Altgeld Gardens. Back then, Kindle had been a bigger deal on the South Side than this skinny organizer all the old ladies loved. They'd all said Obama was going places, but Kindle hadn't seen the potential. Not at the time.

Now that he was working for Obama, Kindle saw it as his job to defend the man's blackness. Kindle was a big blood: nearly a head over six feet tall, with the girth of a man who ate an entire plate of chicken wings as an appetizer. He'd worked with gangs for a dozen years, so he was cool walking into Stateway Gardens or the Robert Taylor Homes. Kindle thought of himself as the street heat, "Darth Vader," the man who knew where the gangs hung out, where the drugs were sold, which cops were on the take. His job, as he saw it, was to make sure the word "defeat" wasn't chiseled on a candidate's tombstone.

When Obama marched in the Bud Billiken Parade—the largest African-American parade in the country and an essential appearance for any South Side politician—Kindle rounded up fifteen supporters to march alongside him. In the projects, he heard the questions that Rush and Trotter were trying to raise.

"Who is this African?"

"Does he live in the neighborhood?"

"Is he tough enough?"

"Is he controlled by the white man?"

"Can we *trust* him?"

Kindle had the same answer for every question.

"If you trust *me*, vote for him."

Obama made Kindle's job difficult. He was an inexperienced candidate who thought he could win by showing the voters his brilliance, as though he were still running for president of the *Harvard Law Review*. He just couldn't—or wouldn't—loosen up. The dignified demeanor that had won him a state senate seat in Hyde Park did not translate to the district's inner-city precincts. His internal rhythm was set to "Pomp and Circumstance." At a nightclub called Honeysuckle's, Obama held an event for black teachers, where he defended his education.

"When Congressman Rush and his allies attack me for going to Harvard and teaching at the University of Chicago, they're sending a signal to young black kids that if you're well educated, somehow you're not 'keeping it real,'" he told his listeners.

The air quotes hung over the silent room.

Obama was simply too inhibited, too embarrassed, to force out phrases like "our community," which rolled naturally off the tongues of Rush and Trotter. Al Kindle and Ron Davis got so fed up with Obama's stiff public speaking they tried an intervention. You're giving a lecture, they told him. The purpose of a lecture is to communicate information clearly so students can take notes. That's not a campaign speech.

Obama brushed off the advice.

"Blackness is not based on what you say," he told his advisers. "It's based on what you do."

Davis thought that was an arrogant statement.

"Motherfucker, you ain't goin' anywhere," he taunted Obama. "You ain't gonna get elected dogcatcher. You're full of yourself. You have to let the air out."

Obama was uptight for another reason. He knew he was going to lose.

Obama had sabotaged his campaign when he failed to come home from a Hawaiian vacation to vote on the Safe Neighborhoods Act, a bill that would have made unlawful possession of a loaded firearm a felony. Obama's vote wouldn't have made a difference, but he had been a strident supporter of gun control, so a lot of Chicagoans thought he was absent when his voice was needed most. Once a year, Obama took his family to Hawaii to visit his grandmother Toot. In 1999, he almost canceled the trip because the fight over the Safe Neighborhoods Act went on until

December 22. The Obamas managed to get out of town on Thursday, December 23, and planned to fly back the following Tuesday, so Obama could be in Springfield when the legislature reconvened the next day.

Kindle, who didn't understand that Obama's grandmother was the only matriarchal figure in his life, had tried to talk him out of flying to Hawaii in the middle of a congressional primary. Michelle wanted to go, Obama insisted. That was a difference between Obama and Harold Washington, Kindle came to realize. Washington was a political automaton with no family, no personal life, and no friends outside Chicago.

On the Monday after Christmas, Obama called Dan Shomon to find out whether Governor Ryan was planning to call the legislature back into session. The governor was, Shomon said.

"We're going to have to go back early," Obama told Michelle.

But on the day of the flight, Obama's eighteen-month-old daughter, Malia, came down with the flu. He decided to stay in Hawaii one more day. If Malia seemed to be recovering, the Obamas would fly home together. If not, Barack would fly out alone. Governor Ryan's office was frantically trying to get Obama back to Springfield, even offering him a private plane from Chicago. Obama sensed the vote was symbolic. Unless Republican senate president Pate Philip agreed to a compromise, the bill was going to flunk out of the senate and go back to committee for further negotiations. Despite that, Obama's presence was important to his political career. If you supported a bill, you couldn't skip the vote. Especially not for a Hawaiian vacation.

On Wednesday, December 27, Malia was well enough to fly, and the family returned to Illinois. (If they hadn't made that flight, they wouldn't have been able to get out until January 8.) The bill came up for a vote that day and failed by three votes. Obama was missing from the tally. Governor Ryan, grumpy even when he was in a good mood, was especially unhappy.

"I'm angered, frankly, that the senate didn't do a better job," he said.

Shomon wasn't happy, either. He taunted his candidate with this vision of a negative ad: a man in a beach chair sipping a mai tai as ukulele music played in the background and a deep-voiced narrator sneered, "While Chicago suffered the highest murder rate in its history, Barack Obama . . ."

Obama never apologized for putting his daughter's health above politics. Once he got back to Chicago, he called Abner Mikva, who supported his decision.

"Barack," Mikva said, "when I was in Congress, there were times when you don't want to, but your family is an issue, and we put our families through so many things, so many sacrifices in this process, anyway, that every once in a while, we have to make decisions in terms of what you think is best for your family, and I think that this was one of those decisions."

Even more than the murder of Bobby Rush's son, the Safe Neighborhoods Act vote convinced Obama that his campaign was a lost cause.

"Each morning from that point onward I awoke with a vague sense of dread," he would write in *The Audacity of Hope*, "realizing that I would have to spend the day smiling and shaking hands and pretending that everything was going according to plan."

Obama's opponents didn't need to run that Hawaiian ad. The callow state senator was castigated in the *Tribune*'s "Inc." column (the headline: D-U-M) and by callers to WVON. He had to answer for his missed vote during a candidates' forum with Trotter in the dank basement of a park field house.

"If you initiate a lot of ideas and at the time of a vote you're not there, how can we count on you?" a voter asked.

Obama answered curtly. "If you look at my record in Springfield, I don't miss votes. I missed one as a result of my daughter being sick. That's an exceptional situation that doesn't arise often."

The man didn't buy Obama's excuse.

"If you tell me this is one of your issues, and then you miss the vote, that concerns me," he said afterward. "With that in mind, I'm very reluctant to support him for anything. I think he's biting off a little more than he can chew. He's got some good issues, but he's too green."

That was the debate where Obama finally lost his cool. Even his body language signaled it. He sat with his lanky legs crossed, chin cocked at a heroic angle. He wasn't even trying to conceal his impatience with Trotter, a mere state senate peer, or with this grungy necessity of campaigning.

Trotter was a traditional Chicago politician, a cloakroom operator who knew how to pass a bill. He liked to brag about the pork he brought home to his district—$26 million for a library at Chicago State University, $75 million for resurfacing Lake Shore Drive. He'd been an architect of the state's child health care system. Like many senators, Trotter thought Obama considered himself too cool for the chamber and disdained the hard work of digging up votes. That evening, he shared his perception with the voters in the folding chairs. Trotter hunched over his microphone, taking digs at his increasingly irritated rival. When he needled Obama for failing to corral enough votes to override Ryan's veto of the child support bill, Obama's calm finally dissolved.

"Senator, that's a distortion!" Obama snapped. His baritone went full fathom five, but he never unbent from his patrician pose.

When I interviewed Obama at his downtown law office, in early February, his answers only reinforced the accusation that he was arrogant. Obama had always seen himself as a special figure, bound for a bigger destiny than the people around him. In *Dreams from My Father*, even the portraits of his family members—a dreamy, hippie-ish mother, an ineffectual grandfather—were a little patronizing. He *was* bound for a big destiny, but that's no way to portray yourself to the voters, especially in one of the nation's poorest congressional districts.

Obama had been a golden boy for so long: embraced by the Ivy League, profiled in the *New York Times*, a published author at thirty-four, a state senator a year later. For the first time in his life, his ambitions were being blocked. The world was pushing back. His impatience showed in a condescension to his surroundings.

Why, I asked him, should the voters choose a newcomer to the South Side over two men who had grown up in Chicago?

Obama struggled for an answer, then joked that his willingness to move from Balmy Hawaii to frozen Chicago showed he was more committed to the city than many natives.

"I really have to want to be here," he said. "I'm like a salmon swimming upstream in the South Side of Chicago. At every juncture in my life, I could have taken the path of least resistance but much higher pay. Being the president of the *Harvard Law Review* is a big deal. The typical path for someone like myself is to clerk for the Supreme Court, and then basically you have your pick of any law firm in the country."

Didn't the people appreciate the sacrifices he'd made? To grind out a voter registration drive when he could have been earning $200K a year at a white-shoe firm? To pick his way over an ice-glazed Chicago sidewalk when he could have been body-surfing back home in Honolulu?

Bobby Rush understood the struggles and aspirations of the high school dropout or the hotel maid trying to raise three children in a way that was impossible for Obama. Obama's blackness had been an advantage with his *Law Review* colleagues and his New York publisher. Rush's blackness had been another handicap to overcome, like his stutter or his poverty.

When Rush was invited to speak from the pulpit of Southwestern Baptist Church, on South Michigan Avenue, he urged the congregation to buy computers and hook up to the Internet, so knowledge would flow into their homes. Using his seminary training, he made a religious connection for his audience, comparing the Web to the Gutenberg Bible, which allowed all Christians to read what only the "high-class, super-elite" priests had seen.

"At one time, the Bible was only read and understood by a very few people," Rush told his listeners. "These folks intimidated those that didn't have access to the Bible. God in his wisdom created the printing press. Then the Bible was mass-produced, so common ordinary folk snatched the power from the elite. I look at the Internet the same way. If we are computer literate, we are on the same level as Bill Gates, the richest man in the world. We are on common ground with the wealthy and powerful. You can bring the libraries of the world to your living room, whether your living room is on South Michigan Avenue or in the richest suburbs."

Obama had gotten some good press for a proposal to spend $50 million on computers for South Side schools, but he'd never expressed the need that eloquently, in the language of black empowerment.

Rush's success in the churches—he held a "Clergy for Rush" rally at which over a hundred ministers gathered in front of a WE ARE STICKING WITH BOBBY! banner—revealed another of Obama's miscalculations. He had assumed that Rush's mayoral defeat meant he was vulnerable in his congressional district. But Rush was clobbering Obama for the same reason he'd lost the mayoral race—he was a South Sider to his bones. Rush had flopped as a citywide candidate because he couldn't see beyond the needs of his community. As a congressman, he didn't have to.

Trotter's campaign had no money, but he could use his family name, and his neighborhood background, to connect with audiences. Trotter had been a Boy Scout with Ralph Metcalfe's son and later worked on one of the congressman's campaigns. At fifty, he was old enough to remember the heyday of Bronzeville, when the Palm Tavern was the hangout for Billy Eckstine and all the jazz greats, and when apartments since chopped up into flophouses were home to writers and teachers.

When Trotter shook hands at a senior citizen center, an old man asked, "Are you related to Reverend Trotter?"

"He was my grandfather," Trotter responded proudly.

"I *know* the Trotter family," the old man noted after the senator had moved on. "The Trotter name is well-known in Chicago. His auntie was the wife of Joe Louis."

Obama's state senate district encompassed empty black neighborhoods with abandoned shopping centers and brownstone row houses standing alone among fields of weeds. But as a congressional candidate, his forays outside Hyde Park rarely addressed serious ghetto problems. Once, he called a press conference to condemn bidi cigarettes—hand-rolled, highly carcinogenic smokes from

India. He was joined by Father Michael Pfleger, a rabble-rousing white priest who led a mostly black congregation, and Alderman Terry Peterson, one of the few black politicians who supported Obama's congressional run. Only one reporter showed up.

One-third of the First District's residents were white, and Obama aggressively courted their votes, opening a campaign office in Beverly, a neighborhood that was home to Irish cops and firemen who did not appreciate being represented by a former Black Panther.

"I think it sends a message to our young people that you can be a big-time rabble-rouser and be in a position of importance later," said a Beverly accountant who shared the anybody-but-Rush sentiment of so many South Side whites. "What incentive does that kid have to behave? He went way beyond the bounds of legitimate dissent. If we're going to say the seat should be occupied by a black person, I've got to believe there's someone better."

A month before the election, death once again halted the campaign. Bobby Rush's seventy-two-year-old father, Jimmy Lee Rush, took ill in Georgia. Rush canceled his appearances and flew down south. He wouldn't return for a week, until after the funeral, where he read a poem he had composed himself. Rush's father was eulogized in the *Tribune*, and the congressman's office issued this statement: "With less than six months between the burying of my son, Huey, and my father, I know my faith is being tested. However, it is only that faith and the loving support of my wife, family, and friends that supplies me with the strength to keep going."

Obama made his first use of electronic media during the congressional campaign: a pair of thirty-second radio ads. He didn't have much money, and in Chicago, it was too expensive to buy a TV ad for a race that concerned only a small percentage of the viewers. Instead, Obama advertised on black-oriented radio stations, with spots that emphasized issues and barely mentioned his biography. When they did, he was a "civil rights lawyer" and "head of Project Vote!," not a Harvard grad. The first ad, aimed at senior citizens, promised that Obama would fight for cheaper prescription drugs in Congress.

VOICE-OVER: State senator Barack Obama, candidate for Congress, speaking with a group of frustrated South Side seniors.

SENIOR CITIZEN: Senator Obama, because the prescription drugs have gotten so high, sometimes I can't afford the medicine I need.

SENIOR CITIZEN: You know, I've always backed Bobby Rush, but I don't see him doing anything about these high prices.

OBAMA: Let me tell you something. The profits of drug companies are at record levels. Meanwhile, we've got seniors who are having to choose between their food, their rent, and their prescription drugs. That's not right. I'm running for Congress to fight for First District families and our seniors on prescription drugs and HMO reform.

VOICE-OVER: Barack Obama. Civil rights lawyer. The head of Project Vote! As our state senator, Barack Obama has taken on the drug and insurance companies with his fight for affordable health care.

OBAMA: America's health care system locks out too many people. I'm fighting to change that.

SENIOR CITIZEN: Barack, we need a congressman like you who will do more than just talk.

[Applause]

VOICE-OVER: Barack Obama, Democrat for Congress. New leadership that works for us.

OBAMA: Paid for by Obama for Congress 2000.

The second ad attempted to burnish his black credentials by pointing out that he had sponsored a bill to ban racial profiling in traffic stops.

COP: Hand over your driver's license!

MOTORIST: But, officer, I wasn't speeding.

COP: Don't talk back to me. Get out of the car.

MOTORIST: But what did I do?

COP: I'll worry about that. Now open the trunk.

VOICE-OVER: It could happen to you. Or to someone you love. Stopped by police for no apparent reason, except that you fit a racial profile secretly used by police. It's called racial profiling, and it's an unethical and dangerous practice that needs to end.

Now state senator Barack Obama, candidate for Congress in the First District, is leading the fight to end racial profiling.

OBAMA: This is state senator Barack Obama. Racial profiling is not only wrong and degrading, it's dangerous and can lead to unexpected confrontations. Not only that, it erodes confidence in law enforcement. That's why I've introduced legislation to address the problem of racial profiling and protect you from those who would abuse your rights.

VOICE-OVER: Barack Obama, Democrat for Congress. New leadership that works for us.

OBAMA: Paid for by Obama for Congress 2000.

Primary day is always cold in Chicago, but Obama stood dutifully in front of elementary schools and park field houses, shaking hands with voters. He cut a lean, handsome figure in his black topcoat and gray scarf. Over and over, the old ladies shuffling to the polls told him the same thing: "You seem like a nice young man, but Bobby hasn't done anything wrong."

If Obama had known in his bones that he was going to lose, now he was hearing the bad news to his face. The local TV stations called the race even before Obama arrived at his Election Night party. The final tally was 61 percent for Rush, 30 percent for Obama, and 7 percent for Trotter. Obama barely won his own neighborhood, taking 55 percent of the vote in Hyde Park.

"There's no more difficult play in politics than running against an incumbent," Obama told his supporters in a concession speech at the Ramada Inn Lakeshore. "I think we did it very well."

But later, talking to a reporter at the party, Obama sounded fed up with politics. He wasn't sure whether he'd ever run for office again.

"I've got to make some assessments about where we go from here," he said. "We need a new style of politics to deal with the issues that are important to people. What's not clear to me is whether I should do that as an elected official or by influencing government in ways that actually improve people's lives."

Obama was dejected, demoralized, and bitter about his opponents' personal attacks.

"Me being president of the *Harvard Law Review*, I never thought it could be a liability," he told Jesse Ruiz, "but it was a liability in this race."

Obama didn't lose because he was "too white." He lost because he was a presumptuous young man challenging a popular incumbent. If anything, his whiteness spared him a bigger beating. He ran strongly in Beverly and the southwest suburbs. Obama also hemmed and hawed too long before committing himself to the campaign, and once he was in, he didn't devote enough time to building a grassroots organization or raising money. Calling his Harvard classmates was no substitute for cultivating donors on the South Side.

Winning the seat in the historic First Congressional District would have added Obama's name to a lineage of powerful black leaders: Oscar DePriest, William Dawson, Ralph Metcalfe, and his own political inspiration, Harold Washington. It would also have put him in line for the job he had coveted ever since arriving on the South Side: mayor of Chicago.

Defeat always smarts for a politician, especially one who has never before failed at anything.

It stung Obama to have his credentials as a black man questioned, and it stung him even more to lose. But in losing, he absorbed a lesson that would carry him far higher than he could have risen as the First District's congressman. Obama was never meant to be a voice of black empowerment, in the way that Rush and Jesse Jackson were. It wasn't just a racial thing. It was generational, too. Confrontational sixties-style politics were not his bag. With his biracial heritage, Obama was born to reconcile the interests of blacks and whites. He tried to sell that message in 2000, but he was running against a civil rights icon in the blackest congressional district in America. It was the wrong race, and the wrong time, for the emergence of Barack Obama.

The week of his defeat, Obama returned to Springfield, where he sat down to his regular poker game at Terry Link's house. The same words were on the lips of every pol at that table: "I told you so." Obama didn't need to hear it. He knew he'd blundered.

Around that time, Obama also had a soul-searching drink with Rich Miller, the publisher of *Capitol Fax*, a Springfield newsletter. During the campaign, Miller had told me, "Barack is a very intelligent man, but he hasn't had a lot of success here, and it could be because he places himself above everybody. He likes people to know he went to Harvard."

Obama was upset about the way Miller had characterized him, but "he took that criticism the right way," Miller would remember years later.

"A lot of politicians, they know that they're smart," Miller said. "They know that they're capable. It messes with their minds. Politics is not a game of qualifications. It's a game of winning. That congressional campaign really showed that to him."

Losing that race helped Obama in another way: It humbled him. Before his encounter with Bobby Rush, Obama was a cocky young pol in a hurry. He needed the deepening experience of defeat to learn who he was as a politician. It wouldn't be enough to present himself as Barack Obama, first black president of the *Harvard Law Review*. He was going to have to stand for something, too.

After the primary, Obama was broke—he had neglected his law practice for six months—and he was persona non grata in a party that had closed ranks around Rush. That summer, Obama flew to the Democratic National Convention in Los Angeles, at the urging of friends who still believed he had a political future. When he landed, he had trouble even renting a car. Hertz rejected his American Express card. Obama eventually got his car but then couldn't get a pass for the convention floor. Sorry, the chairman of the Illinois delegation told Obama. I'm getting a ton of requests. So Obama watched the speeches on TVs in the Staples Center concourse. Once in a while, he sneaked into a skybox by tagging along with friends. Lesson: In Chicago, you wait your turn, young man. Dispirited, Obama returned home before Al Gore was nominated.

Chapter 10

"I'LL KICK YOUR ASS RIGHT NOW"

AFTER HIS FAILED CAMPAIGN against Bobby Rush, Obama's reputation in the black political community was worse than ever. First, this young punk had knocked a little old lady schoolteacher off the ballot and taken her senate seat. Then, he'd tried to beat an incumbent congressman who'd been marching in the streets for civil rights when Obama was a kindergartener in Hawaii.

On Election Night, Rush called Obama and Trotter "very important individuals" and invited them "to work together on the issues that are of concern to the residents of the First Congressional District": "Let's work on the transportation issues. Let's work on the health issues. Let's work on the economic development, and I think we can accomplish a lot together," he said.

Those were just the words of a winner who wanted to sound gracious in the press. In reality, Rush had developed a deep grudge against Obama. Rush had mortgages and children in college, and Obama had tried to take away his livelihood. (Of course, Rush himself had won the seat by beating an elderly incumbent in an election that was also about generational change, from the preachers and funeral directors of the civil rights era to the militants of the black power movement.) When the congressional districts were redrawn after the 2000 census, Obama's condo was a few blocks outside the First District. Rush claimed he'd had nothing to do with the gerrymandering, which divided Hyde Park between himself and Jesse Jackson Jr. Obama pretended not to care, telling the *Tribune* he had no plans to run for Congress again.

In fact, Obama was thinking of quitting politics altogether. During what friends would call his "pity party" after losing to Rush, he almost accepted a job as executive director of the Joyce Foundation. He didn't want to leave politics, he told Ab Mikva, but it was a six-figure job, and Michelle was worried about the family's finances, especially since the congressional campaign had put the Obamas even deeper in debt. The Joyce Foundation had supported the Developing Communities Project, so it was a place where Obama could work to improve the inner city, maybe more so than a politician could. If he couldn't beat Bobby Rush, how was he ever going to get out of the state senate?

Mikva urged Obama to stay in the legislature. If he couldn't afford to do that, Mikva said, he should take the professorship the law school was pushing on him. That would pay as well as the foundation and offer more freedom to keep his hand in politics.

Obama spent the first few months after the primary stewing over his defeat. Once he got over it, he realized that if he was going to have a political future, he would have to repair his relationship with the black community. Bobby Rush's crowd—the nationalists, the militants, the folks who wanted to rail against the white man—would never embrace him now. During the campaign, Obama had made it clear he considered their brand of politics self-defeating.

"On issues of job creation, education, health care, we have more in common with the Latino community and the white community than we have differences," he'd said. "And we have to work with them, just from a practical political perspective. It may give us psychic satisfaction to curse out people outside the community and blame them for our plight, but the truth of the matter is if we want to get things accomplished politically, then we've got to be able to work with them."

There was a segment of black Chicago that was ready to hear Obama's vision of pan-racial politics: the business community. Although Obama was not wealthy—at best, the family was upper-middle-class—he already socialized with members of the city's black bourgeoisie. John Rogers was a close friend, as was Marty Nesbitt, a vice president of the Pritzker Realty Group. (Nesbitt's wife, an obstetrician, delivered both of Obama's daughters.) Obama was also a member of the East Bank Club, a downtown gym/networking salon popular with Chicago's professional class. He played pickup basketball with Jim Reynolds, CEO of Loop Capital Markets, an investment banking firm. Reynolds knew only that Obama was a state senator, which wasn't enough to impress him. Then, one day, he was browsing at Borders and found *Dreams from My Father* in the discount bin. Surprised that one of his basketball partners had written a book, Reynolds bought a copy. The next time he saw Obama on the court, Reynolds mentioned *Dreams*.

"Hey, you know, I read your book," he told Obama. "You're a pretty good writer. You had an interesting background."

"Well, I know I'm a good writer!" Obama shouted back.

After that, Obama and Reynolds became regular teammates. They also met up for golf at the South Shore Country Club, where Obama always won by keeping the ball in the fairway and hitting no errant shots. When Reynolds was in Springfield, he used Obama's state senate office as his own.

Reynolds, who was one of the buppies on the Obama for

Congress finance committee, also helped Obama plot his next political move: a run for the U.S. Senate. On the night Obama lost to Rush, Reynolds tried to buck up his friend by assuring him there would be other races, for bigger offices.

"Hey, man, don't feel bad," he told Obama. "Let's figure out what we're going to do next."

It wasn't long before they did. Obama and Reynolds sat down with Marty Nesbitt and ran through the list of statewide offices. Attorney general would be open in 2002, but Obama's fellow state senator Lisa Madigan had her eye on it. And Madigan was the daughter of the state's most powerful Democrat, House Speaker Michael Madigan. The Senate looked more promising. The Republican incumbent, Peter Fitzgerald, was seen as a one-term fluke. Fitzgerald had not so much beaten Carol Moseley Braun (herself a one-term fluke) as been in the right place to benefit from her missteps. Once in office, he alienated his party by appointing a U.S. attorney from out of state. Unfamiliar with the Chicago Way, Patrick Fitzgerald (no relation) prosecuted corrupt Republicans and Democrats with equal ardor. Senator Fitzgerald had even tried to block funding for a new Lincoln museum in Springfield, figuring it was just pork for Governor George Ryan and his lobbyist pals. As a result, he had no friends in the Illinois GOP, and the word was he would either step down or face a primary challenge from a Republican more willing to play the game.

Reynolds began bringing Obama to meetings of the Alliance of Business Leaders and Entrepreneurs, an all-black business group that met for a monthly luncheon at the Chicago Club. Obama was one of the few politicians among a crowd of investors, bankers, publishers, and attorneys. Whenever anyone questioned his presence, Reynolds made one thing clear: "If you want to be a friend of mine, you have to be a friend of his." While Obama never gave a speech at the ABLE meetings, he was meeting people whose money he would need to run for higher office.

Chicago's black business community has a history as long and rich as that of its black political class. Like the politicians, the entrepreneurs got their first opportunities because of segregation. Whites wouldn't bury blacks or sell them life insurance policies, so storefront funeral parlors and insurance offices sprang up in the ghetto. Whites couldn't cut African hair, so blacks opened their own barbershops and beauty parlors. The downtown dailies ignored life in the Black Belt (*Tribune* editors ordered reporters not to write "blue" news—a code word for African-American.) So blacks communicated with each other through their own network of newspapers, magazines, and radio stations.

Some of America's first black millionaires were Chicagoans, operating businesses that catered only to other blacks. John H. Johnson published *Ebony* and *Jet* magazines from a Michigan Avenue office tower that now bears his company's logo. Ed Gardner sold his Soft Sheen and Ultra Sheen hair care products in drugstores across the nation.

In Chicago, business and politics are inseparable. Wealthy blacks have always been expected to contribute a share of their fortunes to black politicians. In return, they benefit from pinstripe patronage, the practice of handing out big government contracts to big political donors. And, of course, some of that big money ends up back in the campaign funds of the politicians who handed out the contracts.

When Harold Washington was running for mayor, he was backed by the city's black grocers, auto dealers, undertakers, and tavern owners. Once he got into office, he tried to create a new class of black professionals by cutting his people into city business that had once been reserved for the Irish and the WASPs. Washington made sure that blacks got a bigger share of city contracts than they'd received from white mayors. This was a huge boon to black developers and contractors. Once they'd proven they could build a school in the city, why couldn't they build a shopping center in the suburbs? The mayor also made it clear that he would steer more of the city's lucrative bond counsel business to law firms with black partners. Maynard Jackson, who later became mayor of Atlanta, was then a partner with Chapman and Cutler, the city's premier bond firm. After Jackson left to start an Atlanta office in the mid-1980s, the firm needed another black bond lawyer to stay on city hall's good side. It trained a young partner named Stephen Pugh, who eventually started his own public finance law firm, Pugh, Jones, and became an ABLE member.

Washington's campaign to bring blacks into traditionally white businesses was so important because black entrepreneurs had actually been damaged by the civil rights movement. Once blacks could shop downtown at Marshall Field's, they didn't need the clothing boutique on Forty-seventh Street. Once they could go to the show at any movie theater, the neighborhood picture palace shut down (or started screening kung fu or porno movies). Black dollars were leaving the community, but white dollars weren't coming in. The next generation of black millionaires couldn't depend on the ghetto trade; they would have to do business with all races.

As a state senator, Obama was valuable to the members of ABLE. Along with Emil Jones (who was also invited to ABLE meetings), he worked to open up the state's pension fund to minority investment firms.

"We wanted to, as black businessmen, have a relationship with everybody, so they would know our needs and where we were coming from, and be responsive to us," Pugh would say. "In the public finance area, I'm sure that as he went down and looked at the deals that were coming through the state, he made sure that firms like Pugh, Jones were at least put on the list so that we could bid or be selected if we won the competition. It was never a thing that I knew him to say, 'Pugh, Jones needs to get this next bond deal.' Nothing like that. But the state workers knew we were out there. There were people like Emil who were making sure that they just didn't ignore, as they had in the past, minority business in the process."

However Obama and Jones worked, Pugh, Jones got more business from the state of Illinois. In 2002, Pugh's firm was involved in a $10 billion bond deal to support the state retirement system. It also worked on a deal to privatize the state lottery. When the time came, Pugh would find a way to help Obama in return.

During the congressional campaign, Obama had been caricatured as an ineffectual state senator, a man so consumed with his own ambition, so eager to use Springfield as a stepladder to Washington, that he didn't bother to learn the ins and outs of legislating. Despite his success with welfare reform and child support, Obama was still seen as an idealist who thought cloakroom negotiations were beneath his dignity.

When Obama returned to the capitol, he began taking his work—and his colleagues—more seriously. Before, he'd been a résumé in search of an office. Now he was determined to make a name for himself on issues important to his urban district. Some senators thought that Obama had been humbled by his loss to Rush. Donne Trotter didn't quite see it that way. He had to admit his fellow senator was working harder, but humble? Barack

Obama? Obama was a competitor, and competitors don't like to lose. The once-impatient young man immersed himself in the legislative process, learning the "get-along" qualities necessary to pass a bill. No longer a loner, Obama was taking advice from colleagues he'd ignored during his first four years.

Obama, Trotter, and Rickey Hendon cosponsored a racial profiling bill that would have required police to record the race, age, and gender of every driver they pulled over. (It never got out of the Judiciary Committee.) Obama also argued, unsuccessfully, against a bill that made gangbangers eligible for the death penalty if they committed a murder as part of gang activity. It's never popular to look as though you're sticking up for the Vice Lords, so Obama voted "present" on the bill, but only after insinuating it was racially motivated.

"I'm concerned about us targeting particular neighborhoods or particular types of individuals for enhancements, as opposed to others," he said on the senate floor.

The bill was more or less symbolic. Governor Ryan had declared a moratorium on the death penalty after thirteen death row prisoners—one more than the state had executed since 1976—were proven innocent. Unlike many black legislators, Obama never declared himself an opponent of capital punishment, but he supported Ryan's moratorium, and he always supported death penalty reform, such as allowing DNA evidence to review cases.

Obama did pass two women's health bills. One required all hospitals to tell rape victims about the morning-after pill. (It passed after the sponsors made an exception for Catholic hospitals, who didn't have to provide the information if the victim was ovulating.) He also passed a bill expanding Medicaid to cover breast and cervical cancer screening.

But Obama's biggest success in the year after the congressional race was an affordable-housing bill that ended up exposing his relationships with South Side developers and slumlords. Having worked in Altgeld Gardens, Obama saw the folly of housing projects: how they corralled the poor into isolated communities where joblessness, drug dealing, and shootings became ways of life, passed on from one generation to the next. Obama believed private developers could do a better job of managing low-income apartments than the Chicago Housing Authority. The profit motive made them superior landlords, and their buildings were more likely to be located in middle-class neighborhoods.

Obama's bill, which he sponsored with William Peterson, a suburban Republican, gave a 50-percent tax credit to donations toward developing affordable housing, setting aside $13 million a year from the state's coffers.

Throughout his career in Chicago, Obama took hundreds of thousands of dollars from developers. Some, like Tony Rezko and Allison Davis, were guilty of building low-cost apartments that almost instantly deteriorated into slums: rat haunted, freezing in winter, occupied by squatters and drug dealers.

As an associate at Davis, Miner, Obama had worked with nonprofit groups that helped developers win government grants to build affordable housing. Among them was the Woodlawn Preservative and Investment Co., which was headed by Bishop Arthur Brazier, a Saul Alinsky protégé and influential black pastor who preached on television every Sunday morning. Brazier's group partnered with Rezko in redeveloping slum properties. Rezko was so closely associated with Davis, Miner that Allison Davis eventually left the law firm to go into the real estate business with him. In all, Davis, Miner represented three community groups in partnership with Rezko's company, Rezmar Inc. Through those groups, the firm helped Rezko obtain $43 million in government funds. Obama did only five hours of legal work for Rezko, under the supervision of more experienced attorneys, but he had met the developer even before joining the firm.

During his rise through Illinois politics, it was inevitable that Obama would encounter a suckerfish like Rezko. Illinois has more governments than any other state—over five hundred in Cook County alone—and therefore more opportunities for grafters. Antoin "Tony" Rezko arrived in Chicago from Syria in 1971. He barely spoke English, and he belonged to an ethnic group—Arab Christians—too small to elect even an alderman. There's only one way a guy like that can obtain political power. He has to buy it.

Rezko began his career as a civil engineer but was soon investing in real estate and fast food restaurants. He built houses on the South Side and opened Subway sandwich shops and Papa John's pizzerias. Those deals provided Rezko with the money to connect with his first powerful patron: Muhammad Ali. In 1983, at the urging of Ali's business manager, Jabir Herbert Muhammad, Rezko held a fund-raiser for Harold Washington. After that, he was invited to join Ali's entourage as a business consultant. Rezko put together endorsement deals for the Greatest and was executive director of the Muhammad Ali Foundation, a group devoted to spreading Islam.

Rezko used his connection with Ali to expand his fast food holdings. After Washington became mayor, Jabir Herbert Muhammad's company, Crucial Concessions, won the contract to sell food and drinks at the Lake Michigan beaches. Rezko took over the company's operations. In 1997, Crucial opened three Panda Express restaurants at O'Hare, under the city's Minority Set-Aside Program. It would be stripped of those franchises in

2005, when investigators determined the company was a front for Rezko.

In 1989 Rezko and a business partner founded Rezmar Inc., a real estate company that aimed to rehabilitate South Side apartment buildings. Partnering with community groups, Rezmar purchased thirty properties. The company's work was done on the cheap, but that was at the urging of the city, which figured rehabbers could develop more units if they installed low-grade appliances and cabinetry. When boilers and refrigerators wore out after six or seven years, Rezmar hadn't banked enough money to repair them. Eventually, the city stepped in and forced Rezmar to turn up the heat on six properties, including one that went unheated for five weeks.

Rezko's partner oversaw day-to-day maintenance. Rezko's job was to raise equity and cultivate politicians. He was a master at leveraging political contacts for contracts and grants. Rezko scouted young talent as skillfully as a basketball coach sitting in the stands of a high school field house. In 1990, a Rezmar executive read an article about Obama's election as president of the *Harvard Law Review*. Intrigued by Obama's interest in housing issues and his plans to return to Chicago, the executive phoned the young law student and struck up a friendship. When the executive learned that Obama was interested in politics, he introduced him to Rezko, who was as blown away as everyone else Obama lunched with in those years.

"He's great," Rezko raved to the executive. "He's really going places."

Around the same time he was courting Obama, Rezko was also cultivating an ambitious young state legislator named Rod Blagojevich. Like Obama, Blagojevich was a self-made politician—his immigrant steelworker father raised the family in an apartment. Guys like that were easy targets for Rezko, who could provide the money they hadn't inherited. The day Obama announced his campaign for state senate in 1995, he received $2,000 from two of Rezko's fast-food businesses.

When Davis and Rezko wanted to build a senior apartment house in Obama's senate district, Obama wrote letters to the city and state supporting loans for the project. Both developers would later hold fund-raisers for Obama at their homes.

Rezko built part of his fortune by exploiting the black community Obama served in the state senate. But Obama took Rezko's money, even after the businessman was sued by the city of Chicago for failing to heat his low-income apartments, even after he was caught using a black business partner to obtain a minority set-aside for a fast-food franchise at O'Hare Airport, and even after he was under grand jury investigation on charges he had demanded kickbacks from investment firms seeking money from the Illinois Teachers' Retirement System.

During his first year in the U.S. Senate, flush with the book advance for *The Audacity of Hope*, Obama and his wife would decide to trade up from a condo to a bigger, more secure home in Kenwood, a neighborhood of Edwardian piles popular with U of C econ professors looking to blow their Nobel Prize loot. They found a $1.65 million house with four fireplaces, a wine cellar, and a black wrought-iron fence. The doctor who lived there also owned the vacant lot next door and, although the properties were listed separately, wanted to sell both at the same time. Despite their new income, the Obamas could not have afforded both parcels. The Obamas closed on their house in June 2005. On the same day, Rezko's wife, Rita, purchased the vacant lot for $625,000. They later sold a portion of the lot to the

Obamas, for $104,500, so the family could expand its yard. The Rezkos then paid $14,000 to build a fence along the property line.

At the time, Obama knew that Rezko was under a legal cloud but told the *Tribune* "as long as I operated in an open, up-front fashion, and all the T's were crossed and I's were dotted, that it wouldn't be an issue."

Obama believed so strongly in his own integrity that he thought he could associate with a grifter while maintaining his Senator Galahad self-image. "A lot of people ask me, 'Why would you want to go into a dirty business like politics?'" he often said in his speeches. So the business will have one less corrupt, cynical politician, was the implication. He was convinced he could work alongside Chicago politicians while not becoming one himself, as long as he maintained a sense of higher purpose. This is a common delusion among officeholders, especially those as idealistic as Obama.

"In the state senate, he had a real sense of personal mission," said James L. Merriner, author of several books on Illinois politics. "I think he thought he was just above it. He seemed to think he was on a plane above that."

Tony Rezko taught Obama that you can't go into a dirty business like politics—especially Chicago politics—without losing some of your innocence.

Obama also took contributions from condo developers. Every South Side politician did. If you want to run for office, you need money, and who has more money than a real estate tycoon? Those donations were controversial, too, because Obama's district was being gentrified from two directions. On the northern end, whites who enjoyed downtown living were moving into the South Loop, which had once been a Skid Row district of taverns, men's hotels, and missions. (The South Loop's Second Ward had been represented by a black alderman since Oscar DePriest won there in 1915. Bobby Rush lived in the Second Ward. Before the decade's end, it would elect a white alderman.) On the southern end, middle-class whites and blacks were pushing out of Hyde Park, redeveloping run-down areas around the University of Chicago campus. Despite the urging of preservation groups, Obama did not object to a plan to demolish Geri's Palm Tavern, a historic Forty-seventh Street nightclub, and replace it with an upscale restaurant. Harold Lucas, who ran tours of Bronzeville through his company Black Metropolis Convention and Tourism, tried to get Obama involved in the fight to save Geri's, but "that was too controversial," he would recall. "He did not step up to that fight."

Obama didn't want to step on the toes of the local alderman, Dorothy Tillman, who favored the demolition. Tillman, an outspoken politician known for wearing broad-brimmed Sunday-best hats and carrying a gun in her purse, had a strong following among black nationalists.

"There's nothing that jumps out in my mind that he did to risk political capital for my community," Lucas would say years later. "I don't recall anything he did as state senator that empowered the black community."

In that respect, he was the completely opposite of Bronzeville's state representative, Lou Jones. Jones was indigenous to the South Side, having begun her political career as president of the resident council in the T. K. Lawless Gardens housing project. As a politician, Jones never forgot where she had come from; Obama never forgot where he was trying to go. Appearing too black might cost him the white votes he needed for statewide office. As Obama's political career advanced, Harold Lucas came to understand the tricky course Obama was following and always supported his campaigns. Obama might not have been the voice of black empowerment, with a raised fist and a copy of *The Wretched of the Earth* on his bookshelf, but he was at least in a position to bring the community's concerns to the white mainstream.

Toni Preckwinkle, who represented a portion of Bronzeville on the city council, also believed that Obama neglected the neighborhood for purposes of political ambition. Every state senator is given a budget for "member initiatives." It's a goodie fund to spread around the district however he sees fit. In the early 2000s, as Obama was recovering from his loss to Rush and incubating his Senate ambitions, he gave the largest chunk of his member initiative money—$1.1 million—to the Seventeenth Ward, in the southeastern corner of his senate district. The money went mainly for park improvements. Preckwinkle's Fourth Ward got $275,000.

Obviously, every alderman wants more money for her ward, but Preckwinkle was incensed because Obama represented the entire Fourth Ward, while he only represented a small corner of the Seventeenth. She concluded he was trying to score points with Seventeenth Ward alderman Terry Peterson. Like Preckwinkle, Peterson had endorsed Obama in his run for Congress. But Peterson was close to Mayor Daley, whose support could guarantee Obama victory in a Senate primary. (Daley would later appoint Peterson to head the Chicago Housing Authority.) Preckwinkle had backed Obama in his dispute with Alice Palmer *and* his challenge to Rush, and now she was getting leftovers while Obama fattened up a new friend. Using member initiative money to advance his career was evidence of the disloyalty and opportunism that were becoming Obama's modus operandi as he grasped for higher office.

Preckwinkle was particularly frustrated because Obama claimed he didn't have the money to help the city buy and relocate a church that was standing in the way of a proposed pedestrian bridge across Lake Shore Drive.

"We asked him to do things, and it didn't happen, and, subsequently, we discovered that his resources were going other places," she would later complain. "To people who would be useful to him in the future versus people who had helped him in the past."

Even though she considered Obama a social-climbing ingrate, Preckwinkle continued to support his campaigns, lending him staff members and putting his name on her ward organization's Election Day palm cards. As an alderman, she had learned to make a distinction between candidates she liked personally and candidates whose politics she liked. A black U.S. senator would be important to her community.

As a committeeman, though, Preckwinkle was in a position to take some revenge. After Obama won the U.S. Senate seat, he would personally ask Preckwinkle to support Will Burns—his former student and legislative staffer—as his successor in Springfield. Preckwinkle would refuse. Instead, she voted to appoint a lawyer named Kwame Raoul. (Burns eventually won a seat in the state house, representing Bronzeville. There, he finally gave Preckwinkle the money to move that church.)

Obama didn't make the daily papers often during his early years in the senate. He wasn't in the leadership, so he was never involved in budget negotiations, which is always the biggest story out of Springfield. If Barack Obama and Emil Jones walked out of a room together, reporters were going to ignore Obama and surround Jones. Occasionally, he was mentioned in a page 5 metro section story about a bill to crack down on payday loan operations. Like any ambitious politician, though, he cultivated the media. There was an affinity between Obama and journalists. He was a published author, so he had a literary sensibility and knew the toil that went into writing. Obama also shared the press corps's political outlook: He was a liberal reformer who believed in open government. His bill to post campaign contributions on the Internet was a boon to investigative journalism in Illinois. Beyond that, he was articulate, quotable, and accessible, willing to leave the senate floor to talk to a newsman waiting by the Rail, the reporters' and lobbyists' nickname for the third-floor rotunda.

Obama took whatever media attention he could get. He was a frequent guest on *Public Affairs*, a one-on-one talk show that aired on public television stations around the state. Al Kindle put him on a public access show in Chicago. In other words, the name "Barack Obama" was unknown to anyone except wonks who read the *Illinois Blue Book*, a legislative directory. Illinois is a state with a vibrant political culture, but that's still a small following.

At the time, the journalist who covered Obama most closely was Todd Spivak, a twenty-five-year-old cub reporter for the *Hyde Park Herald*. As the neighborhood state senator, Obama was on Spivak's beat, and Spivak usually made a story out of the press releases politicians faxed into their local papers. CURRIE AND OBAMA BILLS SEEK TO CLEAN UP COURTS. SENATOR OBAMA HELPS DEFEAT A CANCELED FIREARM BILL. Or simply, OBAMA BILL PASSES SENATE.

Spivak also covered city hall, where he was used to encountering evasive, antagonistic aldermen. Obama was the complete opposite. He gave Spivak his cell phone number and always returned phone calls the same day, even if it was late in the evening.

Whenever Spivak tried to call Obama "senator" or "sir," he'd hear, "Please, call me Barack." Most politicians become curt or hostile when asked about campaign contributions. They take the questions as affronts to their integrity. Not Obama. It was his style to bemoan the seamier aspects of Chicago politics while at the same time benefiting from them, so he would complain to Spivak that raising money was a necessary evil, but yes, he'd held a fund-raiser, and yes, developers were there, but no, they hadn't gotten anything from him in return. Even worse, Obama was usually right. Spivak was used to writing about hinky South Side pols, but he couldn't dig up any dirt on Obama. One of the few times he tried, by crashing an Obama fund-raiser at Allison Davis's house, he was thrown out by the host.

A year after the congressional primary, I interviewed Obama again for the *Reader*. It was early 2001, and he was trying to pass a bill to ensure that what had happened to Al Gore in Florida would never happen in Illinois. After the 2000 election, Cook County installed ballot-counting machines that spat back overvotes and undervotes, allowing voters a chance to correct their mistakes. In some inner-city precincts, this reduced spoiled ballots by 90 percent. Republicans objected. Kicking back undervotes, they complained, would violate the privacy of people who chose to skip a race. Looming precinct captains might order voters back into the booth to complete the ballot. A Republican senator introduced a bill to turn off the ballot-checking software, thus preventing machines from identifying undervotes. Obama saw that as an effort to suppress the big-city vote. Suburbanites were voting on fill-in-the-bubble ballots, which were hard to screw up. Chicagoans were still punching out chads.

Obama countered with his own bill, which would have given counties the option of kicking back undervotes. After it died in the Elections Subcommittee, he came up with an ingenious compromise: add a "None of the above" line to every race. That would allow voters to skip a race without undervoting. (The issue became moot when a judge allowed Cook County to identify both overvotes and undervotes.)

Ever since Florida had replaced Illinois as the election fraud capital of America, I'd been writing about what our state was doing to avoid taking back the title. So I called Obama. I suspected he was unhappy about my *Chicago Reader* story on the First Congressional District race, which had been full of his enemies' accusations that he wasn't black enough for the South Side. But he returned my phone call.

"The principal reason is partisanship," he told me, in his clipped diction, when I asked about the Republican bill. "Privately, I don't think any of the Republican legislators would deny that. Why would they want to encourage an additional ten percent in Cook County? That's a direct blow against them in statewide races."

When I thanked Obama for his time, he responded with an icy "You're welcome"—the iciest I'd ever heard from a politician. (Curtness is Obama's favorite method of displaying anger.) My first thought was, That guy's got some great ideas. If he ever learns how to act like a human being, he may go someplace in politics. Later, I realized that Obama's "You're welcome" was a smooth move. Blowing me off would have done him no good. The *Reader* had a following among white liberals, an important constituency for Obama in a statewide race. Berating a writer would have invited more bad publicity. Just by using a peevish tone of voice, he'd let me know he was unhappy with my work and ensured his displeasure didn't make the paper. Obama was the most media-conscious politician I had ever met. During the congressional race, whenever I showed up at a campaign event, he always made a point of walking up to me, touching my arm, and asking, "How are you doing?" in a manner that came off as collegial rather than desperate for publicity. Politicians rarely pursue reporters. Most have to be chased across the room or approached as though they are living altars. Obama tried to bond with the press. When it mattered, the press would return the compliment.

In the spring of 2002, Obama's testy relationship with Ricky Hendon finally blew up into an angry, shoving, profane brawl, right on the senate floor.

After five years of working together—even sponsoring some bills together—Hendon was still needling Obama about his blackness.

"Hey, Barack," he'd taunt, "you figure out if you're black or white yet?"

Obama tried to brush it off. Once, in a black caucus meeting, Hendon told him, "You have to stay black all the time. You have to be black on all issues."

"This is not a black or white issue," Obama responded tersely.

Obama had nominated Senator Kimberly Lightford, a young woman from the western suburbs, as chairman of the black caucus. They were allies. After Lightford's first race, Obama wrote her a $500 check to cover campaign debts. Lightford and Emil Jones tried to keep the peace between Obama and Hendon, but there were days when Obama didn't show up for meetings because he didn't feel like being hassled.

On the senate floor, Obama sat alongside three white Democrats from the Chicago area—Terry Link, Carol Ronen, and Lisa Madigan. Their arrangement was called Liberal Row, and it only deepened Hendon's conviction that Obama's true home was in the white progressive community.

On June 11, the senate voted on a proposal to close a Department of Children and Family Services office in Hendon's district. Anguished that the state was snatching another social program from the impoverished West Side, Hendon stood up to speak. He delivered an emotional plea for the children of his neighborhood.

"It just bothers me that you're cutting education to the core, you're destroying lives of the—of the children of this state and nobody's even paying no damn attention," Hendon said. "It's like you don't even care. Well, I care. And it makes a difference what we do here in this chamber out there in the real world . . . stop cutting everything from the children of this state."

When the roll was called, every Democrat voted to keep the office open—except the four liberals. Hendon was furious. He stalked down the Row, demanding answers at every desk. Madigan explained that she was running for attorney general and needed to appear tough on government spending. Link admitted he had voted with the rest of Liberal Row. Ronen apologized and asked for Hendon's forgiveness. Then Hendon confronted Obama.

"Well, we have to be fiscally prudent," Obama said.

"What that mean?" Hendon demanded.

"Tight economy," Obama replied. "We need to watch our coffers."

When the next round of budget cuts came up—including a million-dollar grant to the Chicago for Summer Youth jobs—Obama rose to speak. He acknowledged that budget cuts were necessary but chided the Republicans for portraying themselves as pork busters while keeping alive a $2 million program to train students in video production and $250,000 for suburban recreation.

"It is not true that somehow that side of the aisle has been purely above politics or pork or partisanship in this process," Obama said. "In fact, I think when we start looking at the votes, we'll—it'll turn out that the governor's office has its favorites, and it's looking after the—its favorites. And that's fair. That's the nature of the political beast, but I don't want the—the public to be fooled into thinking that somehow, you-all have a monopoly on responsible budgeting."

That was too much sanctimony for Hendon to bear. Obama, he was sure, was building a record to present to white voters when he ran for higher office. He needed a few "fiscally conservative" votes, so he was selling out the poor folks on the West Side to secure his political future. Hendon pressed his light, demanding recognition from the chair.

"I just want to say to the last speaker, you got a lot of nerve to talk about being responsible and then you voted for closing the DCFS office on the West Side, when you wouldn't have voted to close it on the South Side," he raged. "So I apologize to my Republican friends about my bipartisanship comments, 'cause clearly there's some Democrats on this side of the aisle that don't care about the West Side either, especially the last speaker."

Then Obama pressed *his* light. He apologized for the vote, but he also made it clear he didn't take kindly to being called out in front of the entire senate.

"I understand Senator Hendon's anger at—actually—the—I was not aware that I had voted no on that last—last piece of legislation. I would have the record record that I intended to vote yes. On the other hand, I would appreciate that next time my dear colleague Senator Hendon ask me about a vote before he names me on the floor."

The words were acid with sarcasm and false collegiality. Once Obama's microphone was off, he confronted Hendon directly.

"You embarrassed me on the senate floor," Obama hissed. "If you ever do it again, I'll kick your ass."

"Really?" Hendon retorted.

"You heard me, and if you come back here by the telephones, where the press can't see, I'll kick your ass right now."

At five foot seven, Hendon was half a head shorter than Obama, but he was also from the toughest district in the senate. He couldn't go back to the West Side and tell his constituents he'd backed off a fight with a Harvard grad—from Hyde Park.

"OK," Hendon said. "Let's go."

Hendon led the way to the telephone area, where he dared Obama to hit him. The Illinois senate chamber was designed in the nineteenth century, with as much flourish and pomposity as that era's oratory: marble Ionic columns capped with gilded scrolls rose behind the rostrum. Glass chandeliers dangled from the ceiling. A thick burgundy carpet, patterned with goldenrod accents, absorbed the loafers of senators as they walked to their polished wooden desks, which were arranged in expanding semicircles. Obama and Hendon were treating this noble room like the sidewalk outside a tavern. The two men shoved and swore at each other until Emil Jones noticed the fight and sent Donne Trotter to break it up. Jones told Hendon, an assistant minority leader, to go back to his seat and start acting like a member of the leadership. He told Obama that a major misconduct penalty wasn't going to look good on his legislative record. Even that didn't end the dispute. A TV reporter had seen the donnybrook and asked Obama about it. It had been no big deal, Obama insisted. He and Hendon had worked out their differences.

Hendon wouldn't talk about the fight on TV, but he denied making up with Obama. There was nothing to apologize for. This was relayed to Obama, who wasn't happy to hear it. Those long legs strode back to Hendon's desk, and that long, lean face loomed in to say something. Before Obama could speak, Hendon shouted for Jones, sitting three seats away.

"Get this guy out of my face!"

Jones dragged Obama off the floor.

After that day, the two senators never discussed their showdown, but Hendon began treating Obama with more respect, less antagonism. The name-calling stopped. Obama had shown the West Sider that he was a fighter, not just a passionless lawyer/professor who wouldn't stand up for himself. Some senators, who could never imagine Obama losing his cool, wondered if the entire fight had been calculated to make just that point.

Chapter 11

"YOU HAVE THE POWER TO MAKE A U.S. SENATOR"

BARACK OBAMA'S BIGGEST PROBLEM in running for the Senate was money. He didn't have any. In fact, he had less than no money. His credit cards were still maxed out, because of the congressional race, and he and Michelle were paying off student loans so steep they exceeded the mortgage. One day, after he became famous, *Dreams from My Father* would hit the bestseller list, but in the early 2000s, it was an out-of-print book that generated no royalties for its author. On his trips to Springfield, Obama drove a Dodge Neon, one of the smallest, cheapest cars a patriotic American politician could own.

Of course, thanks to his attendance at ABLE meetings, Obama knew people with money. When he finally decided to run, in 2002, he approached black business owners for help.

Black Chicago wanted that Senate seat back. And many members of the city's Talented Tenth saw Obama as the ideal candidate. The city's bankers, lawyers, and investors weren't interested in simply catering to the ghetto trade, like the generation of black entrepreneurs before them. They wanted to do business with whites, too. In Obama, they recognized a character with the same crossover dreams.

There were intraracial politics at work, too. In the black

community, preachers had always been the leading power brokers. They had money, and they had voters. Many successful
black politicians, such as Adam Clayton Powell Jr., had used a
pulpit as a platform to achieve office. During segregation, that
had been essential, because the church was the center of black life,
the only place blacks could gather to express their aspirations. But
segregation was long gone, so it was time to replace that old model.
White politicians got their money from businesspeople. Blacks
should do the same, especially if they wanted to win among the
wider electorate. It was time to follow the American way of politics. The ministers could be a source of money, but not the leading source. Let them focus on the clergy role, while businesses
took over the financial role.

Throughout 2002, Obama held a series of lunches and meetings with black professionals. He told Hermene Hartman he was
thinking of running for the Senate but would step aside if Jesse
Jackson Jr. or Carol Moseley Braun decided to run. Both had bigger followings in the black community, and Obama didn't want
to be part of another primary in which the "black enough" issue
might come up.

John Rogers first heard about Obama's Senate plans during a
Sunday brunch at the home of Valerie Jarrett, who had been
close to the Obamas for a decade. As Mayor Daley's chief of staff,
she hired Michelle to work in city hall. Jarrett, who went on to
become chairwoman of the Chicago Transit Authority and vice
president at the Habitat Company, wasn't just well connected in
the black professional world, she was its center. When Obama
told Jarrett, "There's something I want to bounce off you," she
also invited Rogers and Nesbitt to the meeting, knowing that he
was going to entertain them all with his fool dream of being a

United States senator. Obama came to Sunday brunch at Jarrett's house, with Michelle in tow.

Jarrett thought running for the Senate was a terrible idea— Obama just lost to Rush, he was broke, he had two toddlers at home, and Michelle didn't like him traveling all over the state. So Obama went to work on the small gathering, begging for one last chance to satisfy his addiction to politics. This race would be different from the last, he promised.

"I've talked to Emil Jones," Obama said. "He's a huge political force, and he's prepared to support me. When I ran for Congress, I didn't have that kind of support. And if I lose, then, Michelle, I'll give up politics. If I can't do it this time, I promise I'll get a normal job in the private sector, so this'll be the last time I ask you to do this, unless I win. And money's a problem, so, Valerie, I think you should help me, because you're in the business community, you and John. You two should think about helping me do this."

"So what if you lose?" Jarrett challenged him.

"If I'm not worried about losing, why are you?" Obama said. "If I lose, I lose. But I think I'll win."

Jarrett wasn't convinced Obama could win, but she was convinced she should support him. Rogers was an easier sell. His friend was about to take a huge chance, so how could he do anything but throw all his personal and financial resources behind the campaign?

Rogers's first task was to get Carol Moseley Braun out of the race. He'd been finance chairman of her successful Senate campaign, so he could tell her the truth: She didn't have the support to run again. Black Chicago's excitement over Moseley Braun's 1992 victory—she was the first African-American Democrat in the

Senate's history—had turned to disappointment during her six years in Washington. Carol had been given the chance to become the most respected black politician in America, and she'd blown it. Paul Simon, her Senate seat mate for four years, summed up Moseley Braun's problems in one sentence: "She fell in love with the wrong person." Her campaign manager/boyfriend, Kgosie Matthews, earned $15,000 a month while other staffers weren't getting paid. After the election, Moseley Braun and Matthews jetted off on a monthlong trip to Africa. Worst of all, he took her to visit Nigerian dictator Sani Abacha, a trip she made without informing the State Department.

Obama insisted, publicly and privately, that if Moseley Braun was in, he was out. How could he win? Her name recognition in Illinois was 92 percent. His was 18 percent. And they would both be competing for black votes, which would be decisive in a primary sure to be full of white politicians.

"If Carol runs, I won't run," he told a reporter. "I just won't have a chance. We're too similar, or we're seen as too similar: two potentially nonthreatening black politicians from the South Side of Chicago."

To give Moseley Braun a reason not to run, Rogers called Jamie Dimon, CEO of Bank One, and asked if he would give her a job. Dimon wouldn't. Obama invited Moseley Braun to his district office to discuss the race. With the same high-handedness that caused her to run through five chiefs of staff in six years, Moseley Braun made it clear that running for her old Senate seat was her prerogative. Obama would just have to wait for her decision.

But Moseley Braun wouldn't make one. Todd Spivak of the *Hyde Park Herald*, Moseley Braun's neighborhood paper, talked to her nearly every week.

"She always talked about she's waiting for this, she's looking at this, and she would not come out," Spivak would recall. "She put everything on hold. Carol became more and more paranoid and upset with me. She came to my office once to yell at my editor for a story I wrote where I was pretty much just parroting what the dailies were saying. She wasn't being embraced by her old supporters. It took her a while to realize, 'My political career is really over.'"

Obama was having better success asking his senate colleagues for support. As he'd told Valerie Jarrett, he started by approaching Emil Jones. If the Democrats took over the state senate in 2002, as they seemed likely to do, Jones would become senate president.

"You know," Obama told his caucus leader, "you're a pretty powerful guy. You have the power to make a U.S. senator."

"Oh, yeah?" Jones said. "Who?"

"Me," Obama told him.

Jones agreed to help. He had opposed Obama in his races for the state senate and the U.S. Congress, but this time the young man was playing by the rules: He wasn't challenging an incumbent Democrat. Obama's poker buddies were on board, too. In the spring of 2002, Obama met Larry Walsh for breakfast at the Renaissance Center in Springfield.

"I want to ask you some very difficult questions," he told Walsh. Then he laid out his plan for a Senate run and asked if Walsh would support him.

"Absolutely," Walsh said.

Not only had the two senators served together—and played cards together—for five years, but Obama had once done Walsh a big political favor. In 1998, Walsh won a difficult primary against an African-American opponent. To mend fences with the black community, he organized a luncheon for African-American leaders in Joliet. Obama had once told Walsh, "If you ever need me, if you'd like me to speak to black ministers or business leaders or whatever, I'd be more than glad to come down." So Walsh invited Obama to keynote the luncheon. Obama's speech resonated with the audience. That fall, Walsh received strong black support.

Walsh, Link, and Jacobs all represented districts that were anchored by a city with a significant black population. Obama was going to do well in Chicago, but to win the entire state, he also needed to do well in Joliet, Waukegan, and Rock Island. Those three old white guys could help.

While Obama waited for Moseley Braun to announce her plans, he started a fund-raising committee. Raising money couldn't wait. Winning the Senate seat was going to cost at least $4 million, most of it for TV ads to introduce himself to Illinois. Peter Fitzgerald had spent $14 million of his family wealth, an amount Obama considered obscene.

Once he had his inner circle behind him, Obama made an appeal to the ABLE crowd. At a gathering at Jim Reynolds's house, he told a group of forty wealthy blacks that he was running for the Senate. He didn't talk about money that night. Instead, he talked about making the campaign a group effort.

"Don't let me get lost," he implored his fellow buppies. "You are my friends. Tell me the truth, keep me real. Don't let me get out there and get the big head. Let's still kick off our shoes and talk."

Everyone at the party agreed that Obama was the right candidate for the Senate. They also agreed his stump speech was terrible. It was all about local issues—he sounded like he was throwing his hat in the ring for alderman—and Obama was *still* using that stilted, professional style that had bored the First Congressional District.

"You've got to broaden it," Martin King, the chairman of Rainbow PUSH, urged him. "You've got to speak larger. You should go see Jesse."

Obama took King's advice and began attending the Saturday morning rallies at "Jesse's Place," the Grecian-temple Rainbow PUSH headquarters on Drexel Avenue in Kenwood. There will always be some tension between Barack Obama and Jesse Jackson. By becoming president, Obama eventually succeeded where Jackson failed. Jackson's politics of black empowerment made him a candidate for one race only. Obama, who was trying to build a multiracial coalition, couldn't associate himself too closely with that message. But before he could reach out to whites, he needed a base in his own community. Jackson and his son Junior, who had enough cred to cover the South Side, the West Side, and the south suburbs, would become important allies in Obama's effort to sell himself to blacks.

Obama's black friends weren't the only ones urging him to be a little more pulpit and a little less lecture hall. Abner Mikva was on his case about it, too. Preaching wasn't Obama's natural style, but he was going to have to learn if he wanted to light up black audiences outside Hyde Park.

"You've got to get into those black churches," Mikva ordered Obama. "You've got to spend more time there. You know, Dr. King never pulled his punches, but he said it in a way black people understood."

Then Mikva told a story from his own day, about something Cardinal Richard Cushing, Archbishop of Boston, said to John F. Kennedy after the 1960 West Virginia primary.

"Jack," Cushing had said, "Jack, from now on be more Irish and less Harvard."

Obama, he was suggesting, needed to be more black and less U of C.

Even by mid-2002, Obama was getting an idea of whom he'd be facing in the Democratic primary. Gery Chico, a Latino lawyer who had served as president of the Chicago Board of Education, was talking about running. So was Cook County treasurer Maria Pappas. His most formidable opponent looked to be state comptroller Dan Hynes, the scion of a Southwest Side Irish political family. Hynes would be the Machine candidate: His father, former Illinois senate president Thomas Hynes, had served with the current Mayor Daley in Springfield. They'd even shared an apartment. The labor unions, ward bosses, and Downstate county chairs, with their battalions of door knockers, would be backing Hynes, who was only thirty-three years old but already having a political midlife crisis as he tried to escape his second-tier state office.

Obama could see the constituencies he'd need to win: blacks and liberal whites, the same folks who'd elected Harold. That fall, as President George W. Bush began threatening Iraq with war, Obama got his chance to impress the latter crowd.

There were already plenty of connections between Obama and the white progressives who'd learned their politics in the 1960s antiwar movement. Jerry Kellman liked to joke that he'd "majored in protesting" at the University of Wisconsin. Judd Miner practically embodied white liberalism in Chicago. And, of course, there was Bill Ayers. Although Obama was an Alinsky organizer, many of the community groups he worked with had been formed during the sixties, as expressions of the era's People Power ethos. The Progressive Chicago Area Network, born from the demonstrations at the 1968 Democratic National Convention, produced some of the biggest players in Harold Washington's campaign, including Al Raby, another of Obama's mentors.

The Democratic convention and the election of Harold Washington had been left-wing Chicago's greatest moments. After Washington died, the movement became dormant, its members concentrating on their careers as journalists, professors, lawyers, politicians, and foundation presidents. They kept up with each other through the pages of the *Reader*, an alternative weekly founded in 1971. (And, of course, the first citywide paper to notice Obama.)

While at Davis, Miner, Obama had met an advertising/PR professional named Marilyn Katz, who had run the media campaign for Harold Washington's mayoral run. Katz was a friend of Bettylu Saltzman, the daughter of a megamillionaire real estate developer. A former aide to Paul Simon, Saltzman had used her family fortune to become one of Chicago's most benevolent Democratic donors. She was also acquainted with David Axelrod, Chicago's number one political consultant, who had begun his career on Simon's 1984 Senate campaign. Saltzman was exactly the kind of white person Obama wanted to meet.

In late September, Saltzman called Katz to talk about Bush's drive for war. Chicago hadn't seen a big demonstration in years. In January 2001, only a few dozen people showed up in Daley Plaza to protest Bush's inauguration. But the president's talk of weapons of mass destruction sounded as bogus as Lyndon Johnson's Gulf of Tonkin incident. Maybe, Katz suggested, they should apply the lessons they'd learned from Vietnam and protest the war *before* it started.

A few days later, fifteen middle-aged activists met at Saltzman's house to plot an antiwar strategy. Some were scared. Bush's approval ratings were in the eighties. Speaking out against the president might be seen as unpatriotic, might lose them work. Others feared they'd look foolish if nobody showed up.

"Look," Katz argued. "In 'sixty-five, there was nobody against the war. I remember going to demonstrations as a kid and there were, like, ten people. If we only get fifty people, so be it. The space for public dissent is really narrow, and if we don't take action against the war now, there won't be any space left."

The group agreed to hold a rally on Sunday, October 2, in Federal Plaza. Saltzman called Obama that Friday and asked him to speak. She also called Jesse Jackson and County Clerk David Orr.

Obama was the only state senator at the rally. Some of his friends warned him against attending. As a legislator, he wasn't expected to have a position on foreign policy. As a Senate candidate, he could hurt himself Downstate by speaking out against what might be a quick, popular war. Obama, however, understood that you win a primary—especially a crowded primary—by motivating special interests. He was already the most liberal candidate in the field. An antiwar, anti-Bush speech would make him even more appealing to Democrats who were feeling distraught and powerless over the country's race to war and were still angry about the 2000 presidential election. These were the activists who wrote checks, stood in front of supermarkets with petitions, made phone calls, and always voted.

Obama had less than two days to write the speech, but it was the first great address of his career. He challenged his audience. Even though he was speaking to an antiwar crowd, he made it clear that he was not a pacifist. In fact, he told them, some of America's wars had made the world a better place. Obama was talking to people who sported PEACE IS PATRIOTIC stickers on the bumpers of their rusty Audis, but he wanted them to know life wasn't that simple: Sometimes war was patriotic, too.

Good afternoon. Let me begin by saying that although this has been billed as an antiwar rally, I stand before you as someone who is not opposed to war in all circumstances.

The Civil War was one of the bloodiest in history, and yet it was only through the crucible of the sword, the sacrifice of multitudes, that we could begin to perfect this union and drive the scourge of slavery from our soil. I don't oppose all wars.

My grandfather signed up for a war the day Pearl Harbor was bombed, fought in Patton's army. He saw the dead and dying across the fields of Europe; he heard the stories of fellow troops who first entered Auschwitz and Treblinka. He fought in the name of a larger freedom, part of that arsenal of democracy that triumphed over evil, and he did not fight in vain.

I don't oppose all wars.

That last phrase demonstrated that Obama had been listening to the preachers, just as his advisers had told him. He would repeat it over and over again as he built to the speech's climax. It was actually more of an evangelical's trick than anything he'd heard in his own church: Jeremiah Wright was a storyteller, not a shouter. But Obama, who would surpass Wright as an orator, was discovering how to use emotion to sell an intellectual point. And he was adding concrete images that had been missing from his earlier, legalistic speeches.

After September 11, after witnessing the carnage and destruction, the dust and the tears, I supported this administration's pledge to hunt down and root out those who would slaughter innocents in the name of intolerance, and I would willingly take up arms myself to prevent such a tragedy from happening again.

I don't oppose all wars. And I know that in this crowd today, there is no shortage of patriots or patriotism. What I am opposed to is a dumb war. A rash war. What I am opposed to is the cynical attempt by Richard Perle and Paul Wolfowitz and other armchair, weekend warriors in this administration to shove their own ideological agendas down our throats, irrespective of the costs in lives lost and hardships borne.

What I am opposed to is the attempt by political hacks like Karl Rove to distract us from a rise in the uninsured, a rise in the poverty rate, a drop in median income—to distract us from corporate scandals and a stock market that has just gone through the worst month since the Great Depression.

That's what I'm opposed to. A dumb war. A rash war. A war based not on reason but on passion, not on principle but on politics.

A dumb war. Obama was expressing himself with a simplicity that his old self might have found simpleminded. Most of the three thousand people in the plaza had never heard of this state legislator from Hyde Park, but as he spoke, they nodded and asked each other, "Who is that?" It was, one listener would remember, a "quiet barn raising"—well timed, with cadence. Obama ended with a challenge to the president, suggesting that he'd chosen the wrong enemy in Saddam Hussein, a weakened dictator who posed no threat to the United States. Over and over, he asked, "You want a fight, President Bush?"

You want a fight, President Bush? Let's fight to make sure our so-called allies in the Middle East, the Saudis and the Egyptians, stop oppressing their own people, and suppressing dissent, and tolerating corruption and inequality, and mismanaging their economies so that their youth grow up without education, without prospects, without hope, the ready recruits of terrorist cells.

You want a fight, President Bush? Let's fight to wean ourselves of Middle East oil, through an energy policy that doesn't simply serve the interests of Exxon and Mobil.

Those are the battles we need to fight. Those are the battles we willingly join. The battles against ignorance and intolerance, corruption and greed, poverty and despair.

The consequences of war are dire, the sacrifices immeasurable. We may have occasion in our lifetime to once again rise up in defense of our freedom and pay the wages of war. But we ought not—we will not—travel down that hellish path blindly. Nor should we allow those who would march off and pay the ultimate sacrifice, who would prove the full measure of devotion with their blood, to make such an awful sacrifice in vain.

The speech had its intended effect, not just on Federal Plaza, but on Obama's public profile. In the days afterward, the text was circulated on the Internet, where such sites as Democratic Underground, Truthout, BuzzFlash, and Daily Kos were becoming important forums for opponents of the Bush administration. The speech cemented the support of Saltzman and Julie Hamos, a state representative who also spoke at the rally. After Obama announced his candidacy, Hamos threw him a fund-raiser in her wealthy

North Shore district, and Saltzman lobbied Axelrod to take him on as a client.

In most of the country, 2002 was a Republican year. President George W. Bush used the fear of terrorism to win his party the U.S. Senate and increase its margin in the House of Representatives. It wasn't so in Illinois. The Republicans had occupied the governor's mansion for twenty-six years, but their incumbent, George Ryan, was involved in a scandal shocking even for a state where corruption is a hallowed tradition. The U.S. attorney was investigating driver's licenses issued for bribes when Ryan was secretary of state, including one to a trucker who caused an accident that killed six children. It was time, the voters felt, to throw out the Republican crooks and give some Democratic crooks a chance.

Ryan's unpopularity wasn't all the Democrats had going for them. Illinois was one of the first states to experience the partisan transformation that would, when it spread nationwide, result in Obama's election as president.

As a Midwestern state, near the population center of the U.S., with demographics almost exactly matching the national average, Illinois is as good a bellwether of political movements as any. It's a radically moderate state. Extremists do not thrive in Illinois. The religious right is regularly crushed in Republican primaries, and the activist left is confined to a few neighborhoods of shabby three-flats near the Chicago lakefront. The state's political culture is practical, not idealistic.

Illinois voted Republican for president in six consecutive elections, from 1968 to 1988, an era when Republicans dominated the White House, Jimmy Carter's post-Watergate win notwithstanding. It elected Republican governors for most of that period, too.

The state began to change its colors with the election of Bill Clinton in 1992. You can actually trace the state's movement from Republican to Democrat by following the political journey of Clinton's wife, Hillary, who grew up in the Chicago suburb of Park Ridge. As a young woman, Hillary followed her father's politics, dressing as a Goldwater Girl for the 1964 election. Then she went to Wellesley, where she made the same ideological journey as so many well-educated suburban children who would become the Democratic Party's brain trust: civil rights lawyers, consumer advocates, college professors, political consultants, nonprofit executives, and newspaper editors. She wrote her senior thesis on Saul Alinsky. In 1968, she staffed a Rockefeller suite at the Republican convention and was appalled by Richard Nixon's hustling of the Southern conservative vote. After sneaking out of her parents' house to witness the riots at the Democratic convention, Hillary became convinced the Vietnam War was a mistake.

Hillary Clinton didn't just presage suburbia's shift to the Democrats—she helped make it happen. The Clinton administration's moderate politics—signing NAFTA and reforming welfare—helped make well-to-do homeowners more comfortable with the party. The Clintons were seen as fiscally responsible, a timeless suburban value. The classic battle line of Illinois politics—Democratic Chicago versus Republican suburbia—was disappearing, one voter at a time. In 2002, the authors of the book *The Emerging Democratic Majority* used Illinois as a case study, identifying the Chicago area as an "ideopolis" whose professionals had benefited from the prosperity of the Clinton years, especially the shift from a manufacturing economy to a knowledge-based economy. The Cook County suburbs where Hillary Clinton had grown up were now "irretrievably Democratic." Obama, who would do very well among rich suburbanites in his U.S. Senate campaign, had his future rival for the presidency to thank for making some of those people Democrats in the first place.

The governor's scandals and blue-ing of suburbia put the Democrats in a good position to take over state government in 2002. But a lucky break, based on a quirk in the state's constitution, made it a certainty. Split between a Republican senate and a Democratic house, the General Assembly failed to draw a new legislative map based on the 2000 census. So Secretary of State Jesse White appointed an eight-member committee, with four Democrats and four Republicans. The committee also stalemated. White asked each party to submit a candidate for a ninth member. He placed the slips in a replica of Abe Lincoln's stovepipe hat and drew the name of Michael Bilandic, the former Democratic mayor of Chicago.

That meant the Democrats got to draw the map. Obama had a very specific idea of what he wanted his new district to look like: a narrow band following the Lake Michigan shoreline from Ninety-fifth Street to downtown. Obama got rid of Englewood, the poorest neighborhood in Chicago, and added the Gold Coast, the richest and one of the most Republican. No longer would he be a South Side senator. He'd be a lakefront senator. Along with Hyde Park, Obama would represent most of Chicago's monuments—Soldier Field, the Adler Planetarium, Grant Park—as well as its priciest shopping district, the Magnificent Mile, and its multimillion-dollar high-rise condos. Mayor Daley would be a constituent. So would Oprah Winfrey. This suited the Democrats' mapmaking strategy. Population growth on the South Side had been stagnant. So the districts had to move north and west, and, of course, the mapmakers wanted to corral as many Republicans as possible into Democratic-leaning districts. It also suited Obama's personal strategy for political advancement. Losing to Bobby Rush had taught Obama that his natural constituency wasn't inner-city blacks but well-educated eggheads of all races. Also, he'd be representing some of the most generous Democratic donors in the state. Abner Mikva had already introduced him to those rich folks, but now they'd see his name on a ballot and his face on the "Legislative Update" every senator sends home. For a politician who was still in debt from law school and past campaigns, their money would be essential.

The Democratic takeover was such a sure thing that the *Illinois Times*, a Springfield alternative weekly, ran a cover story titled "The Great Thaw." Blagojevich was elected governor, and Democrats won a majority in the state senate, increasing their membership by five seats. In the new General Assembly, Obama would be chairman of the Health and Welfare Committee, putting him in a position to advance his most cherished political goal: universal health care. Emil Jones would be senate president, the second African-American to occupy that post. The president decides which legislation reaches the senate floor. For years, the black caucus had suffered the Republican Party's indifference as its pet issues—racial profiling, death penalty reform—ended each session sine die, the legislative term for "dead." Jones would make sure they passed, and he'd make sure Obama, who'd co-sponsored the bills, got plenty of credit. Already, Jones was describing himself as the fatherless young man's "godfather."

Chapter 12

THE GODFATHER

OBAMA HAD BEEN MOVED to go into law, and ultimately into politics, by his failure to pry more funding out of
Emil Jones for the Career Education Network, one of his South
Side community organizing projects. After Obama requested
half a million for the dropout prevention program, Jones delivered $150,000. Pocketing that chump change convinced Obama
that the place to be was on the inside, where the money was
handed out.

Now, fifteen years later, he was inside—but he wanted to go
farther. And because of Jones, he was in a position to do so. The
senate president had a paternal fondness for Obama and was ready
to do whatever he could to make the young man a U.S. senator.
Obama was the only legislator in the Democratic primary, so
Jones planned to use his newly acquired power to provide him
with the record he'd been unable to build while the Democrats
were in the minority. They had fourteen months to make up for
six years of frustration.

The day the new senate was sworn in, Obama's political side-
kick Dan Shomon worked the room at a postinauguration party
thrown by Denny Jacobs and Terry Link. Shomon was handing
out business cards that read "Obama for Illinois. Dan Shomon,
campaign manager."

"Obama's going to be the guy," he insisted to the politicians and reporters present. "Obama's going to be the guy."

Yeah, thought a skeptical journalist at the party, call me when he beats Dan Hynes.

In *Dreams from My Father*, Obama had mocked Jones as "an old ward heeler" begging to introduce Harold Washington at the opening of the Mayor's Office of Employment and Training in Roseland.

Jones had "made the mistake of backing one of the white candidates in the last mayoral election," Obama wrote. Desperate to be seen alongside Washington, he "promised to help us get money for any project we wanted if we just got him on the program."

It was true. Emil Jones had endorsed incumbent mayor Jane Byrne over Harold Washington. He was a man who owed his entire career to the Machine, and he didn't believe in challenging the powers that be. Jones's father had been a truck driver and precinct captain who used clout to land his boy a job as a sewer inspector in the Department of Streets and Sanitation, an arm of city government that's practically an employment service for the sons and nephews of the politically connected. From those subterranean beginnings, Jones rose to state representative, then state senator, but after losing his race for Congress to Jesse Jackson Jr., he realized that Springfield was as far from the South Side as he would ever go. Jones was not an inspiring speaker, and he didn't think much of anyone else's oratory, either. His advice to new senators was, "You pass more bills when you're brief." The ward heeler had worked to defeat Obama in his races against Alice Palmer and Bobby Rush because the kid had broken the wait-your-turn rules of Chicago politics. But there was no incumbent Democrat in the Senate race. (In fact, there was no incumbent at all. The unpopular Senator Fitzgerald wasn't running for reelection.) And Obama was young, educated, articulate, and beloved by white liberals—strong in all the areas where Jones was weak. Dark, heavyset, phlegmatic, Jones had only one touch of flamboyance about him: His first name, which he pronounced ay-MEEL, in the Gallic style.

In the same month that Emil Jones became senate president, Carol Moseley Braun finally accepted the fact that her old supporters wouldn't be with her if she tried to reclaim her Senate seat. Instead, she decided on a symbolic campaign for the presidency of the United States, which no one would expect her to win. That was Obama's cue. On January 29, in a ballroom at the Hotel Allegra (a step up from the Ramada Inn Lakeshore), Obama announced his entry into the Democratic primary, still more than a year away. As he stood on the podium before a few curious newspaper reporters, Obama was flanked by Chicago's most powerful black politicians. Jones was there. So were U.S. representatives Jesse Jackson Jr. and Danny Davis, a West Side progressive. The only black congressman missing was Bobby Rush, who still hadn't forgiven Obama for 2000. To show this was a multicultural campaign, Obama brought along Terry Link and Denny Jacobs.

"Four years ago, Peter Fitzgerald bought himself a Senate seat, and he's betrayed Illinois ever since," Obama said. "But we are here to take it back on behalf of the people of Illinois."

He wasn't the favorite. Not only would he have to beat Hynes, winner of two statewide elections, he had a new opponent: Blair Hull, a blackjack player turned options trader who was prepared to put down $30 million—twice Peter Fitzgerald's "obscene" expenditure.

Comparing himself to David, fighting Goliath with a slingshot and a stone, Obama said, "I don't have wealth or a famous name. But I have a fire in my belly for fairness and justice."

When he made his announcement, Obama had so little money on hand that he could barely afford to open a campaign office. In need of a loan, he went looking for someone with wealth—and maybe a famous name. He called Hermene Hartman, whose office was not far from Oprah Winfrey's Harpo Studios.

"Do you know Oprah?" Obama asked. "Can we get Oprah to give $50,000?"

"Are you crazy?" Hartman said. "I don't know Oprah, but I can call her."

Hartman got through to one of Winfrey's assistants.

"Do you really expect Oprah to meet with a state senator?" the staffer asked.

"That's exactly why I called," Hartman said. "Let me tell you about this guy. He's different. He's going all the way."

Miss Winfrey was unable to spare $50,000. So Hartman went to a more traditional source of money for black politicians: Al Johnson, a wealthy car dealer who had donated to Harold Washington's campaigns. Johnson agreed to meet Obama for lunch at the East Bank Club the following Monday. He was impressed enough to lend the new candidate fifty grand—which the campaign eventually paid back. That covered the rent and the phone bill for a two-room office on Michigan Avenue, which was run by Dan Shomon.

As hard as Obama was working to get into the bank accounts of Bettylu Saltzman and Penny Pritzker, the money that launched his Senate campaign came from a black businessman.

Hartman also tried to help Obama with a less tangible problem: what came to be known as his "Uncle Leland" issue. Just before the Senate announcement, *Chicago Sun-Times* columnist

Laura Washington wrote a piece contrasting how her white and black relations reacted to Obama. Muriel, her Jewish aunt by marriage, met Obama on the set of the *Public Affairs* TV show and thought, Wow. Her uncle Leland "Sugar" Cain, a retired railroad worker from the South Side, was skeptical. At a family dinner, he called Obama an "elitist" who'd visited a housing project in "a thousand-dollar coat." (Obama was not the kind of guy who would spend $1,000 on an overcoat, but he was the kind of guy who could make an overcoat *look* like it had cost $1,000.)

"Whether that's true," Washington wrote, "perception can be reality. The charge is a challenge that Obama will have to overcome if he is to snare the Senate nomination. His weakest appeal is to the working class. He has to balance his time between the shops and community centers of Bronzeville, the churches in Chatham and the diners in Cairo, and the money pitches in the boardrooms of the Loop.

"Getting Aunt Muriel's vote is a damn good start. Uncle Leland is going to take some work."

Obama tried to reach Uncle Leland by sitting in as a guest host on Cliff Kelley's popular WVON radio program. But most of Chicago's black media were suspicious of this new Senate candidate. Hartman and Melody Spann-Cooper, WVON's owner, organized a meeting of neighborhood newspaper editors and radio program directors at a restaurant called Sweet Mabel. They heard hostile questions about Obama: "Is he black enough?" "Who is this stranger in town?"

"Hey, guys, you all aren't supportive," Hartman told the gathering. "Why can't we support our own? He's got a real opportunity to go all the way. You guys are saying, 'Because he wasn't born in Chicago, because he's of mixed parentage, because he's from Harvard, he's not black.' You want to talk about mixed parentage? That's everyone in this room! What I'm hearing is he's not the traditional Chicago politician. He's not Harold Washington. It's true. He can cross over. Let him go!"

After that, the black press gave Obama a pass. And Hartman put him on the cover of *N'DIGO*. That got his story out to the middle-class blacks whose votes he needed. Eight years before, Hartman had declined to review *Dreams from My Father* because she'd thought Obama's life story was too exotic for her readers. Now she saw how that could be an advantage—not just for Obama, but for black Chicago, which wanted another senator.

"The key element for an African-American candidate seeking to run successfully statewide," Obama told *N'DIGO*, "is to be rooted in the African-American community, recognize it as your base, and yet not be limited to it."

Rickey Hendon had been trying for years to get a racial profiling bill through the state senate. Hendon had been pulled over by the police himself, so he'd shared the humiliation of black drivers who were treated like criminal suspects because of their color. But Hendon's proposal—which would have mandated sensitivity training for officers guilty of profiling and yanked state funds from departments that wouldn't comply—never won the support of Republicans or police chiefs. At the beginning of the new session, Emil Jones approached Hendon with a demand.

"I want you to give Barack that bill," he said.

"Bullshit," Hendon shot back. "I've been working on that bill forever. When the Republicans were in charge, we couldn't pass it."

Hendon saw what was about to happen. He'd carried the ball ninety-nine yards on the racial profiling issue, and now Obama was going to score the touchdown. But Hendon gave up the bill.

As he would later tell a reporter, "Mama didn't raise no fool." Going along with the senate president could only help his political career.

Obama began his lobbying campaign with the Fraternal Order of Police. The FOP and the black caucus had an antagonistic relationship. Whenever they'd tried to discuss racial profiling in the past, the blacks had accused the cops of racism, and the cops had folded their arms, refusing to even consider a bill. Ted Street, the FOP president, was still irked about a meeting in Chicago when 125 black ministers crowded into a small conference room: an obvious ploy to intimidate the police, he thought. Street's organization saw Emil Jones as a cop basher more interested in playing the race card than working out a deal with law enforcement.

When Obama arrived at the FOP's office, Street realized immediately that this was a different kind of black legislator. Obama wasn't hostile, first of all. He wasn't there to accuse the cops of targeting black motorists. He was there to draft a bill that would satisfy law enforcement *and* the black caucus. Street wasn't used to that approach. During a series of meetings in Chicago and Springfield, Obama tempered Hendon's bill, making it easier for the cops to accept. The state would conduct a four-year study of traffic stops, keeping records of every driver's race. All police officers would go through diversity training. The punishments were gone. The cops were happy. They were sure the study would prove they'd been engaged in law enforcement, not racial profiling.

"From a layman's perspective, Barack was able to reduce the sting to make it palatable," Street would say. "He was able to get it down to where our view in the end was, 'It's another piece of paper to fill out.'"

Obama lobbied hard for the bill. His senate desk was in the back of the chamber, near the bathrooms. Whenever a senator came out, Obama would ask for a moment. Once, Obama got into a heated argument *in* the bathroom with a black colleague who demanded to know if he *really* understood what it was like to be a young black man getting a pat-down from the police just because he'd been standing on a street corner. The implication was that he didn't understand the streets or the black experience. So Obama talked about the tough neighborhoods he'd seen as a boy in Honolulu and the projects he'd worked in as a community organizer.

Three months into the session, the bill came up for a vote. Kirk Dillard, Obama's most devoted Republican admirer, rose to speak in favor.

"About two to two-and-a-half years ago, Senator Obama and myself began working with Senator Hendon on this particular topic," he said. "Barack and I had many, many early morning, seven A.M., breakfast meetings with former attorney general Jim Ryan, who along with a cast of—of—of—of hundreds from law enforcement from throughout America, helped us understand the difficult issues which Senator Obama has put together so well to make this difficult subject workable."

The bill passed unanimously. While Hendon thought it was watered-down, he would come to see that it was effective. Random stops of black motorists decreased, because the police knew someone was counting.

(On the other hand, Obama's success intensified the antipathy some black legislators still felt toward him. State representative Monique Davis, who had spent years working on a racial profiling bill in the house, felt "snubbed" and "shut out of history." Davis and Obama both belonged to Trinity United Church of Christ, but she was so infuriated by his bill-jacking that she endorsed Dan Hynes in the Senate primary.)

After he passed the racial profiling bill, Obama was able to use his new relationships with law enforcement on a far more important issue: death penalty reform.

No one disputed that Illinois's system of capital punishment needed an overhaul. After thirteen death row prisoners turned out to be innocent, Governor George Ryan halted all executions and appointed a task force to study the problem. (In January 2003, during his final week in office, Ryan commuted every death sentence.) Even law-and-order types had an interest in reform. Unless there were changes, Illinois would never execute another murderer.

The task force came up with eighty-five recommendations, including banning executions of retarded prisoners and requiring police to videotape interrogations of accused killers. Obama seized on the videotape proposal and determined to make it law. At first, almost everyone opposed taping, from police groups to the new governor, Rod Blagojevich.

"A criminal spends more time avoiding capture than sometimes we can spend [capturing them]," one prosecutor complained. "So if he lies for hours upon hours during his interview, now we've got eleven hours of videotape when finally the facts are so compelling that the defendant, the accused, says, 'Okay, I did it,' and tells us what happened. What happens then is that the prosecutor now has eleven hours of videotape, ten hours of lies. Am I to show that to a jury?"

But the bill was important to Obama. Video cameras would train an electronic eye on the Chicago police, whose detectives had obtained murder confessions by smothering suspects with typewriter covers, walloping them with telephone books, jolting them with cattle prods, and burning their flesh with cigarettes. The interrogations were so painful that innocent men confessed to murders they'd never committed. Four police torture victims were freed by Governor Ryan's last-minute amnesty.

Obama met with the state police, the county prosecutors, the Illinois Sheriffs' Association, and the FOP to answer every objection to videotaping. The state would offer grants to strapped cities, Obama promised. His bill would allow audiotaping. If the police forgot to turn on the equipment, the confession could still be used as long as there was, as Obama put it, "reliability and voluntariness shown." Obama even dug up a Florida case in which videotape helped the cops nail a lying suspect. The man claimed he couldn't have committed the crime because he was blind. When his interrogators left the room, he pulled out a sheet of notes.

Obama's arguments even impressed the senate's grimmest cheerleader for the death penalty, Edward Petka. As a state's attorney, Petka had put so many criminals on death row he was nicknamed "Electric Ed." The year before, Obama and Petka had offered opposing points of view for a PBS *NewsHour* report on death penalty reform. Petka was against nearly all the commission's recommendations.

"The net effect, in my point of view, is simply to make it impossible for any prosecutor to seek the death penalty," Petka had said.

Yet even Electric Ed voted for videotaping and for the death penalty reform package.

Emil Jones was reveling in his exalted position in Springfield. To celebrate his newly acquired power, he changed his cell phone ringtone to the *Godfather* theme. From his office suite behind the senate's Victorian chamber, Jones orchestrated his campaign to make Obama a senator—or, who knew, maybe more than a senator. That's how much the senate president thought of Obama's talent. Jones made sure Obama's bills passed through the Rules Committee and on to the full senate. And he leaned on other senators to support his boy, offering perks in exchange for their endorsements.

Jones had to work over some of the Downstaters. "Barack Obama?" they'd say. "That's a tough name down in Southern Illinois. How are we gonna sell him? An African-American is enough of a problem. But an African-American with a Muslim name? That's a *big* problem."

Sparta, Illinois, got a $29 million gun range as a way of encouraging its senator to support Obama. When black senators complained about voting for guns, Jones told them to suck it up.

"You want six million dollars for after-school programs, there's gonna be a gun range in Southern Illinois," the president rumbled.

Jones had to work just as hard on members of the black caucus, who resented Obama's preferential treatment. There wasn't much Jones could do about a house member like Monique Davis, but he called Hendon and Trotter into his office, over and over again, asking them why they couldn't support a fellow senator, a fellow black man. Hendon finally gave in after hearing Obama speak at a West Side church. The rally was packed, and Michelle Obama sat next to Hendon the entire time, assuring him that she wouldn't let her husband forget about issues important to black Chicago.

"I've got him," Michelle told Hendon.

Hearing a homegrown black woman say "I've got him" was enough for Hendon. He stood up, walked to the front of the church, and endorsed Obama. The folks in the pews went wild. Obama's staff left piles of literature at the church, and Hendon pledged his street organization to his senate colleague.

Obama chalked up his colleagues' resentment to jealousy. They'd failed on racial profiling and death penalty reform. Once he took over, the bills passed within months. Todd Spivak, Obama's chronicler at the *Hyde Park Herald*, joined the *Illinois Times* around the time the Democrats took over the senate and witnessed Obama's ascendance there.

"He didn't think too highly of Rickey Hendon and some of those older black legislators," Spivak would recall. "'They couldn't get it done' was the message. 'They had it for years. They couldn't get it done. I got it done. What does that tell you? If they have something against me, that's their problem. They were ineffective in their position.'"

Nearly every Democratic state senator ended up endorsing Obama. It was just practical politics. If he won, with their support, they'd have a friend in Washington. And if he lost, without their support, he might make life uncomfortable when he came back to the capitol.

The Health and Human Services Committee, which Obama chaired during his last term in Springfield, was the most liberal body in the senate, a popular assignment for blacks, Latinos, and big-city whites. It was the perfect platform for Obama to advance his cause of guaranteeing health care to everyone in Illinois.

Two weeks after the 2002 elections, Obama phoned Jim Duffett, the executive director of the Campaign for Better Health Care. Duffett had spent over a decade fighting to expand health care in Illinois.

"You might know this or not," Obama told him, "but I'm now going to be the chair of the senate health committee. I'd like to sit down with you."

The Campaign for Better Health Care had chapters in most of Illinois's cities: Rock Island, Bloomington, Peoria, and Carbondale, among others. Obama wanted to hold town hall meetings to build support for universal health care. Illinois had just elected a Democratic senate and its first Democratic governor in twenty-six years, so this was the moment.

"You guys have these local committees all around the state," he told Duffett. "I want to go out there. I want to use this as a tool, as a chairman."

Duffett pitched him on the Health Care Justice Act, a bill that would require the legislature to come up with a plan for covering the 1.4 million Illinoisans who still didn't have health insurance. Obama loved the idea. In the winter of 2003, they hit the road. To Obama, this was another community organizing project. On cold weeknights, dozens of people shuffled into libraries or union halls to hear the senator from Chicago speak.

Obama described the act, and then, hearkening back to his days as an organizer, he told the gatherings, "You have to put political pressure on these politicians and you've got to keep on pushing and pushing. If they say no, don't give up. If they're a Republican, and they don't support this thing, keep on putting pressure on them, because they go back to the district and they say, 'Oh, my God, I'm really getting beat up on this issue. What's going on?' Same thing with Democrats."

Afterward, Obama went out to dinner with the local chapter's executive committee, telling its members, "We need you as leaders for this movement." That not only built support for the Health Care Justice Act, it built a network of union brass and liberal activists who would back Obama's just-announced Senate campaign.

The insurance industry was adamantly opposed to the act. Its lobbyists found the bill's fatal flaw: It *required* the legislature to come up with a universal health care plan. That was unconstitutional. A General Assembly can't dictate to a future General Assembly. Obama shelved the act and brought it back in 2004, with less demanding language that "strongly urged" a plan to cover all Illinoisans and created a task force to come up with a proposal.

Even the softened version was a tough sell. Conservative Democrats resisted. Denny Jacobs was an old friend of Obama's, but he was an even older friend of the insurance companies. Obama lobbied hard in the cloakroom. He forced Duffett's group to sit down with insurance lobbyists and overcome their mutual loathing to craft language both groups could tolerate. Obama even changed the panel's name from the Health Care Justice Task Force—which sounded like a left-wing pressure group—to the moderate Bipartisan Health Reform Commission.

Unlike his efforts to end racial profiling or reform capital punishment, Obama did not win bipartisan support for the Health Care Justice Act. Republicans saw it as a back-door attempt to bring single-payer coverage to Illinois. The bill contained no specifics, and the commission could only offer recommendations, but the GOP compared it to President Bill Clinton's failed health care plan. During the final debate, Peter Roskam, the Republican spokesman on health care, led his party's attack on the Senate floor.

"The Illinois Life Insurance Council is opposed," Roskam argued. "The Illinois State Association of Health Underwriters is opposed, the National Federation of Independent Business is opposed, and the Illinois Chamber Employment Law Council is opposed. You know, this concept was one that Hillary Clinton took on in 1994 and it created such a stirring that there was a sea change, ultimately, in the politics of the United States. And it's a bill that—while it is not as draconian as what the Clinton administration tried to do, which was basically a nationalization of health care, it is a bill that you're being asked to consider today that has a lot of similar characteristics."

Obama was taken aback and angered by the accusations, especially the suggestion that he was trying to push a single-payer plan on the state. Obama favored a single-payer plan—he'd said so at an AFL-CIO forum in December 2003—but his bill left the details up to the task force and the legislature. Although he never raised his voice—shouting was not his style—Obama defended his integrity passionately.

"The original bill on the house side, I think, would have legitimately raised some concerns with respect to some who might have been fearful that it was a mandate to introduce a single-payer plan," he said. "I modified this. Insurance lobbyists here in Springfield have been engaging in such fearmongering among its agents, suggesting that this was a single-payer bill, that, in fact, a lot of concerns were raised that had nothing to do with the bill that was before the body today."

Obama, who was campaigning for the U.S. Senate by then, told of meeting a Galesburg man who was about to be laid off from the Maytag plant after thirty years. The man didn't know how he could afford $4,500 a month for the drugs his son needed to survive after a liver transplant.

"The majority of people who do not have health insurance are not welfare recipients who are covered by Medicaid," Obama said. "They're folks who work every single day, doing their best to make ends meet and try to raise a family, and the single biggest cause of bankruptcy is when they get sick."

All his bill would do, he argued, is say, "Let's all sit down and try to figure out how to solve a problem."

The Health Care Justice Act passed on a party-line vote, 31–26, but it ultimately accomplished very little. It certainly didn't bring universal health care to Illinois. After more than two years of meetings, the commission issued a report recommending a "hybrid" health care model that would require individuals to obtain coverage, either through their employers (who would have to provide health care) or by taking advantage of a state-funded subsidy. A minority of the members recommended a single-payer plan. The minority group included Dr. Quentin Young, who had supported Obama since his first run for the state senate. Young had always considered Obama a single-payer advocate, so he was disappointed that Obama had stripped the universal health care requirement from the bill.

John Bouman, who had worked with Obama on poverty and health care legislation, was more forgiving. "I think he was in favor of universal, affordable, comprehensive care for all, and not necessarily a disciple of one means of doing it over another," Bouman would say. "He's ever the pragmatist, and single payer is ever the ideal. That's his particular genius, and it causes him to take it in the neck from the left as well as the right."

By the time the commission reported back to the legislature, Obama had gone to the U.S. Senate. Some of its recommendations were adopted by Governor Blagojevich, for a plan he called Illinois Covered. But Illinois Covered never passed. It became a casualty of Blagojevich's inability to work with the legislature (as, eventually, did his entire governorship).

During his last two years in the state senate, Obama did achieve some expansions of health care. He passed a bill to change the eligibility for the Children's Health Insurance Plan—AllKids—from 185 percent of the federal poverty level to 200 percent. The new rules added twenty thousand children to the state-run health insurance program. Obama's bill also lowered the threshold for low-income parents to 90 percent of the poverty level—double where it had stood during the past two Republican administrations. That brought health care to sixty-five thousand poor people and helped solve the problem of welfare recipients refusing jobs or raises because they were afraid of losing Medicaid.

Through his committee chairmanship, and the patronage of Emil Jones, Obama sponsored twenty-two bills that became law that session, one of the highest success rates of any senator. Making the earned income tax credit permanent. Providing HIV testing for pregnant women. Requiring insurers to cover colorectal cancer exams. Forcing public bodies to tape-record closed meetings. None were as glamorous as reforming the death penalty, but it was still an extraordinary achievement for a senator who, a year before, had been an unknown backbencher. Now Obama had more than a résumé and a biography to sell the voters. He had finally done something.

Chapter 13

THE OBAMA JUICE

LIBERTY BAPTIST CHURCH, at Forty-ninth Street and Dr. Martin Luther King Jr. Drive, is an inspiring combination of the modern and the eternal. Its parabolic roof, supported from within by rust-colored beams that soar over the congregants, looks like a quonset hut or an airline terminal designed by a Scandinavian architect. Behind the altar is a stained glass mosaic of a risen Christ, attended by angels and apostles of all races. Despite its modish design, Liberty is one of Chicago's oldest African-American congregations. Its pastor, D. L. Jackson, inherited the pulpit from his father, who had in turn inherited it from *his* father. With a vast sanctuary that accommodates over a thousand worshippers, Liberty is an essential Sunday-morning stop for any South Side politician.

Liberty was where Obama finally showed he could connect with an audience—a *black* audience. For years, his friends and advisers had been beating up on him about stepping out of his professor's gown and putting on a preacher's robe, and now the stubborn SOB was finally doing it. The flip-down seats were filled with black folks, all excited to hear the tall, good-looking young brother running for the United States Senate. They'd been primed by their pastor, and by their alderman, Dorothy Tillman, who'd been fighting for black empowerment so long she could sign a hood pass for a half-white lawyer from Hyde Park.

Obama mounted the red-carpeted steps to the pulpit with his long-legged stride, pointing and waving. When he began to talk, he didn't use bureaucratic, academic terms like "bring together institutions from various sectors." That was the Obama of 2000. The new Obama had studied his audience—hardworking, churchgoing blacks—studied their aspirations, and the way they liked to hear those aspirations expressed every Sunday morning. This was going to be a sermon, not a lecture. It was going to quote Jesus, not the Brookings Institution.

"My name is Barack Obama, and everywhere I went, I would always get the same two questions. Didn't matter where I went. First question was 'Where did you get this funny name, "Barack Obama"?' Though people wouldn't always say it right. They would call me Alabama. They'd call me 'Yo Mama.'" Here, the congregation laughed. "And those were my supporters who called me that. I won't even talk about the folks running against me. The second question was 'Why would you want to get into a dirty business like politics?' There is another tradition of politics, and that tradition says we are all connected. If there is a child on the South Side that can't read, that makes a difference in my life, even if it's not my child."

The pews murmured with approval.

"If there is a senior citizen on the West Side that can't afford their prescription medicine, having to choose between buying medicine and paying the rent, that makes my life poorer, even if it's not my grandparent."

They were standing and clapping now, responding to the rhythms of his oratory.

"I believe that we can be a better nation," Obama shouted. "I believe that we can provide homes to the homeless and food to the hungry and clothes to the naked. I believe that we can defeat George Bush."

There were moments when he sounded like a parody of a jackleg preacher, his voice dipping into a guttural approximation of street talk, as though he were about to add "mm-hmm!" to the end of every sentence. Obama never spoke that way in private, but as a candidate, he wanted to be black when he needed to be black and white when he needed to be white. (Only whites were embarrassed by Obama's attempts to sound ghetto. "It can be painful to hear Barack Obama talk jive," wrote Todd Spivak in the *Illinois Times*, ridiculing Obama for using the word "homeboy" in church. Obama responded to Spivak's article with a wrathful phone call, which suggested that racial identity was still a touchy subject with him.)

Al Kindle was at Liberty that day, and he thought, This is the candidate I've been trying to bring out for years. This Obama is a black man who can go to the Senate—and maybe beyond.

Kindle realized how much was at stake, not just for Obama, but for Chicago's black political movement. Before he even announced his candidacy, Obama had confided, "Once you get elected senator, who knows where you can go? You can even get to president."

Black Chicago had already lifted its politicians higher than any minority community in the country, but this was the guy it could lift to the highest office of all. He was an African-American who could govern for everyone. It was the perfect match of a man and a city. As Kindle would put it much later, "We were looking for someone to do it, and he was looking for a place to do it in." If Obama had to be taught to sound like a black man, that was part of the lifting.

David Axelrod was just as high on Obama. A University of Chicago graduate, Axelrod had begun his working life as a reporter for the *Hyde Park Herald* before moving up to the *Chicago Tribune*. He quit journalism to manage Paul Simon's 1984 U.S. Senate campaign. In the two decades since, he'd become one of the best-known political consultants in the country. Axelrod had worked on Hillary Clinton's 2000 Senate campaign, but his specialty was big-city races, especially those that involved selling black candidates to white voters. Every consultant wants to discover the next John F. Kennedy, but Axelrod had another motivation for finding a candidate who could go all the way. As a political pro who chose to live in Chicago, he felt he wasn't taken seriously by the D.C. wonks. It was the Second City complex, caused by a different city than usual.

Ax, as everyone called him, was also being courted by big-spending millionaire Blair Hull, but he was getting the hard sell on Obama from Bettylu Saltzman, an organizer of the antiwar rally in Federal Plaza. Axelrod agreed to meet the candidate and was immediately smitten. Most white liberals lost it during their first encounter with Obama. Dan Shomon had a term for this phenomenon: "drinking the Obama Juice."

Axelrod got drunk easily. Right after agreeing to work for Obama, he received a phone call from Pete Giangreco, a Chicago media consultant who was helping organize John Edwards's media campaign.

"Listen," Axelrod asked Giangreco, "while I've got you on the phone, what are you doing in the Senate race?"

"Well, Dan Hynes is a former client," Giangreco said. "I

haven't heard from those guys, but it looks like he's gonna go. He's ahead in the polls, and he's going to have labor and the county chairmen behind him."

"You know, all that's probably true," Axelrod said, "but I've got to tell you, I think there's something special about this guy Obama. This guy's the real deal. This is the guy we try to make all our candidates sound like, this really genuine and heartfelt appeal to people's sort of reclaiming their citizenship, and the value of people coming together behind a set of ideals to get things done. There's some *there* there."

Giangreco knew Obama slightly. As a consultant to Rod Blagojevich's gubernatorial campaign, he had given a poll briefing to a group of state senators. Obama had been very inquisitive about the numbers and offered unsolicited advice about death penalty reform and other criminal justice issues. Smart guy, Giangreco had thought. Now, after hearing Ax so excited about Obama—more excited than Ax had ever been about a candidate—Giangreco said, "You know, I've only met him once or twice, but I kind of feel the same way."

Axelrod replaced Dan Shomon as Obama's political alter ego. As much as Ax and Obama had in common—their U of C backgrounds, a love of pickup basketball, a calm demeanor—they still fit the classic roles of candidate and consultant. Axelrod was tall, hangdog, and walked with a slow, heavy, splay-footed shamble. Every year, his unkempt forelock grew thinner, his droopy mustache grayer. But those who had worked with both men considered them equals in discipline, intelligence, and temperament—"a match made in heaven."

Once he was hired as chief strategist, Axelrod also replaced Dan Shomon as Obama's campaign manager, bringing in Jim Cauley, a Kentuckian he had worked with on a mayoral campaign in Baltimore. Shomon was given the job of Downstate coordinator. He had been reluctant to spend nearly two years managing a Senate campaign and suggested that Obama find a new right-hand man. That was fine with Obama's new crew of professionals. They didn't think Shomon had the policy or organizational skills to run a statewide race.

Loyalty to old allies is not one of Barack Obama's long suits. Unlike Bill Clinton, whose White House chief of staff was a kindergarten classmate, or Lyndon Johnson, who was served as an aide for three decades by a high school debate student he'd coached in Houston, Obama has no deep native ties to the state where he made his political career. Throughout Obama's rise, most of his relationships were expedient: Once he had no more use for supporters, he dropped them from his circle, sometimes telling perplexed functionaries to stop calling his cell phone and start calling his people. There was no one he could point to and say, "We've been tight for twenty years." It was the unflattering side of Obama's detached intellectualism. Johnnie Owens was Obama's closest friend during the community organizing days and a best man at his wedding. But once Obama began moving among lawyers, politicians, and professors, the old compatriots rarely saw each other. Obama lost touch with Jerry Kellman until a reporter reconnected them during his U.S. Senate run. Carole Anne Harwell, Obama's first campaign manager, had no significant role in his subsequent races. During Obama's run for president, Shomon would attempt to exploit the Obama connection to benefit his lobbying business. The campaign scolded him publicly.

"There were a number of people who worked for Barack in the early days, then found Barack was working with a different group of people," as one old supporter would put it. "They felt kind of squeezed out."

While that suggests a coldness to Obama's ambition, it did help him avoid the corruption and cronyism that would have ensnared a traditional Chicago politician, brought up in the code of fidelity to the ones that brung him. Obama needed Chicago to put him in a position to run for president, but he couldn't be *too* Chicago if he wanted to win.

When Axelrod took over the campaign, in mid-2003, Obama was polling at 9 percent among the few Illinoisans paying attention to the Senate primary. The front runner, Dan Hynes, was supported by a quarter of the primary voters and had already enlisted the great majority of the state's 102 county chairmen. Still, Axelrod believed that Obama could crank his numbers as high as 43 percent by Election Day if he swept the black community in Chicago, captured wealthy suburban whites, and won Downstate counties with colleges or large black populations. If the campaign met its goal of raising $4 million, they'd be able to start airing television ads in January, two months before the primary—just enough time to transform Obama into a Prairie State idol.

At the time, though, he was still an obscure state senator (a redundancy if there ever was one) with a name uncomfortably close to that of the leader of al-Qaeda. Shortly after 9/11, a Chicago political consultant who'd been sizing Obama up as a Senate prospect told him, "The name thing is going to be a problem." (*Capitol Fax* publisher Rich Miller once teasingly told Obama that he should change his name to "Barry O'Bama" if he wanted to run for statewide office.) When Representative Jan Schakowsky wore an Obama button to the White House, President George W. Bush did a double take on first seeing his successor's name.

"I've never heard of him," Bush explained.

"You will," Schakowsky promised.

Even some well-educated voters were declaring, "I want to vote for someone with an American name." Axelrod had not yet succeeded in spreading Obamamania to the suburbs. The foundations of Obama's campaign were black professionals and the black church. At the District, a West Loop nightclub, he threw a fund-raiser for the kinds of rich young folks who hung Alpha Phi Alpha paddles in their lofts and had their weddings featured in *Jet*.

"The crowd of 500 people were dressed to the hilt, sporting chic natural and relaxed hairdos, Prada, Gucci and Louis Vuitton accessories," the *Hyde Park Herald* wrote of the event, which raised $50,000. "Party goers, including Hyde Park Ald. Leslie Hairston (5th) and Illinois Senate President Emil Jones, grooved to live jazz, R&B oldies from Chic and current neo-soul hits from Jill Scott, while munching on California rolls and fried chicken."

Obama had always professed his distaste for fund-raising, but under pressure to collect $4 million, he was overcoming any reluctance about asking people for money. In fact, he was taking political style tips from Governor Blagojevich, who was well known for his two-handed approach to politicking: The right hand shakes while the left goes for the wallet. Obama and Blagojevich had little use for each other personally. Both wanted to be president, and Blagojevich, raised in a dreary Northwest Side apartment by a steelworker father, thought Hyde Parkers were pampered elitists. But as a loyal Democrat, Obama had sat in on Blagojevich's campaign strategy sessions and came to envy his skill at glad-handing donors while pestering them for cash. Blagojevich's charm, combined with Illinois's no-limit campaign contribution laws, had enabled him to suck up $24 million for his gubernatorial campaign.

As a Senate candidate, Obama was operating under federal funding laws, but Blair Hull's personal wealth meant that Obama could take advantage of the "millionare's exemption," which allowed individuals to donate up to $12,500 to a candidate running against a self-financed swell. Steven Rogers, a business professor at Northwestern University, met the newly aggressive Obama at a golf outing for a West Side charter school. When Obama joined his threesome, on the second hole, Rogers had no idea who the new player was. He quickly found out.

"Look, man," Obama told him. "I want to talk to you because I want to run for the U.S. Senate."

"Look, man, you need to go sit your ass down somewhere," Rogers said, finally recognizing the name. "You just got your ass beat by Bobby Rush. You can't win. You got two damn African names. You need to be like my children: Akila Rogers. Or, instead of Barack Obama, you need to be Steven Obama or Barack Jones."

They had a good laugh, but on the fourth hole, Obama again said, "I want to run for Senate."

"Jesus Christ, man!" Rogers exploded. "What can I do for you?"

"My wife wants me to clear up debts from running for Congress."

"How much debt do you have?"

"Eight thousand dollars."

"I'll tell you what," Rogers said. "I don't know you, but Greg White knows you. Greg brought you to my foursome. I'm gonna give you $3,000."

After that, Rogers heard from Obama every week. As a man who believed that well-off blacks had a duty to support black political talent, Rogers ended up donating tens of thousands of dollars to Obama's campaigns. During the general election, when Obama was running away from Alan Keyes and didn't need the money himself, Rogers wrote five $2,000 checks to Democrats in close Senate races so Obama could collect chits in his new workplace.

The most important financial help Obama received came from a June 2003 fund-raiser held by attorney Stephen Pugh in the lobby of his LaSalle Street office tower. Obama needed to top $1 million by the July 1 campaign filing disclosure to prove he was a serious candidate. LaSalle Street is the main drag of Chicago's business and legal worlds, so Pugh was the ideal host. He introduced Obama as a future president of the United States, then said with a chuckle, "Let's not get ahead of ourselves." With most of Pugh's fellow ABLE members in attendance (as well as Emil Jones), the event raised several hundred thousand dollars, more than enough for Obama to meet his goal. Pugh had been given a hand up by Harold Washington and Emil Jones, and now he was offering a hand up to Obama. It was the unspoken contract between black politician and black businessman, its terms fully executed.

Outside of Chicago, Illinois's largest concentration of African-Americans is in the region known as Metro East—the trans-Mississippi suburbs of St. Louis. East St. Louis, hometown of Miles Davis and Jackie Joyner-Kersee, is the blackest city in the United States—97 percent African-American.

Through his old friend Reverend Alvin Love, president of the Developing Communities Project, Obama had an in with the area's black pastors. As Obama had risen in politics, Love had advanced in ecclesiastical influence. By 2003, he was head of the state's Baptist Convention, which covered four hundred churches. That spring,

Love invited Obama to address the convention's annual meeting, in Danville. After giving a biblically-themed speech—"A lot of people say this campaign is impossible, but with God, all things are possible"—Obama collected business cards from two hundred preachers.

Obama's Metro East coordinator was Ray Coleman, a state park supervisor who had been recruited to the campaign by Michael Pittman, a Springfield real estate developer Obama knew through a lobbyist. Downstate blacks never questioned Obama's racial authenticity. They had other reservations about his candidacy. Living in communities where whites were openly bigoted (the 1909 Springfield Race Riot is still a divisive issue in the state capital), they doubted their Caucasian neighbors would vote for Obama, and some even worried they'd look "too black" by supporting him. Springfield isn't Chicago, where blacks have their own machine-within-a-Machine. Dan Hynes and Rod Blagojevich controlled thousands of state jobs in Springfield. The first time Pittman met Obama, he thought, This guy is sharp. Then he thought, If this guy wasn't black, he could be president. Pittman held a fund-raiser for black professionals, which raised several thousand dollars, and he called black political junkies all over Central Illinois, spreading the word about Obama.

When Ray Coleman heard from Pittman, he, too, was skeptical.

"Mike," he said, "the guy can't win with a name like that. It's too close to 'Osama.' It's still close to Nine/Eleven."

"I'm gonna send you an article from the *Chicago Sun-Times*," Pittman replied. "It says if eighty-five percent of African-American voters support Obama, he'll win."

Coleman read the article, was impressed with Obama's credentials, and agreed to run the local operation. When Obama and Shomon arrived in Metro East, Coleman took them around to the churches. At St. John Missionary Baptist, in Centerville, Obama got a few minutes in the study of Reverend Robert Jones. His first words to Jones were, "How are you doing? Alvin Love is a friend of yours. He said you're a good man to meet in this part of the state."

Black pastors are used to politicians using their churches for campaign speeches. They usually allow it, but they're not always enthusiastic. Obama, though, had the endorsement of Reverend Love. That went a long way with the Baptist clergy. Jones invited Obama to speak at a youth revival at Mt. Zion Baptist in East St. Louis—the church where Jesse Jackson began his first presidential campaign in 1984. A crowd of fifteen hundred, Jones promised.

The church was packed. Obama started with his shopworn stump joke—"Some people call me Yo Mama, some people call me Alabama"—and the crowd roared with laughter. When he told them, "I'm not asking you to work for me because I'm African-American, but don't we deserve to have at least one in the Senate?" they nodded, and when he talked about folks who'd grown up in the age of Jim Crow but believed America could be a better place, they stood and cheered.

The powerful St. Clair County machine was supporting Hynes, and Hull was paying workers $10 an hour to staple his signs to every telephone pole in the American Bottom, as the area's alluvial lowlands are known. But Obama and Shomon thought the campaign could do at least as well as Carol Moseley Braun had in Metro East. Shomon asked Coleman if he could turn out four thousand votes in St. Clair County, which includes East St. Louis. It seemed like a reasonable goal, since Obama's only important local supporters were the state senators James Clayborne and Bill Haine.

"Dan, I'll get you that," Coleman promised. "I think we're going to do better. I think we can get six or eight thousand."

When Coleman started talking up Obama, in September 2003, people were asking him, "Who is this guy? Omar?" As the election drew closer, he was hearing from a lot of people who weren't supposed to be for Obama but had decided that electing a black senator was more important than obeying the county machine. East St. Louis precinct captains were ignoring the party line by asking for Obama yard signs and instructing printers to place "Obama" on their palm cards instead of "Hynes." In most elections, the voters followed the precinct captains. But this was shaping up to be a people's election. The voters wanted Obama, so the precinct captains were following.

All over the South Side of Chicago, billboards were going up: Barack Obama and Jesse Jackson Jr., standing side by side, looking like a pair of cardboard cutouts. It was a message from the Jacksons to black Chicago: We've got him. Junior was developing one of the most powerful political organizations in the city—his wife would soon be an alderman—so Obama needed him for votes as well as cred.

Only one black congressman refused to support Obama: Bobby Rush. Still sore about 2000, Rush endorsed Blair Hull, assuring the millionaire that "blacks won't vote for Obama." The endorsement wasn't motivated by payback, Rush insisted. After all, Rush was an independent, and Hull was the only candidate with the resources to beat the Machine's boy, Dan Hynes. (Hull was also the only candidate with the resources to hire Rush's half brother as a $12,000-a-month campaign adviser.)

Motivated by bitterness, Rush was misreading the black electorate as badly as Obama had done four years earlier. Elders who had supported Rush in 2000 were now behind Obama, for the very same reason: He was the black candidate with the best chance to win. Bishop Arthur Brazier endorsed Obama. So did historian Timuel Black, who publicly scolded the holdouts, asking, "Why can't we support one of our own?"

The black politician who most worried Obama was his fellow Senate candidate, Joyce Washington. A health-care consultant who had never held office, Washington was polling in the low single digits. But all her support was coming from the black community. In a close election, 1 or 2 percent might cost Obama the nomination. At one point, Obama, Giangreco, and Axelrod held a conference call to discuss whether to challenge Washington's petitions. Remembering Alice Palmer, Obama was reluctant. He didn't want to look like he was bullying another black woman off the ballot. He was supposed to be the inspirational candidate in this race, not the hack. The ill will over a petition challenge might end up costing him more votes than Washington, an innocuous candidate with no money. After a long discussion of the pros and cons, Obama finally said, "Guys, we're not gonna do it."

Obama's Senate campaign office was in a suite near the top of a low-rise office building on South Michigan Avenue. The view of Lake Michigan was inspiring, but the walls were nearly bare. Obama's only adornments were a framed copy of his *Chicago Reader* profile and a poster of Muhammad Ali looming over Sonny Liston, which hung behind the candidate's desk.

I visited the office in January 2004, to interview Obama for the *Reader*. I hadn't seen him in four years, so I was expecting another preening, insecure performance. When I'd called to set up the meeting, Obama's press secretary, Pam Smith, had expressed her displeasure with the "negative comments" in my article on his congressional campaign.

If Obama was still dissatisfied, he didn't act that way. This was months before he became famous, so he was dealing with the press one-on-one. He greeted me outside his office.

"Good to see you again," he intoned casually, gliding across the floor like Fred Astaire playing Abe Lincoln. His tie was firmly knotted, but he'd doffed his suit coat for shirtsleeves.

We walked into his office, where Smith sat by his side as note taker and timekeeper. I told him I'd seen a picture of Michelle in that morning's *Sun-Times*. "She was looking awfully cute," Obama said, grinning.

It was only January, but Obama was already developing the themes he would use at that summer's Democratic National Convention. He gave me some of the same lines he'd used on the congregation at Liberty Baptist.

"There is a tradition of politics that says we are all connected," Obama recited. "If there is a child on the South Side who cannot read, it makes a difference in my life, even if it's not my child. If there's an Arab-American family who's being rounded up by John Ashcroft without benefit of due process, that threatens my civil liberties. Black folks, white folks, gay, straight, Asian—the reason we can share this space is that we have a mutual regard. That's what this country's all about: E pluribus unum. Out of many, one."

That was the mission statement of twenty-first-century Obama. As a black candidate, he'd been too inhibited, too embarrassed, to force out such phrases as "our community." Finally, he was comfortable in his own skin, now that he'd accepted that the skin was half white. As a multicultural politician trying to find a unified theory of racial politics, he was rolling like Tiger Woods at the Masters. The aloofness was gone as well. Intently, he laid out his plan for a federal children's health insurance program.

"I think it'd be a good opportunity to lay the groundwork toward expanding health care to all the uninsured," he said.

Obama was no longer selling himself. He didn't mention Harvard once. This time, he had a legislative goal and a strategy for making it happen. Or maybe, because he knew I'd been one of his skeptics, he was selling me on the idea that he wasn't selling himself. Just as he was looking two moves ahead politically, I'm sure he was two moves ahead of my expectations. It was working. I was impressed that he finally seemed to believe in something more than the fact that being president of the *Harvard Law Review* is a pretty big deal. He was a big-government liberal, and he was unafraid to confess it.

"How would you have voted on the Iraq war resolution?" I asked.

"I would have voted no." And then, repeating his assertion from Federal Plaza, he said, "I'm not opposed to all wars. I'm opposed to dumb wars."

Finally, we got around to his race against Bobby Rush.

"I got a good spanking," Obama said evenly. He'd obviously thought out that response. "I think that was youthful impatience on my part."

Later, when I called his office for follow-up questions, Obama jumped on the line to drill me with more details of his health care plan. He also repeated his "E pluribus unum" speech, tweaking a few words. He was proud of that one.

In a *Chicago Tribune* poll taken that month, Obama was the choice of 14 percent of Democratic voters, tying him for the lead with Dan Hynes and Maria Pappas. Blair Hull was just behind, with 10 percent.

"Statewide, the poll showed some gains for Obama, who was the choice of only 9 percent of Democratic voters in October," the *Tribune* reported. "Most of the growth in his support was among black voters, with 29 percent backing him."

These were meaningful gains, but with two months until the primary, Obama had not broken out of the pack. He hadn't united the black vote behind him, either.

In the fall of 2003, Obama's campaign had been cultivating an endorsement that would have put him in the lead for good. Paul Simon had retired from the Senate in 1996, but his name and his word were still golden among Illinois liberals. Simon had even handpicked his successor, Dick Durbin. In this contentious primary, his blessing would be decisive.

Simon had worked with Obama on the ethics reform bill and served on the death penalty task force that recommended videotaping interrogations. Obama showed courage and skill in promoting that, Simon thought. Illinois had a tradition of progressive senators going back almost to World War II: Paul Douglas, Adlai Stevenson III, Simon, Durbin. Obama fit that lineage. Simon's only reservation about making an endorsement was his long friendship with Dan Hynes's father, who had served in the state senate when Simon was lieutenant governor.

Abner Mikva also thought Obama fit the state's senatorial tradition. At a private fund-raiser on the North Side, Mikva heard Adlai Stevenson III give a powerful speech about Obama's virtues as a candidate. That gave him an idea. Excitedly, he called Simon.

"You know, it would be a great press opportunity and marvelous publicity for Barack if we could have a press conference with you and Adlai endorsing him," Mikva said, giving him the pitch.

It would, Simon agreed.

"If you can get Adlai, I obviously will do it," Simon told Mikva. "I've tried to avoid a public endorsement because of Dan, but if you get Adlai, I'll absolutely help you."

So Mikva called Stevenson. So enthusiastic at the fund-raiser, Stevenson now hemmed and hawed about making a public statement.

"Well, I know the Hynes family so well," he said. "They've been so good to me."

"Adlai," Mikva responded, "Paul's in the same position. He's going to do it."

"I'm going to have to think about it some more," Stevenson said finally.

While Stevenson dithered, Simon checked into a Springfield hospital for open heart surgery. He was still hale enough for a press conference. In a phone call to reporters, Simon endorsed Howard Dean for president from his sickbed. Mikva phoned Stevenson every day but couldn't get him off the fence. Then, suddenly, it didn't matter. On December 9, 2003, Simon died on the operating table at age seventy-five.

It was a tremendous blow to the Obama campaign, both politically and personally. Simon's endorsement would have validated the reformer image Obama was trying to project. It would have impressed suburban liberals, the white faction of his hoped-for coalition. Simon's death was a personal loss because so many of Obama's staffers and fund-raisers had begun their careers with him. Axelrod and Bettylu Saltzman were attracted to Obama for the same reasons they'd loved Paul Simon: intelligence, integrity, and a progressive spirit.

After enough time passed, Axelrod approached Simon's

daughter, Sheila, a Carbondale city councilwoman and guardian of her father's political legacy. Would she be willing to film an ad saying her father had planned to endorse Obama?

Simon had reservations. She didn't want to speak for her late father. On the other hand, she knew how he'd felt about Obama, and she was an Obama supporter herself, eager to help him win.

"I don't know if I'm really comfortable with that," she told Axelrod. "I don't know if I want to say who Dad endorsed."

"Why don't we just talk about the parallels of the things they worked on together?" Axelrod suggested.

To that, Simon agreed. In the ad, she talked about her father's career, over film clips of Paul Simon campaigning throughout Illinois.

"For half a century, Paul Simon stood for something very special in public life: integrity, principle, and a commitment to fight for those who most needed a voice," Simon said. "State Senator Barack Obama is cut from that same cloth. With Paul Simon, Barack led the fight to stop wrongful executions and to pass new ethics and campaign finance laws to clean up our politics."

In the final ten seconds, Sheila Simon appeared on camera. She had her father's dark hair, his rubbery smile. The resemblance was unmistakable. As Sheila herself once admitted, neither father nor daughter was much more than plain. A homely face, horn-rimmed glasses, and a bow tie were all part of Paul Simon's appeal. Like Lincoln, he wasn't handsome, but he was honest.

"I know Barack Obama will be a U.S. senator in the Paul Simon tradition," she said. "You see, Paul Simon was my dad."

The Sheila Simon ad was one of three TV spots the Obama campaign recorded that winter. Axelrod's strategy was to start airing the ads in late January, six weeks before the primary. With

$4 million, that was the longest window Obama could afford. Hull had already been on TV for months. But Axelrod—who had turned down an offer to run Hull's campaign, for far more money than Obama was paying—was confident that he had a better candidate. He was crossing his fingers that Obama's limited means would give the campaign just enough time to make that case.

While Obama worked the black churches—he was attending five services every Sunday—Axelrod and Giangreco tried to win over white suburbanites. They tested the ads before a focus group on the North Shore, the wealthy, socially liberal suburbs depicted in *Ordinary People, Risky Business*, and *Ferris Bueller's Day Off*. North Shore residents aren't likely to live next door to a black person, but they are willing to vote for one.

As Obama's consultants watched from behind a one-way window, the Democratic voters viewed three advertisements, in the order the campaign planned to air them. The first was a biographical spot. It mentioned (of course) that Obama had been the first African-American president of the *Harvard Law Review*. It touted his record in the state senate—on education, on expanding the children's health insurance program.

"They said we couldn't insure every kid, but we did," Obama said, addressing the camera. Then, for the first time, he uttered his now-famous campaign slogan: "I'm Barack Obama, and I paid for this ad to say, 'Yes, we can.'"

When Obama spoke, the voters—especially the women—leaned forward to listen.

(Al Kindle had an explanation for Obama's appeal to suburban women. "He was so good-looking that they can have him in the bed with them without having him in the bed," he would say.

"He was the dream they wished they could take home. In Glencoe and Evanston, all of these areas where there were rich white females, there were more Obama posters than in Chicago. Once people got past his race, it was cute and niche-y that he was African-American.")

The second ad, designed to emphasize Obama's multiracial appeal, was a dual endorsement by Jesse Jackson and Jan Schakowsky, who represented the northern suburbs in Congress.

Finally, the focus group saw the Simon ad. The campaign intended to run it last. Paul Simon's endorsement, from beyond the grave, would validate everything voters heard about Obama in the first two ads and in a direct mail piece that offered him as "finally, a chance to believe again." After seeing the Simon ad, everyone in the room got the connection.

"He *reminds* me of Paul Simon," one woman said effusively.

During that primary season, there was no better place to see Obama work both his bases at once than the Heartland Café, a restaurant in Rogers Park, Chicago's most integrated neighborhood. Founded by hippies, the Heartland was renowned for its vegan dishes, its folk music concerts, and a magazine rack that carried *Dissent* and the *Nation*. By bringing in Obama, the restaurant was trying to re-create the spirit of 1983, Chicago progressives' greatest year. Harold Washington spoke at the Heartland during his first campaign for mayor. A photo of that appearance still hung on a brick wall.

In the crowded dining room, Obama was awaited by punk rockers, gray-haired war protestors, and dreadlocked West Indians. The local ward organization had been expecting a hundred people. Over three hundred showed up—so many that latecomers were turned away. As Obama moved from whites to blacks, he adjusted his language, just as he adjusted his speeches for a Southern Illinois farm cooperative and a Chicago Baptist church.

"You've got some pretty blue eyes," he said, hoisting a baby boy. "I'm gonna have to introduce you to my daughter. She's a little older than you. You like older women?"

After handing the child back to his father, Obama turned and gave dap to a black guy.

"How are you?" he asked in his deepest voice. "What's goin' on?"

Obama was introduced by the local alderman, Joe Moore, who had also spoken out against the Iraq War in 2002, appearing on the *Today* show to argue for diplomacy.

"Barack Obama is not the son of a powerful politician," Moore said. "He is not a multimillionaire. What he is is a man of courage, a man of conviction, a man who will stand with his principles regardless of which way the political winds were blowing. I was here some twenty-one years ago, almost to the date, the last time this room was as filled as it is today, and that was for Harold Washington. He had this room filled with the same kind of energy that is here today because people in this neighborhood have great political instincts."

Obama's three-syllable name lends itself to a chant, so the candidate mounted the step-high stage to a rolling "O-BA-ma! O-BA-ma!"

"You guys, you guys, you're making me blush," he protested.

Anyone who had listened to the pedantic lecturer of 2000 would have been bowled over by the camp-meeting speech Obama gave that Saturday morning. And anyone who subsequently heard him speak at the convention in Boston would have recognized the rhetoric and felt the same energy, in that small room, that Obama later projected across the Fleet Center.

"I came to Chicago to work among the least of these," Obama began.

Communities that needed help after the devastation caused by the closing of steel mills on the South Side of Chicago. The best education I ever received was working with people in the community on a grassroots level. What it taught me was ordinary people, when they are working together, can do extraordinary things. A lot of people ask me, 'Why would you want to go into politics?' Even in this room that is full of activists, there is a certain gnawing cynicism about the political process. We have a sense that too many of our leaders are long on rhetoric but short on substance. We get a sense that, particularly here in Illinois, that politics operates as a business rather than a mission, and certainly, we have the sense that in Washington, power always trumps principle. What I suggest to you today is what I told people when I first ran: that there is another tradition of politics, and that tradition says that we are all connected. If there is a child on the South Side of Chicago that cannot read, it makes a difference in my life even if it's not my child. If there is a senior citizen in Downstate Illinois that cannot buy their prescription drugs, or is having to choose between medicine or paying the rent, that makes my life poorer, even if it's not my grandparent. If there is an Arab-American family that is being rounded up by John Ashcroft without benefit of an attorney or due process, that threatens my civil liberties, even if I'm not Arab-American. So, it's that idea that we have a set of mutual obligations toward each other. That I am my brother's keeper. That I am my sister's keeper. That I am not an island unto myself. It is that concept that makes this country work. It is why all of us can be in this room together. Black folks and white folks. Men, women, gay, straight, Asian, Hispanic, poor, well-to-do. The reason we can share this space is because we have a sense of mutual regard, and that's the basis for this country. *E pluribus unum.* Out of many, one.

Obama was a fight announcer, a preacher, and a motivational speaker, all in the same lean frame. Full of conviction, he drove his words into his listeners' ears like a carpenter shooting nails. The white folks loved Obama because he was a reformer, and because a multiracial candidate appealed to their ideal of black and white coexistence. The black folks loved him because the white folks loved him.

"We need someone who can reach beyond the race," one woman said after the speech. "He can go to Washington and speak their language."

Axelrod had brought a camera crew to the Heartland Café. (Footage from the speech would be used in some of Obama's ads.) He was thrilled with the turnout.

"When I felt the enthusiasm in that room," Ax later told the local ward committeeman, "that was when I felt the tide had turned for Obama."

Thanks to a quirk of geography and the presidential primary schedule, the Quad Cities are very appealing to an Illinois politician who's already thinking about where he can go from the U.S. Senate. Moline and Rock Island, Illinois, lie across the Mississippi River from Davenport and Bettendorf, Iowa. The towns may be in different states, but they're all in the same media market. The big newspaper—the *Quad-City Times*—and the big TV station, WQAD, are both in Davenport, but they cover Illinois news.

With Denny Jacobs at his side, Obama campaigned in union halls and picnics all over Illinois's half of the Quad Cities. As a state senator from Chicago, he wasn't drawing big crowds, but those who showed up felt the same star power Jacobs had sensed when Obama first walked onto the state Senate floor.

"I don't know what the hell it is about you," Jacobs complained to Obama, "but when we walk into a room, they look at you like you're the greatest, and they look at me like, 'Get out of here, prick.'"

"Jacobs, that's 'cause you're short," Obama explained.

Obama would lose Rock Island County to Hynes, but he got his face on WQAD, and he was endorsed by the *Quad-City Times*. Four years before winning the Iowa caucuses, he introduced himself to Iowa voters, without even leaving his home state.

If Obama could win the primary, he was bound for the Senate. Of that, he was certain. Illinois was a blue state, hostile to George W. Bush's reelection. The Republican front-runner, Jack Ryan, had earned millions as an investment banker but lacked political experience.

"This is my election," Obama told campaign volunteers. "I'm not worried about the Republicans. This is the battle."

To anyone who picked up the *Chicago Tribune* on February 23, the battle must have looked hopeless. According to the paper's latest survey, Blair Hull was now leading the field, with 24 percent. His TV ads were omnipresent. Every hour, on every news channel, Hull was talking about his army service or his plan to improve schools. It was beginning to look as though the Senate seat that had gone for $14 million to Peter Fitzgerald was about to be sold to the man with thirty mil.

Obama was in second place, with 15 percent, but he had the lowest name recognition of any major candidate. Only a third of the voters knew who he was. A year before, Hull had been even more obscure, but he had bought his way into the public consciousness. Maria Pappas was Cook County treasurer, Dan Hynes was comptroller, Gery Chico had run the school district. Those jobs all had bigger constituencies than a state senator.

Once again, though, the disciplined, dispassionate Obama benefited from another politician's weakness. Mel Reynolds couldn't stay away from young girls. Alice Palmer had made the fatal error of giving Obama permission to run for her state senate seat. When Palmer changed her mind, she was unable to organize a petition drive. Against Bobby Rush, Obama had been the one who couldn't control himself, allowing his arrogance and impatience to lure him into a race he couldn't win.

This time, the tragic character was Blair Hull. Hull's relationship with his second wife, Brenda Sexton, had been volatile. The couple married and divorced twice. Before the final breakup, Sexton took out an order of protection against Hull. That was public record, but the nature of the couple's disagreement was sealed in their divorce file. Hull refused to talk about the file, but every political hack in Chicago knew there was something inside that could destroy his megamillion-dollar candidacy.

Kitty Kurth worked briefly on Hull's campaign but quit because he wouldn't come clean about the divorce.

"You need to talk about these records now, in July, because if you don't talk about 'em in July, David Axelrod is going to have somebody talking about 'em in February," Kurth told Hull's staff.

During her career in Chicago politics, Kurth had worked both with and against Axelrod. Ax was the shrewdest operator in town. If Kurth knew the divorce papers were dynamite, Axelrod had to know, too. You can't keep a secret like that in a political campaign.

Axelrod did know. When he interviewed with Hull in 2002, Axelrod forced the millionaire to confess his most sordid secrets. If Ax signed on, he'd have to defend his candidate against anything the opposition dug up, so he wanted the dirt in advance. Hull told Axelrod that his ex-wife had alleged mental and physical cruelty as grounds for divorce.

Illinois was talking about Hull's divorce in February, but it wasn't Axelrod's or Obama's doing. An operative for Dan Hynes slipped the outside sheet of Hull's divorce file to David Mendell, a reporter for the *Tribune*. Hynes thought he had a lot to gain by knocking the other white guy down a peg. The sheet detailed Sexton's request for an order of protection. But when Mendell interviewed Hull for a campaign profile, Hull refused to discuss the divorce.

That only led to more questions. Women's groups demanded details. A week later, Hull admitted the order had resulted from an incident in which he was accused of striking Sexton on the shin. In a televised debate at the Old State Capitol in Springfield, every candidate except Obama attacked Hull's unwillingness to open his divorce records. (Obama attacked Hull for misrepresenting his opposition to the Iraq war: "The fact of the matter is, Blair, that you were silent when these decisions were being made. You were AWOL on this issue.")

"You know, you're responsible for this," Axelrod told Mendell during the debate.

"David," Mendell replied, "if it wasn't through me, you folks would have figured out another way to get the mess out there. I just fired the first bullet loaded into the chamber."

Realizing that his marriage had become the campaign's biggest issue, Hull asked a judge to make the divorce file public. It ended his hopes of becoming a senator. Hull's ex-wife had accused him of being "a violent man" who "hung on the canopy bar of [her] bed, leered at [her] and stated, 'Do you want to die? I am going to kill you.'" According to Sexton, Hull had thrown fake punches in an attempt to make her flinch and punched her "extremely hard in the left shin."

Since the divorce, Hull and Sexton had become good friends. In a touching Chicago gesture, he'd even used his clout to find her a job. As a six-figure contributor to Rod Blagojevich, Hull got the governor to appoint his ex-wife head of the Illinois Film Board. But the tales of domestic violence were more memorable than any of Hull's ads. To the average Illinoisan, Blair Hull, champion of prescription drugs for seniors, was now Blair Hull, wife beater.

The wreck of Hull's campaign ended up benefiting Obama, not Hynes. Although Hynes had won two statewide elections, they were for comptroller, an uninspiring office that pays the state's bills. Hynes was uninspiring in other ways, too. He owed his political career to his father, boss of a powerful Irish ward. At thirty-five, his only apparent signs of maturity were a few gray hairs above his elfin ears. And his airless, colorless, odorless personality was not redeemed by a TV ad in which he wore an apron and cracked an egg to symbolize how Republicans wanted to scramble seniors' nest eggs by reforming Social Security. Hynes had the support of the Daley family and even a few black ward committeemen. In his father's day, that would have been enough to carry a candidate as bland as Dan Hynes. But Hynes's image as a prince of the Machine was a liability against Obama, whose personal story was getting through to voters now that his ads were on TV. Hynes represented Chicago's provincial past—political dynasties, ethnic loyalties, unadulterated Irishness, precinct captains ringing doorbells for a kid from the neighborhood. Obama reflected the modern Chicago, a cosmopolitan city made so by ambitious migrants like himself.

Axelrod's strategy of saving it all for the last six weeks was working. If any one event put Obama over the top, it was the airing of the Sheila Simon ad. State Senator Jeffrey Schoenberg, an Evanston Democrat who by early March was regretting that Hynes had asked him for an endorsement before Obama, thought Simon's endorsement was the most powerful thirty seconds of political television he had ever seen.

"It was a tremendous difference," Schoenberg would say. "It reached into your chest and grabbed you by the heart and never let go."

Hull had been doing well among African-Americans because of his TV ads, his signs in the ghetto, and his support among the black politicians still resisting Obama's ascendance. (Even during the last week of the primary, there was still an "anybody but Obama" sentiment in the capitol, especially among house members.) All those black voters were now shifting to Obama.

Obama's campaign could not afford nightly polling, but Hull's could. His staffers watched their candidate tumble down a hill, while Obama sprinted up a mountain. Even without numbers, Axelrod, Giangreco, and Cauley could sense something big was happening: Suddenly, money was pouring in through the mail, over the phone, and on the Internet. Politicians who had once been coyly neutral were now jumping on Obama's bandwagon. And wherever their candidate went, the crowds were bigger and

louder. Still unsure of the black vote, Obama ran a last-minute
ad titled "Hope," with clips of Paul Simon addressing a veterans'
group and Harold Washington hugging an old white man.

"There have been moments in our history when hope defeated cynicism, when the power of people triumphed over machines," the narrator intoned.

The message to black Chicago was clear: Let's make this like
1983 all over again.

Illinois held its primaries in mid-March for two reasons: to
make life difficult for upstart candidates, who had trouble finding people to ring doorbells all winter, and to coincide with
the St. Patrick's Day Parade, which always showcased the Irish
candidates.

The Irish Machine candidate wasn't getting the help he'd expected that day. There's another tradition in Chicago politics,
summed up by the motto, "Don't make no waves, don't back no
losers." By six A.M., when the libraries, churches, and school
gymnasiums unlocked their doors for the voters, everyone in
Illinois politics knew Obama was going to win.

Hynes was a lost cause. Union heavies in quilted White Sox
jackets were still handing out palm cards with his name, but a lot
more guys would have stood in the cold for Hynes if he'd been a
contender. Where was the reward in working for an also-ran?

On the South Side, the scene was different. The Obama campaign had collected so much money in the last few weeks it was
able to pay people $25 to knock on doors and leave Obama hang-
ers on the knobs. Over a hundred vans sat in the parking lot of
an abandoned department store at Seventy-sixth Street and Stony
Island Avenue, each with room for a supervisor and fourteen
"flushers." Word had gotten around the hood that you could

work for Obama *and* get paid, so the lot was mobbed. Before sunrise, Obama's street organizers worried about finding enough workers. They ended up turning people away. The two-bit door hangers who emerged from the two-flats and housing projects that morning overwhelmed the organizations of the few black bosses who were supporting Hynes out of loyalty to the mayor. This day wasn't quite like the day that elected Harold Washington, when some South Side precincts reported 100 percent turnout, but almost every African-American who voted was voting for Obama. When the first spindle counts came in, around ten A.M., turnout was low everywhere but in the black community, which was showing moderate to moderately high activity. John Kerry had already sewn up the Democratic nomination for president, so many white voters figured the primary didn't matter.

Obama and his family awaited the election results in a suite at the Hyatt Regency, which was owned by the Pritzker family. They didn't have to wait long. At seven o'clock, the moment the polls closed, news anchors began announcing, "Barack Obama has won the Democratic nomination for United States Senate." His victory was that decisive. It was bigger even than Axelrod, who was wonking out on returns at the Cook County clerk's office, could have imagined. Forty-three percent, he'd told Obama. That's the best we'll do, if everything goes perfectly. But now, in a seven-candidate field, against experienced politicians, Obama was winning 53 percent of the vote. In some South Side wards, his margins were running over 90 percent. One Hyde Park precinct cast all 124 ballots for its neighborhood son. Hynes won only the Southwest Side wards controlled by white political dynasties: the Daleys, the Madigans, the Lipinskis, and his own family. Obama ran respectably in all four, which would have been unimaginable for a black candidate when he arrived in Chicago.

Harold Washington had been lucky to win one percent in those neighborhoods. Chicago was changing, and a multiracial candidate was helping to change it.

Obama took two-thirds of the vote in Chicago. Outside the city, he won every county in the metropolitan area. Hynes won most of Downstate, but Obama took a few college towns and Abraham Lincoln's Springfield. In St. Clair County, Obama got eight thousand votes—twice what Carol Moseley Braun had won and just what Roy Williams, his county coordinator, had promised to deliver. Obama's final tally—655,923—was only a few thousand short of all the ballots cast in the Republican primary.

As the night went on and rivals called to concede, Obama gradually revealed himself to a wider and wider circle of supporters. When the polls closed, he was sequestered in his thirty-fourth-floor suite with thirty or so family members and friends. Michelle celebrated her husband's projected victory by slapping him a high five.

"They like you!" she teased. "They really like you!"

An hour later, Obama was hugging and shaking hands with two hundred of his biggest donors in a VIP room. Obama didn't make his victory speech until after ten o'clock, when the late local news airs in Chicago. As he paced back and forth in a hallway behind a ballroom crammed with five hundred supporters, he was introduced by Sheila Simon, who had done as much as anyone to bring about this moment. Simon named all her father's friends who were there that night—Ax, Ab Mikva, Rahm Emanuel—firmly passing on the Paul Simon legacy.

"Barack was a long shot," Simon said. "His campaign was against the odds, but when you've got a lot of guts, you can get things done."

Obama calmly studied his notes until Simon announced his name. Then, the crowd burst into an enormous cheer and an aide threw open the door separating the candidate from his followers.

"You're on, Barack!" the aide shouted. "You're on!"

Suddenly, he was on: the smile, the wave, the smooth stride, the grasping handshake. In an instant, Obama switched from intellectual to politician. In his victory speech, he was both.

"I am fired up!" he shouted. "There's no way a skinny guy from the South Side with a name like Barack Obama could win, but here we are sixteen months later."

Then the room quieted, and he read from notes he had written out by hand.

"At its best," he declared, "the idea of this party has been that we are going to expand opportunity and include people that have not been included, that we are going to give voice to the voiceless and power to the powerless, and embrace people from the outside and bring them inside, and give them a piece of the American dream."

In politics, as Denny Jacobs liked to say, when you are, you are. All of Obama's old supporters were at the Hyatt—Emil Jones, Toni Preckwinkle, and Jesse Jackson Jr., who called Obama "the light that challenges the darkness" in one of the introductory speeches. But Obama's triumph meant that even his most vitriolic enemies were forced to acknowledge that he now stood at the pinnacle of black politics in Chicago.

"I am supportive of Mr. Obama," Bobby Rush told a reporter that week. Despite Rush's endorsement of Blair Hull, Obama won 82 percent of the vote in the Second Ward. "We need everyone to be on board and come around for the Democratic ticket. I will be doing all I can to elect the entire ticket."

It was a victory equal to Oscar DePriest's in 1928, Harold

Washington's in 1983, or Carol Moseley Braun's in 1992. At the age of forty-two, less than two decades after arriving as a stranger, with no money and no roots in Chicago, Obama had joined the roll of the city's great black politicians. That night, he won for the entire community, and the entire community embraced him.

Epilogue

THE BIRTHPLACE OF
POST-RACIAL POLITICS

OBAMA'S VICTORY in the Democratic primary made him a political celebrity. As a man who was likely to become the nation's only black senator, he was interviewed the next day on CNN and *Today*. Bigfoot pencils from the *New Yorker*, the *New Republic*, and the *Wall Street Journal* flew into Chicago to write the first of the fawning profiles that must have made them wonder, What was I thinking? when they saw their prose in the morning papers. (Newhouse News Service called Obama "tall, fresh and elegant." The campaign staff gave him no end of grief over that description.)

Carol Moseley Braun had gotten similar attention after winning her primary, but there was a feeling that Obama might be more than a token black face in an all-white chamber. He might be the guy who finally climbed over the barrier that had blocked African-Americans from power for nearly four hundred years. Race had been the one undying issue in American politics, from the writing of the Constitution, through the Civil War, the Jim Crow era, the civil rights movement, and the white flight from the cities. Maybe Obama could begin to change that, too.

"Obama has the potential to become the most significant

political figure Illinois has sent to Washington since Abraham Lincoln," wrote Mark Brown of the *Chicago Sun-Times*.

It was an apt statement, and not only because it came true. Lincoln's Illinois was a state divided between Southerners who'd migrated up from Kentucky and Tennessee, and Yankees who'd arrived via the Erie Canal and the Great Lakes. Those two factions took up the question of slavery a generation before the rest of the country, settling the issue in 1824 with a bitter plebiscite that banned the sale and ownership of human beings. A generation before Obama became president, his Chicago was led by a black mayor who proved to hostile whites that he wasn't going to turn the city into a Midwestern Zimbabwe. Chicago survived as a multicultural metropolis, evenly divided between whites and blacks.

Obama's belief that the Democratic primary would determine the election was right on the mark. The winner of the Republican primary, Jack Ryan, was forced to withdraw from the race for the exact same reason as Blair Hull: because of embarrassing disclosures in his divorce file. Ryan, who had been married to *Star Trek: Voyager* actress Jeri Ryan, tried to pressure his wife into having sex in front of strangers at swingers' clubs. For the second time that year, the *Chicago Tribune* published the marital secrets of an Obama rival.

Without a general election opponent, Obama was free to work on becoming a star. His campaign lobbied John Kerry's staff for a prime-time speaking slot at the Democratic National Convention. Kerry, who watched Obama own the crowds at two Chicago campaign events, offered him the keynote address. In Boston, Obama delivered the greatest maiden speech since William Jennings Bryan's "Cross of Gold" in 1896, introducing America to the message of inclusion and shared responsibility he had been preaching across Illinois all that winter and spring. As one of his speech coaches later put it, "He walked onto that stage as a state senator, and he walked off as the next president of the United States."

Realizing that Obama was unbeatable, the Illinois Republican Party asked conservative commentator Alan Keyes to serve as its sacrificial nominee. Keyes, who had run two campaigns for president, was thrilled to step into Obama's spotlight. He used the attention to condemn homosexuals as "selfish hedonists" and insist that Jesus Christ would never vote for Obama (a moot point, since Jesus was not registered in Illinois).

In spite of Keyes's clownishness, the general election was significant: It was the first time two black candidates had competed for a U.S. Senate seat.

"Illinois has a record of such innovation," wrote columnist Amity Shlaes, a graduate of the University of Chicago Laboratory School. Neither candidate was campaigning on a black agenda, which meant that Illinois was "yet again emerging as the venue for a shift on race." "The big show of 2004 may well take place in the Land of Lincoln," she added.

It was a race in which skin color was not an issue, won by a black candidate who had shown unprecedented appeal to white voters. That Illinois would become the birthplace of postracial politics was no surprise to Obama. Early in his Chicago years, he realized his adopted home was the perfect training ground for solving America's problems, racial and otherwise. Barack Obama came to Chicago decades after the Great Migration, but for a young black man with political ambitions, it still turned out to be the promised land.

ACKNOWLEDGMENTS

This book would not have been written without the guidance of two editors. The first is Patrick Arden of the *Chicago Reader*, who in 1999 sent me down to the South Side to check out this guy Obama who was trying to take Bobby Rush's congressional seat. "Is Bobby Rush in Trouble?" the story that came out of that reporting, is the basis for chapter 9.

The second is Mark Schone, who was news editor of Salon .com in 2007, when Obama declared his presidential candidacy. I pitched a story about Obama's "lost campaign" and how it helped him mature as a politician to over a dozen national news outlets. Only Mark was interested. Throughout the 2008 campaign, I wrote a number of stories about Obama and Chicago for *Salon*. The essay "Chicago is Barack Obama's kind of town" is where I first developed the idea that certain historical forces made Chicago the perfect home base for a black presidential candidate.

My agent, Jeff Gerecke, responded enthusiastically to my book proposal when I e-mailed him after the 2008 election. Jeff then used his knowledge of the New York publishing world to find the perfect editor: Pete Beatty, who had just moved to Bloomsbury Press from the University of Chicago Press. As a former Hyde Parker, Pete understood exactly what I meant when I said that Obama wouldn't have become president if he hadn't moved to Chicago.

Most of the people I interviewed are named in this book, but there are a few whose help was especially important: Jerry

Kellman, Brian Banks, Alan Dobry, Douglas Baird, and Todd Spivak all reviewed sections of the manuscript for factual accuracy. (Alan also told me I could find Abner Mikva in the phone book, which is the last place someone of my generation thinks to look.) Hermene Hartman, publisher of *N'DIGO*, was an invaluable guide to the worlds of black business, media, and politics. Cheryl Johnson always made me feel welcome when I visited Altgeld Gardens and allowed me to attend meetings of her group, People for Community Recovery.

I also want to thank Eithne McMenamin for serving as my guide at the state capitol in Springfield and Beth Milnikel for showing me around the University of Chicago Law School. Joan Walsh, Alison True, Anne Fitzgerald, and Lucinda Hahn are other editors who encouraged me to write about Obama. (Lucinda, I'm looking forward to seeing your memoir in print.) Jim Dye, my oldest friend, digitized the nine-year-old Obama interview tape I found in a desk drawer.

Finally, I want to thank my mother, Gail Kleine, for typing the manuscript, saving me a lot of time and money when both were in short supply. She worked as an editor after college and used those skills on this book, too. It is a better work because of her.

INDEX

ABLE (Alliance of Business Leaders
    and Entrepreneurs), 172–75,
    198–99, 236
ACORN, 68, 77–79
Addams, Jane, 96
affordable-housing bill, 177–78
Ali, Muhammad, 178
Alinsky, Saul, 8
Alinsky model
    and Clinton, Hillary, 207
    fund-raising, 8, 17
    lobbying, 43–44, 55–56
    Obama's expansion of, 48, 61,
        111–12
Allen, Martha, 42
Alliance of Business Leaders and
    Entrepreneurs (ABLE), 172–75,
    198–99, 236
Altgeld Gardens, 5–7, 9–10, 19, 20–24,
    41–46
Angle, Paul M., 139
Annenberg, Walter, 96–99
antiwar, anti-Bush speech, 202–6
asbestos and CHA, 41–46
Askia, Gha-is, 109, 120
Audacity of Hope, The (Obama), 48, 129,
    139–40, 157, 180
"Audacity to Hope, The" (Wright), 54
Augustine, Loretta
    biographical info, 16, 60
    and CCRC, 9

and DCP, 15–16, 20–23, 59
and Obama, 11–12, 17–18, 51, 74
and Washington, 21–23
Axelrod, David
    biographical info, 201, 230
    and election results, 257
    on Heartland Café speech, 250
    and Hull's character, 252–54
    and Simon, Sheila, 244–46
    See also U.S. Senate campaign
Ayers, Bill, 11, 94–99
Ayers, Thomas, 94–95

Bagby, Margaret, 16, 60, 74
Baird, Douglas, 80–81, 84–85, 105–6,
    136–37
ballot-counting issues, 186–87
Banks, Brian, 71–72, 106–7, 118–19,
    120
Barnett v. Daley, 75–76
Baron, Hal, 107, 115
basketball, 127
Bauler, Paddy, 133
Bennett, William, 56
Bernardin Amendment, 142
Beverly neighborhood, 162
Bilandic, Michael, 37, 208
Bipartisan Health Reform Commission,
    223
Bitter Fruit (Grimshaw), 37
Black, Timuel, 28, 36, 115, 116, 240

Black Belt of Chicago
  and CHA, 41–42, 43
  middle-class moving from, 89
  opportunities for blacks, 173
  overview, 28–29
  See also black political culture
black caucus (Springfield)
  and Democratic majority, 209
  and FOP, 216
  Harold Washington Award, 26
  and Obama, 125–26, 188–92, 220
  and Palmer, 115–16, 122
black churches
  as foundation of Obama's campaign,
    234, 246
  as leading power brokers, 194
  Obama learning about, 13, 51–53,
    199–200, 203
  Rush's success with, 160–61
  and U.S. Senate campaign, 246
Black Metropolis (Drake and Cayton),
  33
Black Panthers, 145
black political culture
  and Daley, R. M., 65–66
  and migrations to Chicago area, 27–29,
    35
  segregation as benefit to, 29, 32–33,
    34–35, 173–75
  and skin color, 35–36
  See also specific politicians
Blagojevich, Rod, 179–80, 209, 225,
  234
Bloody Williamson (Angle), 139
Boss (Royko), 30
Bouman, John, 225
Bowers v. Hardwick, 83
Branch, Taylor, 14
Brazier, Bishop Arthur, 177, 240
Brown, Mark, 261–62
Bud Billiken Parade, 68, 153
Burns, Will, 184
Burrell, Sam, 74, 126
Burris, Roland, 72–73, 139
Bush, George W., 200, 201–2, 204–5,
  233
Byrne, Jane, 37, 38, 107

Cain, Leland "Sugar," 214–15
Calumet Community Religious
  Conference (CCRC), 8–9
Calumet region, Chicago, 6
campaign contribution reporting, 132,
  133–34, 185
Campaign for Better Health Care,
  221–22
campaigns. *See* Illinois First Congressio-
  nal District campaign; state senate
  campaign; U.S. Senate campaign
Canary, Cynthia, 133
capital punishment, 176, 218–19
Career Education Network, 55–57, 209
Carmon, Father Dominic, 9, 24
Cauley, Jim, 231–32
Cayton, Horace R., 33
CCRC (Calumet Community Religious
  Conference), 8–9
Center for Neighborhood Technology,
  102
Cerda, Maria, 20–21
CHA (Chicago Housing Authority),
  41–46
Chicago
  First Great Migration, 27–29
  local attitude toward legislators, 134–35
  misbehaving politicians, 103–5,
    251–54, 262
  as Obama's muse, 4, 24, 100–101
  Second Great Migration, 35
  ward maps, 75–76, 169–70, 208–9
Chicago Annenberg Challenge, 96–99
Chicago Defender, 26–27, 28
Chicago for Summer Youth jobs
  program, 189
Chicago Free South Africa Committee,
  107
Chicago Housing Authority (CHA),
  41–46
Chicago Machine, 36, 131–32
Chicago Maroon, 99
Chicago Reader, 111, 152, 201, 240
Chicago Reporter, 42, 46
Chicago Tribune, 42, 73, 113–14, 157–58,
  181, 242–43
Chico, Gery, 200

Child and Family Services office closure, 189
child care centers, 129
Children's Health Insurance Plan, 225
Cities in Schools, 108
civil rights issues, 63, 77–79, 84–85. *See also* voter registration
civil rights movement, 14, 36–37, 61, 91, 150, 174
Clark, Mark, 36–37, 145
Clinton, Bill, 72, 139, 207–8, 223
Clinton, Hillary, 121, 207–9, 223
Coleman, Ray, 237–39, 258
Community Renewal Society, 41, 42–43
conservative liberalism, 85
"Council Wars," 40, 76
Crucial Concessions, 178
"Current Issues in Racism and the Law" seminar (Obama), 81–82
Currie, Barbara Flynn, 135
Cushing, Cardinal Richard, 199–200

Daley, Barnett v., 75–76
Daley, Maggie, 99
Daley, R. J., 8, 34, 35, 36–37
Daley, R. M., 38, 75, 90–91
Darrow, Clarence, 31
Davis, Allison, Jr., 63, 177
Davis, Danny, 212
Davis, Miner law firm, 63–65, 75–79, 177–78, 201
Davis, Ron, 120, 155
Dawson, William, 31, 33–36
DCP. *See* Developing Communities Project
death penalty reform, 176, 218–19
demeanor, Obama's, 125–26, 138, 154–55, 159–60, 166, 168, 248
Democratic National Conventions, 1–2, 8, 101, 168, 248–49, 262–63
Democratic Socialists of America, 94
Democrats
  and Alinsky, 8
  and Daley, R. J., 37
  and Obama, 21–22
  opposition to school councils, 55
  the "Twenty-nine," 39–40, 145

and Washington, Harold, 39–40
on welfare reform, 128–30
DePriest, Oscar, 30–33
Despres, Leon, 90–91
Developing Communities Project (DCP)
  and asbestos issue, 41–46
  board members, 16
  Challenge support for, 97
  community members taking on projects, 58–59
  meeting of priests and pastors, 14–15
  MET office in Altgeld Gardens project, 20–24
  Obama leaving for Harvard, 59–61
  one-to-one interviews, 13–14
  origin of, 9–10
  and Owens, 50–51, 59–60, 74, 232
  success of, 55
DeZutter, Hank, 111
Dimon, Jamie, 196
discrimination
  Chicago-style, 28
  police brutality toward blacks, 36–37
  racially biased ward maps, 75–76
  segregation, 28–29, 32–33, 34–35, 173–75
Dixie Kitchen & Bait Shop, Hyde Park, 93
Dixon, Alan, 66, 69
Dixon, Bruce, 70
Dobry, Alan, 117–19
Doe, Phyler v., 81
Dohrn, Bernardine, 94–95, 111
Douglas, Paul, 90
Draft Alice Palmer Committee, 116, 119
Drake, St. Clair, 33
Dreams from My Father (Obama), 65, 80–81, 100–101, 105, 125, 171, 211
Dred Scott lawsuit, 83
Duffett, Jim, 221–22, 223
Duneier, Mitchell, 93
Dunham, Ann, 52

East Bank Club, 171
East St. Louis, Illinois, 236–39
Edgar, ACORN v., 77–79
Edgar, Jim, 77, 131
Edwards, John, 230

INDEX

Emerging Democratic Majority, The
    (Judis and Teixeira), 207
EMILY's List, 105
Englewood neighborhood, 109–11, 208
Epstein, Richard, 84
Epton, Bernard, 39
ethics reform, 109, 111, 130–33
Evans, Timothy, 75
Ewell, Marc, 109, 120

Farier, Father Stanley, 7
Farm Service Agency's Diversity Days,
    141
First Great Migration, 27–29
Fitzgerald, Patrick, 172
Fitzgerald, Peter, 172, 198
Fraternal Order of Police (FOP), 216
Fugitive Days (Ayers), 95
fund-raising
    Alinsky model, 8, 17
    community involvement in, 17
    from developers/slumlords, 177–83
    Obama's views on, 186
    for Project Vote!, 70
    questionable sources, 177–82
    shifting from church-based to
        business-based, 193–94
    for U.S. Senate campaign, 198, 213,
        234–36

Galileo Scholastic Academy, 98
Gamaliel Foundation, 48
gangbanger/murderers bill, 176
Gardner, Ed, 70, 173
Geri's Palm Tavern, 182
Giangreco, Pete, 230
Gift Ban Act, 130–33
Golden Gate neighborhood, 16
golf, 127–28
Granger, Bill, 35
Granger, Lori, 35
Grant Park, Chicago, 1–4, 68
Gregorian, Vartan, 99
Grimshaw, Jacky, 47, 48
Grimshaw, William J., 37
gun control issue, 147
Gutenberg Bible, 160

Hairston, Leslie, 234
Hamos, Julie, 205–6
Hampton, Fred, 36–37, 145
Hanrahan, Edward, 37
Hardwick, Bowers v., 83
Hardwick, Michael, 83
Harlem, New York, 32–33
Harold Washington Award, 26
Harold Washington Party, 66, 75
Harper's, 131
Harrison, William H., 31–32
Hartman, Hermene, 194, 213–15
Harvard, 57–58, 59–61
Harvard Law Review presidency, 62,
    63–64, 65, 79–80, 82, 166
Harwell, Carol Anne, 67, 109, 112,
    119–20, 232
Hawaii, vacation in, 155–57
Hawkinson, Carl, 124
Hayes, Charles, 146
Health Care Justice Act, 222–25
health care reform, 128, 142, 221–26
Heartland Café, Rogers Park, 247–50
Hendon, Rickey, 118, 122–24, 188–92,
    215–16, 220
Holt, Barbara, 108, 116
Holy Rosary Church, Roseland, 12,
    14–15, 17
Hull, Blair, 212, 235, 251–54, 255
Hyde Park Herald, 100, 116–17. 135,
    185–86, 234
Hyde Park neighborhood, 18–19, 49–50,
    88–93, 109
Hynes, Dan, 200, 233, 253–55
Hynes, Thomas, 200

Ida B. Wells Homes, 41–46
Illinois
    cultural regions in, 137–39
    demographics, 141–42
    voting record, 206–9
"Illinois Blues" (James), 27
Illinois First Congressional District,
    31–32, 34–36, 38, 92, 146
Illinois First Congressional District
    campaign
    announcing candidacy, 146–47

Kindle's help with, 153–55
networking, 151–52
Obama's response to losing, 169–70, 175
office in Beverly, 162
political sabotage, 149–51, 152–53
public speaking, 148–49, 154–55, 159–60, 170–71
radio advertising, 163–65
results and lessons, 165–68, 209
Rush and, 143–44, 146–47, 149–50, 160–61, 162
Safe Neighborhoods Act, 155–59
speeches, 148–49, 154–55, 159–60, 170–71
Trotter as opponent, 152–53, 158–59, 161
Illinois Issues, 60–61
Illinois Times weekly, 209
immigrants and welfare reform bill, 129–30
independent liberalism, 88–92
Independent Voters of Illinois Independent Precinct Organization (IVI–IPO), 79, 91, 116, 119
Industrial Areas Foundation, 8, 50
Iowa, 250–51
Iraq War, 202–6
Irish "athletic clubs," 28–29
Irish Machine, 40, 256. *See also* Daley, R. J.; Daley, R. M.
IVI–IPO (Independent Voters of Illinois Independent Precinct Organization), 79, 91, 116, 119

Jackson, Jesse, 2–3, 4, 40, 199
Jackson, Jesse, Jr., 74, 107, 112–13, 212, 239, 247
Jackson, Maynard, 174
Jacobs, Denny, 124, 127–28, 132, 133, 142, 198, 212, 223, 251
Jacobson, Walter, 42
James, Skip, 27
Jarrett, Valerie, 194–95
Johnson, Al, 213
Johnson, Hazel, 44
Johnson, John H., 173

Jones, Emil, Jr.
campaign for U.S. representative, 107, 112–14
and Hendon's racial profiling bill, 215–16
and Obama, 56–57, 109, 153, 210
supporting Obama's U.S. Senate race, 174–75, 195, 197, 209, 210–12, 219–20, 234
Jones, Lou, 115, 182
Jones, Rev. Robert, 238
Joyce Foundation, 96–99, 170
judicial minimalism, 85
Judis, John B. (*The Emerging Democratic Majority*), 207
Justice Department, 78–79

Kagan, Elena, 86
Katz, Marilyn, 201–2
Kellman, Jerry, 7–11, 19, 200, 232
Kelly, Edward, 33–34
Kennelly, Martin, 34
Kenwood neighborhood, 180–81
Kerry, John, 262
Keyes, Alan, 263
Khalidi, Rashid, 99–100, 151
Kind and Just Parent, A (Ayers), 95
Kindle, Al, 153–55, 185, 229–30
King, Martin, 199
King, Martin Luther, Jr., 36, 91
Kraemer, Shelley v., 89
Kruglik, Mike, 10
Kurth, Kitty, 252–53

LaFontant, Jewel, 151
League of Women Voters, 78–79
Legal Eagle Award (IVI–IPO), 79
Leo XIII, Pope, 8
Liberty Baptist Church, Chicago, 227–30
Lightford, Kimberly, 188
Lilydale First Baptist Church, 13–15
Lincoln, Abraham, 87, 137–38
Link, Terry, 127–28, 188–89, 198, 212
Little Egypt area, 137–38
Lloyd, Yvonne, 9–12, 16, 46, 60, 74
Lords of the Last Machine (Granger and Granger), 35

Love, Rev. Alvin, 13–15, 22–23, 52–53, 60, 236–37
loyalty, Obama's, 232–33
Lucas, Harold, 182–83

the Machine
    Chicago Machine, 36, 131–32
    Chicago voters against, 90–92
    Irish Machine, 40, 256
    and Jones, 211
    and organizers, 23
    and Palmer, 107–8
    South Side Machine, 37–38, 72–73
Madden, Martin P., 31
Madigan, Jim, 83
Madigan, Lisa, 172, 188–89
Malcolm X (movie), 69–70
Management Services of Illinois, 131
Manilow, Lewis, 70
Matthews, Kgosie, 196
Mayor's Office of Employment and Training (MET), 19–24
McClelland, Edward, 148–49, 186–87, 240–42
McConnell, Michael, 80
McKnight, John, 48, 57
media interviews, 148–49, 184–88, 240–42, 261–62
Medicaid expansion bill, 176
Melton, Steve, 78–79
Mendell, David, 253–54
MET (Mayor's Office of Employment and Training), 19–24
Metcalfe, Ralph, 37–38
Metro East area, 236–39
Mikva, Abner
    on family values, 157
    as Illinois state representative, 91–92, 132
    and Obama, 62–63, 143–44, 150–51, 243–44
    on public speaking, 199–200
    at U of C, 88–89
Miller, Rich, 166
Million Man March, 111
Miner, Judson, 63–65, 136, 200
Minority Set-Aside Program, 178
Minow, Newton, 151

Moore, Joe, 248
Moseley Braun, Carol
    decision on 2004 election, 196–97, 212, 261
    and Hyde Park, 92–93
    and Project Vote!, 69, 71, 73
    U.S. Senate race and win, 66, 69, 72, 139, 195–96
Moses, Robert, 19
Motor Voter law, 77–79
Mt. Zion Baptist, East St. Louis, 238
Muhammad Ali Foundation, 178
multiracial appeal, 17–18, 167–68, 193, 214–15, 241–42, 247

NAACP, 68
National Voter Registration Act "Motor Voter," 77–79
N'DIGO, 101, 215
Nesbitt, Marty, 171, 194–95
New Deal, 33
Newhouse, Richard, 91, 108
Newman, Sandy, 65–66, 67–68, 71
New Schools Multicultural Network, 97
New Ward Committeeman Coalition, 107–8
New York Times, 62, 100
Nichols, Mike, 90
Nixon, Richard, 207
North Shore neighborhood, 92, 246–47

Obama, Barack
    awards and honors, 26, 73, 79, 86, 94
    effect on women, 71, 246–47
    and former associates, 232–33
    overview, 18–19, 51–52
Obama, Malia Ann, 135, 156–57
Obama, Malik, 74
Obama, Michelle Robinson, 63, 73–74, 93, 220
"Obama Juice," 230
O'Brien Lock, Chicago, 58
OLG (Our Lady of the Gardens), 6–7, 20–21, 44–46
organized crime mob "Outfit," 34
organizing, Obama's article on, 60–61.
    See also Alinsky model

Orr, David, 108
Our Lady of the Gardens (OLG), 6–7, 20–21, 44–46
Owens, Johnnie, 48–51, 59–60, 74, 232

Palestinian Identity (Khalidi), 99
Palmer, Alice
  campaign for Congress, 105, 112, 114
  insufficient petition signatures, 119–20
  reneging on deal, 115–21
  as state senator, 118, 123, 124–25
  support for Obama, 106–8, 111, 114–15
Palmer, Edward "Buzz," 115
Palmer, Lu, 68–69, 152
Palmer Park, Roseland, 49
Pappas, Maria, 200, 252
Paretsky, Sara, 151
Parting the Waters (Branch), 14, 19
People's Movement, 31–33
People's Power ethos, 200
Perkins, Stephen, 47–48, 102
Perle, Richard, 204
Peterson, Terry, 162, 183
Petka, Edward, 219
Pfleger, Father Michael, 162
Philip, James "Pate," 128
Phyler v. Doe, 81
Pittman, Michael, 237
poker games in Springfield, 127
police brutality, 36–37, 218–19
political accountability, 111
Posner, Richard, 84
Powell, Adam Clayton, Jr., 32–33, 194
Power Broker, The (Moses), 19
Preckwinkle, Toni, 74, 105, 108, 119, 153, 183–84
Pritzker, Penny, 99
Project Vote!, 65–73
Public Affairs (talk show), 185
public speaking
  adapting for race, 227–30, 248
  antiwar, anti-Bush speech, 202–6
  First Congressional District campaign, 148–49, 154–55, 159–60, 170–71
  Mikva on, 199–200
  on mutual obligations, 248–50
  primary win speech, 259

Pugh, Stephen, 174–75, 236
PUSH/Rainbow PUSH, 68, 70, 199

Quad Cities, Illinois and Iowa, 250–51

Raby, Al, 47, 48
racial profiling bill, 176, 215–17
radio advertising, 163–65
Randle, Linda, 41–46
Ransom, Lou, 26–27
Reed, Adolph, 115
Regional Employment Network job training network, 9, 20
religion, Obama's childhood, 51–53. See also black churches
Republicans, 31, 128
Reynolds, Jim, 171–73, 198–99
Reynolds, Mel, 103–5
Rezko, Antoin "Tony," 151, 177–81
Rezko, Rita, 180–81
Rezmar Inc., 177–78, 179
riots, 1, 8, 28–29, 36, 139
Robbins, Tony, 146
Robert Taylor Homes, 36
Robinson, Michelle, 63, 73–74
Rogers, John, 70, 194–96
Rogers, John, Jr., 151–52
Rogers, Steven, 235–36
Ronen, Carol, 188–89
Rose, Don, 73
Roskam, Peter, 223
Rostenkowski, Dan, 113
Rove, Karl, 204
Royko, Mike, 26, 30
Ruiz, Jesse, 81–82, 105
Rules for Radicals (Alinsky), 43
Rush, Bobby Lee
  after election win, 169–70, 239–40, 242
  as Obama's opponent, 143–44, 146–47, 149–50, 160–61, 162
  support for Obama, 259
Rush, Huey, 147, 148
Rush, Jimmy Lee, 162
Ryan, George, 131, 132, 143, 157, 176, 206, 218
Ryan, Jack, 251, 262

Safe Neighborhoods Act, 155–59
Saints Peter and Paul Church, South
    Chicago neighborhood, 58–59
Saltzman, Bettylu, 70, 201–2, 206, 230
Sawyer, Eugene, 58–59
Scates, Kappy, 140–41
Scates, Steve, 137, 140–41
Schakowsky, Jan, 233, 247
Schmidt, John, 70, 137, 152
school reform issue, 55–57, 96–99
Second Great Migration, 35
segregation, 28–29, 32–33, 34–35, 173–75
Seminary Co-op Bookstore, Chicago,
    18–19
September 11, 2001, terrorist attacks, 203–4
Sexton, Brenda, 252–54
Shlaes, Amity, 263
Shelley v. Kraemer, 89
Shomon, Dan, 137–41, 151, 156–57,
    210–11, 231–32
"Silent Six," 35, 37
Simon, Paul, 79, 130–32, 137, 201, 243–44
Simon, Sheila, 244–46, 247, 258–59
skin color, 35–36
Slim's Table (Duneier), 93
Small Schools Workshop, 97
Smith, Callie, 45
Smith, Pam, 240–41
Smith, Scott, 99
Smith, Zirl, 43–46
social justice teaching, 95
South Chicago neighborhood, 58–59
South Loop neighborhood, 181–82
South Side Africa Village Collaborative,
    97
South Side blacks, 67
South Side Machine, 37–38, 72–73
South Side neighborhood, 68, 90,
    109–11, 125, 153, 256–57
Southwest Side neighborhood, 76, 92
Spann-Cooper, Melody, 214
Spivak, Todd, 185–86, 196–97, 221, 229
Springfield, Illinois, 126. See also black
    caucus; State Senator Obama
state senate campaign
    clearing it with Alice Palmer, 105,
        106–8, 111, 114–15

Mel Reynolds's sex scandal, 103–5
    Palmer's renege, 115–21
State Senator Obama
    ballot-counting issues, 186–87
    budget cuts, 189–90
    budget for "member initiatives,"
        183–84
    death penalty reform, 176, 218–19
    demeanor, 125–26, 138
    first bill hazing, 122–24
    Gift Ban Act, 130–33
    Hawaii vacation, 155–57
    health care reform, 128, 142, 221–26
    and Hendon, 118, 122–24, 188–92
    image damage from campaign loss,
        170, 175
    local attitude toward legislators,
        134–35
    and media attention, 184–88
    overview, 135–37, 176–78, 226
    racial profiling bill, 216–17
    Safe Neighborhoods Act, 155–59
    socializing, 127–28
    tax reform, 142–43
    welfare reform, 128–30, 143
St. Clair County, Illinois, 236–39, 258
steel mills closing near Altgeld Gardens,
    7–8
steelworkers, laid-off, 15–16
steelworkers' union, 15
Stevenson, Adlai, III, 243–44
St. John Missionary Baptist, Centerville,
    Illinois, 238
Street, Ted, 216
Sullivan, David, 143
Sunstein, Cass, 85

Talented Tenth, 53, 193
tax reform, 142–43
Teixeira, Ruy (The Emerging Democratic
    Majority), 207
television advertising, 244–47, 255–56
Tenth Ward neighborhood, 20
Thompson, William Hale "Big Bill,"
    29–30, 31
Tillman, Dorothy, 182, 227–28
Time magazine, 40

Trinity United Church of Christ
  Obama joining, 53–54
  Obama wedding at, 73–74
Trotter, Donne, 116, 125, 152–53, 158–59, 161
Turow, Scott, 151
the "Twenty-nine," 39–40, 145

"Uncle Leland" issue, 213–15
unified theory of racial politics, 241–42
United Neighborhood Organization (UNO), 58
United Voter Registration League, 68
University of Chicago (U of C), 79, 81–87, 89, 99, 106, 136–37
University of Chicago Laboratory Schools, 95
University of Illinois–Chicago, 94–95, 98
UNO (United Neighborhood Organization), 58
U.S. Senate campaign
  advertising, 244–47, 255–56
  antiwar, anti-Bush speech, 202–6
  building a support base, 193–200
  campaign office, 240
  fund-raising, 198, 213, 234–36
  Heartland Café speech, 247–50
  Jones's support for, 195, 197, 209, 210–12, 219–20
  opposition, 200, 212, 251–54
  results, 256–60
  staff, 201–2, 205–6, 210–11, 237–39
  "Uncle Leland" issue, 213–15
  See also Axelrod, David
U.S. Steel, 7

Valois Cafeteria, Hyde Park, 93
videotaping interrogations, 218

voter registration, 38, 40, 65–73, 77–79
Voting Rights Act, 92
Vrdolyak, Edward, 20, 39–40

Walsh, Larry, 127, 142, 197–98
ward maps, 75–76, 169–70, 208–9
Washington, Harold
  and black businesses, 173–74
  influence on Obama, 26
  at MET office ribbon cutting, 21–23
  political career, 25–26, 37–40
Washington, Joe, 56
Washington, Joyce, 240
Washington, Laura, 213–14
Washington Post, 100
Waste Management Inc. landfill, 58–59
welfare reform, 128–30, 143
West Side neighborhood, 67, 124–25, 189
White, George, 32
White, Jesse, 208
"Why Organize?" article (Obama), 60–61
Wickers, Ronnie "Ronnie Woo-Woo," 3
Wilder, Douglas, 35–36
Wilson, William Julius, 94
Winfrey, Oprah, 3, 4, 213
Wolfowitz, Paul, 204
Women's health bills, 176
Woodlawn Preservative and Investment Co., 177
Woods Fund foundation, 96
World War I, 27
Wright, Edward H., 29
Wright, Rev. Jeremiah A., Jr., 53–54, 68
WVON radio, 70, 150, 157–58, 214

Young, Quentin, 225

ABOUT THE AUTHOR

Edward McClelland lives in Chicago. His previous books include *The Third Coast: Sailors, Strippers, Fishermen, Folksingers, Long-Haired Ojibway Painters, and God-Save-the-Queen Monarchists of the Great Lakes* and *Horseplayers: Life at the Track.* A former staff writer for the *Chicago Reader*, he has contributed to the *New York Times*, the *Boston Globe*, *Salon*, *Slate*, and the *Nation*. He is currently working on a history of the Rust Belt, to be published by Bloomsbury Press. Find him on the Web at www.tedmcclelland.com.